# BETWEEN OPERA AND CINEMA

# BETWEEN OPERA AND CINEMA

*Edited by*
Jeongwon Joe and Rose Theresa

Routledge
New York and London

Published in 2002 by
Routledge
29 West 35th Street
New York, NY 10001

Published in Great Britain by
Routledge
11 New Fetter Lane
London EC4P 4EE

Routledge is an imprint of the Taylor & Francis Group.

Copyright © 2002 by Routledge

Printed in the United States of America on acid-free paper.

10 9 8 7 6 5 4 3 2 1

Library of Congress Cataloging-in-Publication Data
Between opera and cinema / edited by Jeongwon Joe and Rose Theresa.
    p. cm. — (Critical and cultural musicology)
    Includes bibliographical references and index
    ISBN 0-8153-3450-8
    1. Motion pictures and opera. 2. Operas—Film and video adaptations—
History and criticism. I. Joe, Jeongwon. II. Theresa, Rose. III. Series.
ML2100.B47 2001
782.1—dc21                                                    2001034879

# Contents

# Series Editor's Foreword

*Martha Feldman*

MUSICOLOGY HAS UNDERGONE A SEA CHANGE IN RECENT YEARS. WHERE once the discipline knew its limits, today its boundaries seem all but limitless. Its subjects have expanded from the great composers, patronage, manuscripts, and genre formations to include race, sexuality, jazz, and rock; its methods from textual criticism, formal analysis, paleography, narrative history, and archival studies to deconstruction, narrativity, postcolonial analysis, phenomenology, and performance studies. These categories point to deeper shifts in the discipline that have led musicologists to explore phenomena which previously had little or no place in musicology. Such shifts have changed our principles of evidence while urging new understandings of existing ones. They have transformed prevailing notions of musical texts, created new analytic strategies, recast our sense of subjectivity, and produced new archives of data. In the process, they have also destabilized canons of scholarly value.

The implications of these changes remain challenging in a field whose intellectual ground has shifted so quickly. In response to them, this series offers essay collections that give thematic focus to new critical and cultural perspectives in musicology. Most of the essays contained herein pursue their projects through sustained research on specific musical practices and contexts. They aim to put strategies of scholarship that have developed recently in the discipline into meaningful exchanges with one another while also helping to construct fresh approaches. At the same time, they try to reconcile these new approaches with older methods, building on the traditional achievements of musicology in helping to forge new disciplinary idioms. In both ventures, volumes in this series also attempt to press new associations among fields outside of musicology, making aspects of what has often seemed an inaccessible field intelligible to scholars in other disciplines.

In keeping with this agenda, topics treated in this series include music and the cultures of print; music, art, and synesthesia in nineteenth-century Europe; music in the African diaspora; relations between opera and cinema; music in the cultural sensorium; music and Marxism; and music, sensation, and sensuality. Through enterprises like these, the series hopes to facilitate new disciplinary directions and dialogues, challenging the boundaries of musicology and helping to refine its critical and cultural methods.

# Introduction

## Rose Theresa and Jeongwon Joe

I believe that in the coming years by my work and that of others . . . grand opera can be given at the Metropolitan Opera House at New York without any material change from the original and with artists and musicians long since dead.

—Thomas Edison (1895)

The world of opera is built upon premises which radically defy those of the cinematic approach. . . Opera on the screen is a collision of two worlds detrimental to either.

—Siegfried Kracauer (1951)

Opera shares with film . . . many of its functions.

—Theodor Adorno (1955)

In significant ways, opera via the media today is more important, more vital than opera done live. . . . But this shift toward mediated opera has a price.

—Sam Abel (1996)

T HE TITLE OF THIS VOLUME, *BETWEEN OPERA AND CINEMA*, REFLECTS ITS purposefully ambivalent and multivalent aim. To focus attention on those spaces between the two—whether aesthetic, cultural, historical, ideological, institutional, phenomenological, or technical—implies questioning both what is shared between opera and cinema and what comes between them.

Within the university, opera and film as academic disciplines share a sense of relative youth. Both fields established their institutional affiliations from the periphery, and both are marked by their involvement in critical and methodological issues that have continually questioned and redefined relations between the centers and margins of the academy. As Marc Weiner points out in chapter 5, the growing field of opera cinema studies, where these two disciplines come together most obviously, is further marked by its diversity and heterogeneity. Perhaps this is as it should be, owing to the myriad ways in which opera and cinema have interacted over the past century. Though this volume reflects the diversity of its interdisciplinary subject, we have nonetheless loosely organized its chapters under three rubrics.

## SILENT AFFINITIES

Thomas Edison's statement points out the special interest of early cinematographers in the possibilities of opera on screen. As Noël Burch has argued, a desire for the reproduction of theatrical, literary, pictorial, and, in some cases, operatic modes of representation was part of a complex cultural fantasy during cinema's early years. Cinema was at once "a series of researches whose ultimate aim remained the reproduction of life. . . an analogue of reality" and, at the same time, a "lyrico-theatrical dream" for a perfectly reproduced "reality" no less than operatic in its effects.[1] Edison's dream of performances given by "artists and musicians long since dead" also suggests some of the strangeness of early relations between opera and cinema. When Edison launched his series of "Grand Operas" in 1909 with a film version of Gounod's *Faust*, the characters onscreen were mute. In his *Music and the Silent Film*, Martin Marks discusses the seeming contradictions of film based on opera during the era before standardized synchronization of sound:

> The mute medium robs such a work of its dramatic essence; and even if the accompanying score were to include vocal as well as instrumental parts (which does not often seem to have been the case), the original theatrical balance has been lost.[2]

And yet, as Marks has discovered, film producers and audiences willingly accepted these mute adaptations of popular operas.

In chapter 1, Rose Theresa situates the appeal of opera in the context of cinema's early modes of spectatorship based on spectacle and narrative procedures. During cinema's first decades, the early "cinema of attractions," which emphasized the spectacle of cinematic technology, gave way to narrative films. With the newer modes of narration, Theresa stresses, spectators were offered new positions of understanding and subjectivity, not so much as part of a particular exhibition or technological event, but rather from a space within the fictional worlds of specific films. Spectatorship became part of the film itself as a point of address and a textual entity that worked to standardize cinematic consumption. In her investigation of early cinematic versions of Gounod's *Faust*, the most frequently filmed opera of the period, Theresa argues that opera provided cinema with a flexible model for negotiating—at times through sexual difference—the contradictory claims of spectacle and narrative during this "transitional" period in cinema's history.

Michal Grover-Friedlander's essay is part of a larger project exploring the significance of silence to opera and operatic representation. At the heart of silent film's attraction to opera, she posits, is the fact that opera derives its force not simply from the extravagance of the singing voice, but rather in its suggesting or approaching the limit of the vocally expressible. What lies at that limit, constituting a hidden focus to which voice is drawn, is that which transcends the operatic voice: the silence beyond song. For Grover-Friedlander, early cinema in its muteness—its fascination with and anxiety about silence—was uniquely suited to revealing opera's tendency to go beyond song, disintegrating into deadly silence. But the silent affinity between opera and cinema that lies beyond the limit of the sensical can be traced in films throughout the history of cinema. In this essay, she turns to the Marx Brothers's *A Night at the Opera* (1935) to question whether or not cinema, now possessing a voice, is still attracted to opera. She explores how cinema, after its transformation into the talkie, looks back at its silent past. She argues that cinema wishes to remember, that it is nostalgic for the absent voice or for a loss in relation to its new voice. What the talkie indeed inherits from its silent past is related in fundamental ways to the medium of opera.

Lesley Stern also locates the encounter between opera and cinema in the practices of silent film. In chapter 3, Stern discusses Michael Powell and Emeric Pressburger's *The Tales of Hoffmann* (1951)—not a silent film at all, but rather what Powell called a "composed film." She argues that *The Tales* dissolves the "real" of its operatic source into a magical display of cinematic trickery and stylized artificiality. Though far removed from the operatic stage in its exuberant display of special effects, it nonetheless conveys a remarkable sense of the operatic through certain operations she defines as "operality." Stern traces a genealogy of these operations through the "grandiose époque of hysterical cinema"—through the silent cinema of the divas—to illustrate the intersections of dancerly, operatic, and theatrically avant-garde practices that find their apotheosis in Powell and Pressburger's film. Conceived within the parameters of a dramaturgy not centered on character but nonetheless charged by an intense investment in acting, this film's multiplication and doubling of operatic and cinematic performative signs produces for Stern a cinema of visceral engagement.

It may have been this multiplication and doubling—the "operality"—of Powell and Pressburger's *The Tales of Hoffmann* that left Siegfried Kracauer quite profoundly ambivalent. Of the film he wrote that "having thrown out the cinema as a means of capturing real life, Powell and Pressburger reintroduce it to evolve an imagery which is essentially stage imagery, even though it could not be staged in a theatre. . . No doubt it is cinema. But it is cinema estranged from itself."[3] For Kracauer, opera was a "monstrous amalgam" laden with values and meanings irreconcilable with the critical and even redemptive potential of a popularly conceived cinema. As Miriam Hansen has argued, Kracauer felt that film should take as its object the material realm of the everyday as it existed at or just below the surface: "the world of things in its habitual, unconscious interdependence with human life, with the traces of social, psychic, and erotic relations."[4] It was not the job of Kracauer's "cinematic approach" to reflect faithfully everyday phenomena but rather to render them strange, to expose the contingency of that which was habitual and familiar. Within the context of his critical economy, opera worked at cross-purposes with cinema, magically transforming the strange and improbable into the spectacularly familiar. Paraphrasing Kracauer, opera does not "penetrate" the material world, it "transcends" it.

As Jeongwon Joe demonstrates in her dissertation "Opera on Film, Film in Opera: Postmodern Implications of the Cinematic Influence on Opera," the exploitation of aesthetic and technical conflicts between opera and film can yield the sort of disruptive effects that Kracauer sought exclusively in cinema. Philip Glass's *La Belle et la Bête* is one of several recent works attempting such a provocative fusion of cinema and opera. In *Belle*, Glass uses Jean Cocteau's film of 1946 as the visual content of his opera, while replacing the original soundtrack with live music. In chapter 4, Joe examines this multimedia opera's dialectical tension between stage and screen, between live bodies and reproduced images, to elucidate how, by re-embodying operatic voices in cinematic images, the cinematic visuality of Glass's *Belle* challenges performing and viewing conventions of the traditional operatic theater. Joe also traces affinities between *Belle* and silent film, focusing on the fact that both explore the mixture of live voices with filmic images. Yet, she argues, the live voice in Glass's opera functions to undo silent cinema's convention of reducing the distance between voice and body.

STRATEGIC MEDIATIONS

Theodor Adorno, like Kracauer, also wrote about relations between opera and cinema. For Adorno, however, the two shared significant aesthetic and historical similarities. In chapter 5, Marc Weiner draws on insights from *In Search of Wagner*—in which Adorno advanced the notorious thesis that Wagnerian music drama is the ideological precursor to modern film—to answer the question "Why does Hollywood like opera?" He observes that in the last twenty-five years, opera has played a central role in a large number of "blockbuster" films intended for a wide popular audience that would otherwise evince little interest in the art form. Applying Adorno's discussion of "phantasmagoria" to the use of opera in Jonathan Demme's *Philadelphia* (1993), Weiner seeks to uncover the ideological assumptions regarding the role of opera in American culture and the often unacknowledged set of associations that attend it. He argues that in terms of its social and psychodynamic function, opera constitutes a labile object rife with contradictions. When opera is strategically deployed in blockbuster films such as *Philadelphia*, the social differences that often accompany the artform—between high and low, rich and poor, homosexual and heterosexual, diseased and healthy, exotic and mainstream—are both evoked and transcended by opera's phantasmagorical efficacy as a sign of the universal.

Mary Hunter addresses somewhat similar issues in chapter 6. She argues that the representation of opera in Frank Darabont's *The Shawshank Redemption* (1994) evokes a world of universality and timelessness where engaged listening and emotional response to aesthetic phenomena transcend arbitrary social divisions. But this is not the only way that mainstream cinema uses opera. John Huston's *Prizzi's Honor* (1985), in stark contrast to *The Shawshank Redemption*, cleverly deploys operatic quotations to articulate an insider culture where hierarchy outweighs universality. In her essay, Hunter offers a comparative analysis of these two films, illuminating how the use of both diegetic and non-diegetic operatic music, as well as the female voice, marshals opera to engage cinematic listeners—through sonic versions of feeling and knowing—even while entering universes that in sociopolitical terms are nearly diametrically opposed.

David J. Levin offers a critique of the recent trend in opera criticism toward the intensely emotive and autobiographical. In their libidinal effusions, such authors as Wayne Koestenbaum, Sam Abel, and Paul Robinson seem to emulate the operatic objects of their affections. In chapter 7, Levin charts the terms of this particularly extravagant style of criticism, which he terms "Neo-Lyricism," through a reading of Jean-Jacques Beineix's 1981 film *Diva*. Like the New Lyricism, this film both suggests and repeatedly performs the notion of "going your own way with your pleasure." Levin suggests that the New Lyricism is in part a product of the media technology that brings operatic experiences into the privacy of the home. What informs this criticism is a love of opera as an undomesticated pleasure of the domestic sphere. But, he argues, there are no innocent pleasures. For Levin, little is gained by purchasing the legitimation of enthusiasm at the cost of nuanced textual analysis.

For Marcia Citron, Jean-Pierre Ponnelle's *Le nozze di Figaro* (1976) is an instance of the mediation between technology and tradition that characterizes the genre of the opera-film itself. Her essay focuses on the alternation in this film between "exterior" and "interior" singing. She argues that interior singing, in which vocal music is presented without the moving lips of the characters, calls into question the status and location of the voice. As a flexible, mobile, and quasi-independent object, it wields considerable power in the narrative and representational economy of Ponnelle's film. Citron's analysis demonstrates that through interior singing and other cinematic techniques, Ponnelle produces an opera-film that is striking in its literary sensibility.

MEDIATED MEMORIES

The last three chapters treat films in which representations of operatic traditions effect significant mediations between past and present. When art music is used in postwar Italian cinema, it is most often the music of Verdi. Deborah Crisp and Roger Hillman read this phenomenon as part of the process of Italy's coming to terms with the prewar fascist era and its ongoing presence in postwar politics. In this context, where both the left and center-right of Italian politics have mythologized the Resistance as a "Second Risorgimento," the use of Verdi, veritable icon of *the* Risorgimento, becomes a powerful device of cultural and historical commentary, both eliciting and refiguring cultural memory. Chapter 9 focuses on two postwar films. Crisp and Hillman argue that in his *Senso* (1954), Visconti draws on parallels between the Risorgimento reception of operas with potentially incendiary plots and Italian "occupation" by the forces of fascism to ignite the political and personal narratives of the film. Leto, in his *La villeggiatura (Black Holiday,* 1973), on the other hand, traces the continuation of bourgeois humanism into the prewar years of fascist ascendancy, with Verdi representing an ideal once shared and now contested. Both exploit the dramatic potential of Verdi's operas to reinforce a historical myth. Bearing a skewed relationship to neorealism, the combination in these films of the operatic and cinematic creates a threatricalized version of Italian history. What Verdi's music evokes in these films—whether tenable or not—is the mythology of the Resistance as a convenient postwar view of Italian history.

Teri Silvio also sees opera—in this case Chinese Opera—as a vehicle for engaging cultural memory. Her essay on Chen Kaige's *Farewell My Concubine* (1993) focuses on how nostalgia is evoked through the tension between the theatrical subject of the film and its "Hollywood" style, particularly the contrast between the charisma of the film's opera actor Cheng Dieye and the international pop star Leslie Cheung who plays him. Silvio argues that the overabundance of Freudian symbolism in the film and the construction of Leslie Cheung's queer star persona are both attempts to find a cinematic correlative of the lost erotic quality of the Peking Opera actor's physical presence. She reads the linking of themes of cultural identity and homosexual desire in this film in light of the ongoing transformation of China's entertainment culture from local and stage-based to international and screen-based.

In Mary Wiles "Sounding Out the Operatic," opera is seen to mark personal rather than cultural nostalgia in the work of filmmaker Jacques Rivette. Wiles demonstrates that, in the film *Noroît,* Rivette pays tribute to the memory of his friend and mentor Jean Cocteau, who was planning a filmed version of *Pelléas et Mélisande* shortly before his death. While Rivette's *Noroît* is usually read as an adaptation of Tourneur's *The Revenger's Tragedy,* a seventeenth-century play quoted at strategic moments in the film, Wiles persuasively traces *Noroît's* "phantom source" in the characters, narrative, and mise-en-scène of Debussy's opera. She further situates Rivette's project in the context of theoretical debates of the 1960s and 1970s to argue that Debussy's subtle though radical modernism provided Rivette with an alternative to the prevailing anti-aesthetic tendencies of Brechtian filmmakers. The essence of mystery and ambiguity found in *Pelléas* is captured in *Noroît,* a film inspired by Debussy's opera of uncertainty.

Despite the century-long, mutual attraction between opea and cinema, as evidenced in this collection of essays, there are but a handful of book-length studies devoted to the topic.[5] A fairly recent spate of papers, presentations, and seminars suggests, however, the potential of a growing community of scholars interested at this time in what is at stake in the study of these two forms of representation and their complex interrelations. With the aim in mind to stimulate more dialogue within and beyond this community, this volume offers a mapping out of some of those richly ambivalent spaces yet to be explored between opera and cinema.

NOTES

1. Noël Burch, *Life to Those Shadows*, trans. Ben Brewster (Berkeley and Los Angeles: University of California Press, 1990), 49.

2. Martin Marks, *Music and the Silent Film* (New York and Oxford: Oxford University Press, 1997), 42.

3. Siegfried Kracauer, "Opera on Screen," *Film Culture* 1 (1955), 21.

4. Miriam Hansen, "'With Skin and Hair': Kracauer's Theory of Film, Marseille 1940," *Critical Inquiry* 19 (spring 1993), 442.

5. Marcia J. Citron, *Opera on Screen* (New Haven and London: Yale University Press, 2000); Jeongwon Joe, "Opera on FIlm, Film in Opera: Postmodern Implicationsa of the Cinematic Influence on Opera" (Ph. D. diss., Northwestern Univesity, 1998); Alexander Thomas Simpson, Jr., "Opera on Film: A Study of the History and Aesthetic Principles of a Hybrid Genre" (Ph. D. diss., University of Kentucky, 1990); Roxanne Elizabeth Solomon, "A Critical Study of Franco Zeffirelli's *La Traviata* (EDD diss., Columbia University Teachers College, 1987); Jeremy Tambling, *Opera, Ideology and Film* (New York: St. Martin's Press, 1987); Jeremy Tambling, ed., *A Night in at the Opera: Media Representations of Opera* (London: John Libbey and Co., 1994); the joint issue of *L'Avant-Scène Opéra/Cinéma*, no. 98: *Cinema et Opéra (May* 1987); David Levin, *Richard Wagner, Fritz Lang, and the Nibelungen: the Dramaturgy of Disavowal* (Princeton: Princeton University Press, 1988).

# 1

# From Méphistophélès to Méliès
## Spectacle and Narrative in
## Opera and Early Film

### *Rose Theresa*

D URING THE LAST DECADES OF THE NINETEENTH CENTURY, GOUNOD'S *Faust* was performed more often than any other operatic work, not only at the Paris Opéra, but internationally as well.[1] It was also the opera earliest cinematographers turned to most frequently. During cinema's first decade and a half, *Faust* made its way to the screen time and time again. Why was this so? The appeal of this opera around the turn of the century can be attributed in some part to they way it "combined spectacle and narrative," to borrow a phrase from Laura Mulvey.[2] As Mulvey and others indicate, spectacle and narrative are distinct forms of visual pleasure that realize the circulation of meaning and power with particular force in the cinema. As different ways of seeing, they shape spectators' rapport with the screen. Through spectacle and narrative, we will see how *Faust* offered early filmmakers a readymade, proven, and flexible model for establishing and regulating visual pleasure.

For Mulvey, the pleasures of spectacle and narrative and the experiences of filmgoers are structured through sexual difference. Cinema's ultimate power—particularly in mainstream cinema of the 1930s to the 1960s—is that of the "patriarchal order." Historians of early film, on the other hand, attend to distinctions between spectacle and narrative to elucidate a transformation in the nature of both cinematic language and spectatorship during the earliest decades of the medium. For scholars such as Tom Gunning, Thomas Elsaesser, and Miriam Hansen, cinema during these years effects a gradual shift from modes of engagement predicated on spectacle to those based on narrative continuity. They read this shift as one aspect of the increasing control of an emerging film industry over the cinematic experiences of its audiences. This essay will briefly consider *Faust* the opera in light of Mulvey's feminist analysis of spectacle and narrative before exploring several *Faust* films in the context of changing modes of early cinematic spectatorship.

## MULVEY AND THE GENDERING OF SPECTACLE AND NARRATIVE

In her "Visual Pleasure and Narrative Cinema," Laura Mulvey focuses on spectacle and narrative to discern ways in which sexual difference both structures and is structured by these "two contradictory aspects of looking in the conventional cinematic situation."[3] In her groundbreaking essay, Mulvey analyzes the ubiquitous gaze of the cinema in terms of three secondary "looks," those of the camera, the characters on the screen, and the spectators in the theater. She argues that it is through this powerful apparatus of interchanging looks that masculine-identified positions are more coherently aligned with narrative procedures, while femininity comes to be equated with spectacle.[4]

Though much attention has been given to defining the nature of narrative in the cinema and to analyzing narrative procedures in individual films, similar work on cinematic spectacle—the predominantly feminine side of Mulvey's dichotomy—has been generally limited to studies of early film, pornographic genres, and the American musical. In this context, spectacle is often defined in a negative relation to narrative. In the most general terms, where narrative is understood as the figuring of spatial and temporal movement, spectacle is characterized as static, disrupting the narrative flow through direct confrontation with "the here and now."[5] For example, Paul Willemen characterizes similarities between musicals and pornographic films in just this way:

> In both cases the importance of the generically obligatory sequences makes for a weak narrative as the story is simply there to link the graphic sex/musical numbers with fairly predictably coded transitions from the narrative to its interruptions, with the interruptions functioning as self-contained pieces. Moreover, the need to include such relatively autonomous segments arranged as spectacles "arresting" the look and thus, at least to a significant extent, suspending the narrative flow, makes for films that proceed with a halting rhythm.[6]

Without challenging these notions, Mulvey's essay shows that spectacle and narrative can also be distinguished more instructively as two different modes of address in cinema, two distinct ways in which cinema implicates its spectator.

Although any film may be read as an interweaving of spectacle and narrative, these two ways of seeing structure the ongoing rapport between spectator and screen in different ways. Spectacle is perhaps the more ambivalent of the two, the more unstable in its effects. With spectacle, there is a sense of direct rapport, an immediacy that invites a merging of spectator and screen image. But, at the same time, the experience of spectacle is necessarily predicated on separation: the spectacle is experienced primarily as other than the spectator. It is, after all, only through separation that "the fantasy of merging, the confused boundaries between self and other" may be posited.[7]

Narrative operations, on the other hand, are effected through an initial sense of sameness and belonging. The narrative mode of address establishes and assumes identification of the spectator with a space constructed and shared from within the fictional world of the film itself. In other words, where spectacle addresses the spectator in a way that says "look *at* me and see me from where you are," narrative says "look *with* me and see what I see from where I am." Spectacle invites an immediate, direct rapport with the other. Narrative provides a more vicarious experience, in that rapport with the other is mediated through the same. In Mulvey's words, spectacle "implies a separation of the erotic identity of the subject from the object on the screen." Narrative, on the other hand "demands identification of the ego with the object on the screen through the spectator's fascination with and recognition of his like."[8]

In cinema's gendering of spectacle and narrative, then, the other is female and the same is male. Mulvey exemplifies this gendering of vision through a comparative analysis of specific films directed by Josef von Sternberg and Alfred Hitchcock. She demonstrates that in Sternberg's films starring Marlene Dietrich—particularly *Morocco*—spectacle reigns supreme. Mulvey describes Sternberg's general approach to narrative as one concerned with "situation, not suspense, and cyclical rather than linear time, while plot complications revolve around misunderstanding rather than conflict." In film after film, Sternberg casts Dietrich in the role of a performer such as a cabaret singer, a character whose profession is to provide erotic spectacle. In this context, a liberal use of close-ups overwhelms the narrative with images of Dietrich—of her face, of her legs—presented "in direct erotic rapport with the spectator." At the same time, a consistently shallow depth of field focuses visual interest on the pictorial space of the frame, such that "the beauty of the woman as object and the screen space coalesce."[9]

By contrast, the narrative mode of address dominates the films of Hitchcock, where suspense is expertly generated and resolved through patterns of mystery, intrigue, investigation, recognition, and disclosure. Though female characters provide instances of erotic spectacle, in some films they also embody the narrative's primary enigma or mystery-to-be-solved. The title characters of *Marnie*, for example, or *Vertigo*'s Judy/Madeleine become motivating objects of curiosity not only for the film's male protagonists, but also for the cinematic spectator.

Throughout Hitchcock's films, and irrespective of a female character's status as central enigma, it is predominantly—though never exclusively—from the perspective of male characters that the gaze implicates the spectator. As Mulvey explains, "Hitchcock's skillful use of identification processes and liberal use of subjective camera from the point of view of the male protagonist draw the spectators deeply into his position."[10] *Rear Window* provides a most obvious example of this tendency in that, throughout the film, the spectator generally sees what Jeffries, the male protagonist (played by Jimmy Stewart), sees as he peers through his rear window. In Mulvey's words, the spectator is "absorbed into a voyeuristic situation within the screen scene and diegesis which parodies his own in the cinema." The spectator is thus positioned to share this situation with the protagonist who drives the narrative from within the film's fictional world.[11]

It is remarkable the degree to which Gounod's operatic characters Faust and Marguerite embody, if through quite different means, the visual dynamic outlined by Mulvey: "Woman as Image, Man as Bearer of the Look." Time and again throughout the opera, Faust gazes upon Marguerite who is presented as a spectacular vision to behold. The first appearance of the two characters together onstage provides an obvious example of the opera's gendering of spectacle and narrative. This takes place in the extended middle section of the first-act duo between Faust and Méphistophélès. It is the moment when Faust is about to sign away his soul. Méphistophélès presents him with a black parchment, but Faust balks, his hand trembles, and Méphistophélès responds to Faust's indecision:

> What will it take to persuade you?
> If it is youth that you desire,
> dare to gaze upon this![12]

With a wave of Méphistophélès's hand, the far wall of Faust's study, a painted curtain, rises to reveal Marguerite at her spinning wheel.[13] Faust looks, exclaims "O merveille!" and, after a general pause in the orchestra, the horns introduce "O nuit d'amour," one of the opera's most lyrical melodies to accompany Marguerite's spectacular first appearance.[14]

The visual apparatus of the theater is put into play to accentuate Marguerite's status as spectacle. She appears deeply upstage, removed from the main area of the stage by a sheer blue curtain.[15] From this enclosed space she poses mutely at her spinning wheel, in the manner more of a figure in a painting than a character in an opera. Marguerite's stage space, beyond the study and behind the transparent blue curtain, is also brightly illuminated. Faust and Méphistophélès remain downstage, left along with the audience in relative darkness. The spectator is thus positioned, through staging and focused lighting, to gaze along with the male characters upon the spectacle of Marguerite.[16]

Faust's role here is to look, and look he does until Marguerite disappears from view as magically as she appeared. While she is still onstage, Faust asks for the parchment and signs it. Méphistophélès offers his new conscript a celebratory drink. With goblet in hand, Faust toasts the vision of Marguerite, "to you, charming and adorable phantom," and proceeds to drink.[17] During all the acting out of this stage business, Faust gazes continuously upon the vision of Marguerite, his eyes never wavering from the spectacle. Even with the goblet at his lips, he does not turn away from the apparition.[18] Faust's visual engagement with the female character, here and across the opera, comes to channel the spectator's visual engagement with the opera. As I have argued elsewhere, there are few operas of the nineteenth-century repertory that so "neatly" combine spectacle and narrative through sexual difference.[19] In this opera, the gaze is male.

Was it this gendering of visual pleasure in Gounod's *Faust* that appealed to early filmmakers? I would say yes, but it was more than that, too. For the visual and narrative dynamic provided by the two main characters is generated by a third one, namely, Méphistophélès. From within the diegetic world of the opera, he conjures the female spectacle out of thin air. With a wave of his hand, she appears. If Faust can look, it is because Méphistophélès makes it so. Here and elsewhere throughout the opera, it is through his trickery that spectacle and narrative are combined. Méphistophélès, in other words, embodies a fantasy of mastery over the very technology—the stage, settings, lighting, and even the orchestra—that realizes the opera in performance. Méphistophélès's fictive control over the operatic apparatus was perhaps the *ultimate* pleasure that Gounod's *Faust* had to offer its spectators, and especially the cinematographers who made this opera their own.

## FAUST ON SCREEN: THE MOVE FROM SPECTACLE TO NARRATIVE

> [Narrative] continuity becomes not the attainment of an ideal of narrative efficiency as much as it is a "weapon" in a struggle over control, in which textual authority is the expression of authorship as product control and the ability to impose standards and standardization. . . . Continuity and the question of control can thus be seen to be linked, becoming crucial aspects of the story-telling process.[20]

For many historians of early film, the gradual emergence of a cinematic language based on narrative procedures must be understood in the context of cinema as an emerging industry based on various and shifting interests. The founders of French cinema were concerned above all with the new technology and its manufacture. Films themselves were seen merely as a promotional adjunct for selling cameras, projectors, and unexposed film stock. Although the Lumière company, for example, sent cameramen around the world, their short films capturing slices of local reality were used to publicize the company and its developing technologies. It was not until the nickelodeon era that film production—the making of movies—became a commercial enterprise in and of itself. Charles Pathé began construction on his first studio in 1902. The more cautious Gaumont waited until 1905 to invest in a studio. By the end of the decade, increasing numbers of production crews were churning out the single-reel genres demanded by an expanding international market. From manufacture of the apparatus and production of short films, the industry next moved in the direction of distribution of films, with Pathé abandoning films sales in 1907 to rent out entire weekly programs. At the same time, film companies also began extending their concerns to the actual sites of exhibition. The Omnia-Pathé, Paris's first movie palace, opened its doors on December 15th, 1906. By midsummer of the next year, there existed over fifty newly constructed or converted movie houses in Paris. The French press declared 1907 "the year of the cinema."[21]

Indeed, 1907 was something of a watershed year. In the United States, the nickelodeon market had reached a saturation point, with independently operated storefront theaters attracting audiences in small towns and urban neighborhoods across the country.[22] French production companies provided much of the footage shown during this time; France led the United States in production and international distribution of films until about 1911.[23] The film genres increasingly in demand, from about 1907 onwards, were single-reel story films rather than actualities (films of "real life"). By 1907, market forces were in place and cinema was becoming a much different object than it had been ten years earlier.[24] As a commodity, cinema was no longer the technological apparatus. From apparatus to the individual reel of film and eventually the weekly program, it had now become a cinematic experience the industry offered for sale directly to the spectator.

For Tom Gunning, the true narrativization of cinema occurred with the commodification of a relatively standardized film experience, during the period from 1907 to about 1913. Before this time, films were not dominated by the narrative impulse that later asserted its sway over the medium. They were presented to their audiences as spectacle rather than narrative, and experienced in terms of "exhibitionist confrontation rather than diegetic absorption."[25] Miriam Hansen argues that:

> . . . early films adopted a particular aesthetics of display, of showmanship, defined by the goal of assaulting viewers with sensational, supernatural, scientific, sentimental, or otherwise stimulating sights as opposed to enveloping them into the illusion of a fictional narrative.[26]

Early cinema differed not only in terms of genre and style but, above all, in terms of the way it engaged its viewers.

Gunning stresses that "every change in film history implies a change in its address to the spectator, and each period constructs its spectator in a new way."[27] By his account, the move from spectacle to narrative signals a paradigmatic shift, and this "transformation of filmic discourse . . . bound cinematic signifiers to the narration of stories and the creation of a self-enclosed diegetic universe."[28] Only with the narrativation of cinema were spectators invited to enter the fictional fantasy worlds of the films themselves. Although spectators generally experience films as an interweaving of spectacle and narrative—and there is no doubt that even the earliest actualities and trick films display a narrative component—the relative move from spectacle toward narrative is perhaps the most important aspect of a trend toward more imaginary relations between the spectator and the screen. These relations relied less and less on local contexts as the cinematic experience became more standardized, and at the same time, more fully interiorized.[29]

It is striking that there occurred a substantial increase in the number of films based on operas during this crucial period in the history of cinema. Operatic adaptations were especially popular from 1908 through 1910. Of the more than 150 opera-related titles produced before 1926, nearly half were released during these years.[30] The other striking fact that emerges from an initial investigation of cinematic titles is the number of films based on Gounod's *Faust:* roughly thirty. *Faust* indeed seems to have been the first opera adapted for the screen. In 1897, Lumières produced two short scenes from the first act of the opera. These two shorts are quite anomalous within the context of the hundreds of actualities that comprise Lumière's output.[31] Short travel films made up the bulk of Lumière's production, with more shots of West African dancers than any other single subject. Why French opera amidst all of this African dancing?

The two operatic scenes produced by Lumières were two opportunities Gounod's opera offered for cinematic tricks. The first was the vision of Marguerite conjured for Faust by Mephistophélès, the second Faust's transformation from shriveled up old scholar to vibrant youth. Both are transformation scenes, a relatively popular genre in early cinema.[32]

Although the Lumière company produced very few trick scenes, other filmmakers devoted more energy to this genre. Several of them produced films based on specific stage tricks from Gounod's opera.[33] These are all very short films, generally a couple of minutes in duration, and display little if any sense of narrative. These short, isolated scenes functioned to display technological tricks, and are excellent examples of cinema's early spectacle-orientated mode of address.

Georges Méliès's 1904 *Faust et Marguerite* is a much more elaborate adaptation of Gounod's *Faust.* With the exception of his *Le Royaume des fées* of the previous year, *Faust et Marguerite* was in fact Méliès's most ambitious film to date.[34] Roughly twenty minutes in duration—a long film for the time—*Faust et Marguerite* relates the entire story of the opera, with few departures from the series of events as they occur in the Gounod.

Méliès's approach to cinema is best understood in terms of his involvement with stage magic. Many of his films were first exhibited at the Robert Houdin, a small magic theater he had owned since the 1880s. Like his magic shows of which they were a part, Méliès's films were intended to dazzle his audience with spectacular visual effects. By his own account, the story of a film functioned only to provide a context for the all-important tricks:

> As for the scenario, the "fable," or "tale," I only consider it at the end. I can state that the scenario constructed in this manner has no importance, since I

use it merely as a pretext for the "stage effects," the "tricks," or for a nicely arranged tableau.[35]

Most of Méliès's films bear this out. For example, in *L'Enchanteur Alcofrisbas* of 1903, Méliès stages, in under four minutes, many more tricks than in the twenty minutes of *Faust et Marguerite*.[36] Even the few films longer in duration than *Faust*, such as *Le Royaume des fées* (1903) or *Les quatre cent farces du diable* (1906), are saturated with special effects that are presented in a narrative style amazingly phantasmagoric. In the context of Méliès's general output, *Faust et Marguerite* displays a high level of narrative control, with special effects serving the story, rather than the other way around.[37] This seems to be a direct result of the extent to which Méliès relied on the opera as a model for his film.

Several aspects of Méliès's production are indebted to its operatic model. Most obvious is the "nicely arranged tableaux" of the film. Sets and costumes, as well as the choreography and blocking of the actors were all based on those of the Paris Opéra.[38] *Faust et Marguerite* is presented as a series of twenty tableaux that each function, in effect, as operatic numbers. One might suggest that the film also creates a spectator that is perhaps as much operatic as cinematic. Méliès's exceptionally deep staging in this film, intended to emphasize the elaborate sets, tends to dwarf the characters, who generally occupy little more than a third of the screen's height. Although unusual from a cinematic standpoint, the effect is not unlike that of an operatic performance. The use of an immobile camera moreover positions the spectator to experience the action on the screen as though from a seat in an opera house, as a *l'homme d'orchestre*. The camera, and therefore the spectator, remain positioned in the same fashion from tableau to tableau.[39] Méliès's reliance on a specifically operatic system of tableaux contributes to the exceptionally static quality of this film, a characteristic frequently pointed out by critics.[40]

At the same time, *Faust et Marguerite* represents a step for Méliès in a direction toward clarity of narrative organization and continuity. The opera's series of tableaux offered Méliès a relatively clear-cut sequence of events to follow.[41] But just as important as the underlying temporal linearity of the story is the way in which the *mise-en-scène* of Gounod's *Faust* provides a specific model for negotiating spectacle and narrative—as modes of address—within the space of the tableau. We encounter in *Faust et Marguerite* a demarcation between foreground and background space that takes on more and more significance from tableau to tableau. As in Gounod's opera, the background (upstage) comes to be identified with feminized spectacle, the foreground (downstage) with the more masculine narrative mode of engagement from which the male characters gaze along with the spectators.[42]

Throughout the film, Marguerite tends to appear in the background, where she is presented as a spectacle offered by Méphistophélès to Faust and the audience. It is only after she has been conquered by Faust and cursed by her brother that Marguerite occupies foregrounded space, and then only for the church and prison scenes. After her death, she is restored to the background, in a tableau of angels and saints. (Méliès's face appears as the second member of the Holy Trinity!) Her lifeless body, however, remains in the foreground space of the screen. Only when mad or dead does she occupy the space of the film's narrative mode of engagement.[43] The effect of this positioning is most obvious in the opening sequence: the vision of Marguerite appears within the frame of a window that becomes, with her appearance, a little tableau within the tableau. In hand-tinted prints of the film, Marguerite appears in color, though framed in black and white within her small, screen-like setting.

As in the opera, Méphistophélès is the producer of this image. Judith Mayne has remarked on the presence in many early films of what she calls a "primitive narrator." Particularly in cinema of the first decade or so of the century, narrative functions were often fulfilled from within the fiction of the film by characters "who appear to direct, mediate, or otherwise act out the visual pleasures of the cinematic scene":

> . . . they are neither omniscient narrators nor the absolute agents of "primitive" narration—i.e., they are objects of the camera's view at the same time that they act out the emerging visual and narrative capacities of the film medium.[44]

These characters prefigured the invisible, interiorized narrator of later cinematic narrative. Mayne points to the conjuror or magician as the most obvious example of a "primitive narrator"—a type of character that was in fact a favorite of Méliès, who often played the magician in his own films.[45]

In *Faust et Marguerite*, Méliès himself plays Méphistophélès, the primitive narrator who controls the space of the screen to conjure Marguerite as a spectacular special effect. This film, following the example of the opera, effectively creates for the spectator a visual and narrative space from which to gaze, in classic fashion, upon the spectacle of femininity. The model provided by Gounod's *Faust* for negotiating the competing claims of spectacle ("look *at* me") and narrative ("look *with* me") operated along an axis of sexual difference. Méliès indeed seems to have been the earliest filmaker so profoundly and so specifically influenced by the lyric stage. And, according to Mayne and others, his are among the earliest films "to confirm the widely held claim that the cinematic apparatus, emergent or otherwise, is made to the measure of male desire."[46]

## MÉPHISTOPHÉLÈS AFTER MÉLIÈS

Though one of the earliest operatic adaptations, Méliès's *Faust et Marguerite* was also one of the most famous, and the most thoroughly documented of the adaptations of Gounod's opera. Less well-known are the opera films directed between 1900 and 1907 by Alice Guy for the Gaumont company.[47] Like Edison, the Gaumonts were involved with sound reproduction before they turned to cinema,

and Guy's operatic adaptations were part of the chronophone series of films, produced and exhibited with synchronized sound.[48] Guy's 1907 production of *Faust*
was the last and most complete of her operatic adaptations. It consisted of twen-
ty-two operatic scenes, each short enough to have had the appropriate music
recorded on a wax cylinder. Longer operatic numbers, such as the quartet in the
garden, were produced in more than one scene. The chronophones, also called
*phonoscènes*, were very popular in France until World War I.[49] Though none of the
prints from this series have survived, the format of these films, autonomous
scenes presenting musical "numbers," implies an approach, like that of Méliès,
based on the operatic tableau for narrative and visual organization.[50]

From 1907, the year of Guy's adaptation of *Faust*, to 1910, there sprang
up several French production companies specializing in the genres of the literary, dramatic, and operatic adaptation.[51] These new companies enlisted the
expertise of established artists to design, direct, and act in their consciously
"artistic" productions.[52] Films based on *Faust* were produced within this relatively specialized context. Film d'Art's *Faust* (1910), directed by Henri
Andreani, is perhaps the most freely adapted of the French productions.
Although Georges Sadoul claims Andreani was inspired more by Gounod than
Goethe, this seems to be the only French adaptation to incorporate scenes from
the Goethe play that do not appear in the opera. The filming of this production
took place somewhere along the Côte d'Azur, and the specific scenes chosen from
the play all take place out of doors, affording Andreani additional opportunities
to take advantage of the beauty of the countryside, a major component of
Andreani's *mise-en-scène* in this film.[53] Although many scenes were shot out of
doors, rather than in a studio, the film still displays an organization indebted to
the tableau, with relatively deep staging, an immobile camera, and little, if any,
crosscutting within each scene.

Unlike the *Faust* of Film d'Art, the version produced by the Cines/Eclair
company was marketed, at least in the United States, specifically as an operatic
adaptation.[54] The opening title informs us that this is *Faust*, an "opera by Charles
Gounod," and some of the intertitles within the film consist of the titles of specific arias from the opera.[55] Although it announces to its audience the use of
Gounod's opera as its model, this version, directed by Enrico Guazoni, represents
a significant departure from the tableau aesthetic that informs so many early
operatic adaptations. There are examples of crosscutting, close-ups, point-of-
view shots, some with peepholes, a narratively significant fade to black, and even
an example of parallel editing, all cinematic operations associated with the
"emerging" classic mode of narration.

The film begins within a point-of-view shot. The aging Faust peers out the
window of his study and spots a couple on the street below, walking arm-in-arm.
The film cuts to a peephole shot of the couple, presented as though peered at
through a telescope.[56] The spectator is thus invited, fairly obviously, to share
Faust's point of view. Similar peephole shots occur throughout the film, in scenes

devoted to the character of Marguerite. Most occur in the garden, which in this film becomes a distinctly feminine domain.[57] Several times Faust spots Marguerite amongst the trees and bushes. In each case, his look precipitates a cut to Marguerite, who is then presented through a peephole. In one case, Marguerite turns to the camera, obviously flattered. In all cases, she gently rebuffs Faust's advances. The one example of parallel editing in this film also occurs in the garden, during the quartet. Here the camera cuts back and forth between the two couples, with short cuts to the comic antics of Marthe and Méphistophélès contributing an element of suspense to Faust's more serious attempts at lovemaking. The scene eventually culminates in a first kiss between Faust and Marguerite. Through means that are more obviously cinematic than those utilized by Méliès, Guazoni achieves very similar ends in this film. Through the parallel editing of the quartet sequence, but even more so through the point-of-view shots that occur over the course of the entire film, the camera mediates the visual pleasure of the spectator by effectively narrativizing Marguerite as a spectacle experienced from the viewpoint of Faust. Here Guazoni's camera work achieves that which Méliès's Méphistophélès, following his operatic counterpart from the Gounod, accomplished in *Faust et Marguerite*.

Production in France of operatic adaptations dropped off by late 1912, and after the war there seems to have been much less interest in opera for the screen.[58] Undoubtedly, silent film—particularly during its period of transformation from engagement based on spectacle to narrative procedures—is especially marked from the so-called classic cinema by its interest in and use of opera. As it was negotiating that transformation from spectacle to narrative—while, in Tom Gunning's words, "cinema's very mutability and fragmented nature (into many practices and unstable hierarchies of importance)" still contrasted with the narrative control that would come to characterize the Hollywood model[59]—cinema found a perhaps more flexible model in opera. That Gounod's *Faust* provided the specific operatic model most frequently employed suggests that the eventual narrativization of cinema during these years was fueled by a fantasy of mastery and control that was realized, at least in part, through sexual difference.

Both Tom Gunning and Miriam Hansen have drawn parallels between early cinema and late cinema. For Hansen:

> . . . both periods are characterized by a profound transformation of the relations of cultural representation and reception and by a measure of instability that makes the intervening decades look relatively stable by contrast, for they are anchored in and centered by the classical system. Both stages of media culture vary from the classical norm of controlling reception through a strong diegetic effect, ensured by particular textual strategies and a suppression of the exhibition context. By contrast, preclassical and postclassical forms of spectatorship give the viewer a greater leeway, for better or for worse, in interacting with the film—a greater awareness of exhibition and cultural intertexts. Both early modern and postmodern media publics draw on the *periphery* . . .[60]

She further characterizes the years between early and late cinema as "a historical interlude, a deep-freeze perhaps." As many of the essays in this volume suggest, we find an accelerated interest in opera for the screen beginning in the mid-to-late 1970s, during the period inaugurating media culture's post-classical meltdown. Opera, it seems, leads both into and out of the frozen interlude of classic cinema.

NOTES

1. Herbert Lindenberger, *Opera: Or, the Extravagant Art* (Ithaca and London: Cornell University Press, 1984), 231–32.

2. Laura Mulvey, "Visual Pleasure and Narrative Cinema," *Screen* 16 (Autumn 1975). Reprinted in, among many other places, *The Sexual Subject: A Screen Reader in Sexuality* (London and New York: Routledge, 1992), 27. Subsequent citations will refer to page numbers of this reprint.

3. Laura Mulvey, "Visual Pleasure," 26.

4. See Stephen Heath's discussion of these three looks in his *Questions of Cinema,* (Bloomington and Indianapolis: Indiana University Press, 1981), 119ff.

5. Patricia Mellencamp, "Spectacle and Spectator: Looking Through the American Musical Comedy," *Ciné-Tracts* 1 (summer, 1977): 29.

6. Paul Willemen, "Letter to John," in Mulvey's *The Sexual Subject*, 182.

7. Judith Mayne, *The Woman at the Keyhole: Feminism and Women's Cinema*, (Bloomington and Indianapolis: Indiana University Press, 1990), 36.

8. Laura Mulvey, "Visual Pleasure," 26.

9. Ibid., 30.

10. Ibid., 31.

11. Ibid. For more detailed readings of *Rear Window* that explore issues raised but not addressed by Mulvey's analysis see: Tania Modleski, *The Women Who Knew Too Much: Hitchcock and Feminist Theory* (New York and London: Methuen, 1988), 73–85; and Jeanne Allen, "Looking through 'Rear Window': Hitchcock's Traps and Lures of Heterosexual Romance," in *Female Spectators: Looking at Film and Television*, edited by E. Deidre Pribram (London and New York: Verso, 1988), 12–30.

12. Que faut-il pour te décider?
   La jeunesse t'appelle;
   ôse la regarder!

13. As indicated in the *livret de mise-en-scène*, when Méphistophélès waves his hand, "le rideau F se lève doucement et laisse voir Marguerite assise sur la chaise D près de son rouet et filant." Note that "F" is a special curtain a "rideau représentant le fond du cabinet de Faust. Ce rideau est en harmonie avec la peinture du cabinet; il doit être équipé pour monter et descendre à volonté pour la vision." See the staging manual for the opera printed in *The Original Staging Manuals for Twelve Parisian Operatic Premières*, edited by H. Robert Cohen and Marie-Odile Gigou (Stuyvesant, New York: Pendragon Press, 1990), 101–35. It should be noted, however, that though Cohen claims the manual he reproduces was used during the work's pre-

mière, this is not the case. This manual contains cues for the later-added recitative, which was not performed in productions staged by the company of the Théâtre Lyrique until September 1866. The version of the opera we find in the manual also places Marguerite's church scene at the end of the fourth act, a practice that began only after the 1862 revival of the work. The Brussels première of *Faust* (February 1861) was also given with spoken dialogue, although recitative was employed the following year. And neither was Cohen's manual used at the Opéra's première because it does not contain the ballet that was a standard feature of all performances there. On information regarding the various versions of the opera, see Fritz Oeser's problematic edition of the work (Kassel: Alkor-Edition, 1992), 354ff., and also Steven Huebner, *The Operas of Charles Gounod* (Oxford: Clarendon Press, 1990), 127–32. It is likely that the particular document Cohen provides in his edition was used for French performances outside of Paris and that it reflects a performance tradition established in Paris only after 1866.

14. The melody associated with the apparition of Marguerite recurs several times over the course of the opera. In the third act it constitutes the lyrical culmination of the first section of her love duet with Faust, where he sings the melody to the words "ô nuit d'amour." In the prison scene of the last act it recurs to underscore Marguerite's hallucinatory reminiscence of the duet in the garden. Several times over, then, this melody represents the relationship Faust and Marguerite share. But the relationship is unbalanced, defined by Faust's gaze and Marguerite as that which he gazes upon.

15. A "rideau de gaze bleue," as indicated in the staging manual.

16. From the beginning of the apparition, when Méphistophélès waves his hand, the stage is to be lit quite dimly, "Nuit partout." Only Marguerite's area receives bright light: "Éclairer très-fort le fond où se trouve Marguerite." *The Original Staging Manuals*, 103.

17. "A toi, fantôme adorable et charmant."

18. The staging manual indicates that from the beginning of the apparition "Faust regardant toujours l'apparition." Even after speaking the words "Fantôme adorable et charmant," Faust "vide la coupe, puis sans quitter Marguerite de l'oeil, il laisse tomber la main qui tient la coupe; Méphistopélès la lui prend et la pose sur la table: sur cette dernière réplique, la vision disparait." Ibid, 104.

19. See Chapter 4 of my dissertation, *Spectacle and Enchantment: Envisioning Opera in Late Nineteenth-Century Paris* (Ph.D. diss., University of Pennsylvania, 2000), 354ff.

20. Thomas Elsaesser, ed., *Early Cinema: Space—Frame—Narrative* (London: BFI Publishing, 1990), 305.

21. See Richard Abel, *The Ciné Goes to Town: French Cinema, 1896–1914* (Berkeley, Los Angeles and London: University of California Press, 1994), 25–32.

22. Charles Musser, "The Nickelodeon Era Begins: Establishing the Framework for Hollywoods' Mode of Representation," in Thomas Elsaesser, ed., *Early Cinema*, 261.

23. The firm of Pathé alone produced eight hundred new film titles in 1907. Abel, *The Ciné Goes to Town*, 34.

24. Abel points out another factor that contributed, especially in France, to cinema's evolving status at this time. Under French law cinema was initially classified as a *spectacle de curiosité*, and as such subject to local censorship. However, in 1906, the French government put an end to censorship restrictions against the theater, and, according to Abel, this provoked efforts to upgrade the status of film to the level of legitimate theater. As he states it, "the consequences of this move to align the cinema with the theater were profound—the theater analogy, at the level of both commercial enterprise and critical discourse, became more deeply engrained in France than anywhere else," lending to the French cinema "a high degree of historical specificity." Richard Abel, *The Ciné Goes to Town*, xiv.

25. "The Cinema of Attractions: Early Film, Its Spectator, and the Avant-Garde," *Wide Angle* 8, no. 3/4 (fall 1986), rpt. in Elsaesser, *Early Cinema*, 59–60. And see as well Gunning's "An Aesthetic of Astonishment: Early Film and the (In)Credulous Spectator," *Art and Text* 34 (spring 1989), rpt. in Linda Williams, ed., *Viewing Positions: Ways of Seeing Film*, (New Brunswick: Rutgers University Press, 1994), 114–33.

26. Miriam Hansen, "Early Cinema, Late Cinema: Transformations of the Public Sphere," in Thomas Elsaesser, ed., *Early Cinema*, 137.

27. Gunning, "The Cinema of Attractions," 61.

28. Ibid., 60.

29. Linda Williams has successfully argued that even Muybridge's physiological studies of human locomotion effectively narrativize the human body, particularly the female body. See her "Film Body: An Implantation of Perversions," *Ciné-tracts* 3, no. 4 (winter 1981): 19–35.

30. Numbers can of course be deceiving, especially in the context of early films, the vast majority of which did not survive. But based on the available filmographies, I can speculate that in France overall film production picked up dramatically in 1907, but then seems to have stabilized and even declined a bit over the years leading up to World War I. The rise in the number of operatic films seems to have been more localized around 1909 and 1910—with a definite spike during those years.

31. See Rittaud-Hutinet, *August et Louis Lumière: Les 1000 premièrs films* (Paris: P. Sers, 1990). Entries for the *Faust* scenes appear on page 197.

32. On the transformation scene, see Abel, *The Ciné Goes to Town*, 61ff.

33. Méliès's *Faust et Marguerite* (1897), Smith's *Faust and Mephistopheles* (1898), Méliès's *Damnation de Faust* (1898), Porter's *Faust and Marguerite* (1900), and presumably Alice Guy Blaché's *Faust et Mephistopélès* (1903). Some of the later titles are blow-by-blow copies of the earlier ones. The earliest filmakers seem to have had no qualms about copying the work of their competitors. This relates to the lack of authorial investment in films during the first years of cinema.

34. Earlier films of similar length include Méliès's *L'Affaire Dreyfus* (240 meters) and *Cendrillon* (120 meters), both from 1899; *Barbe-bleue* (210 meters), 1901; and *Le*

*Voyage dans la lune* (260 meters), 1902. *Faust et Marguerite* was 270 meters. Note that all of these, with the exception of the remarkable film on the Dreyfus affair, were based on operas or operettas. *Le Royaume des fées* (335 meters) of 1903 was based on a popular pantomime of the late nineteenth century, *Biche au bois*. According to John Frazer, there was a musical score available to accompany this film, as well as all of the films based on operas and operettas. See his *Artificially Arranged Scenes: The Films of Georges Méliès* (Boston: G. H. Hall, 1979), 118.

35. Georges Méliès, "Importance du scenario," in Georges Sadoul, *Georges Méliès* (Paris: Editions Seghers, 1961), 118, as translated and quoted in Gunning, "Cinema of Attractions," 57.

36. This short film begins in a deep underground cave where the magician Alcofrisbas, one of Méliès's favorite characters, prepares for a series of revelations for the benefit of a young dandy dressed in Renaissance costume. The conjurer holds a footed vase in the air in front of the dark recess of the cave. A flame sprouts from the vase, turning into the head and torso of a young woman. In another transformation, a larger vase is turned into a standing woman. The woman is mesmerized by Alcofrisbas and her rigid body is suspended over two sawhorses. Assistants place a flaming brazier beneath her. As the fire is fanned by a bellows, the woman rises into the air. The visions that follow include a cascade of water, three nymphs gesticulating in midair and a Saint Catherine's wheel. The mirage accomplished, the magician thumbs his nose at the young man and disappears in a puff of smoke. The young man, surrounded by five shrouded, threatening phantoms, flees for his life. See Frazer, *Artificially Arranged Scenes*, 128.

37. As Abel remarks, "despite its dependence on a series of autonomous tableaux, with whatever kind of musical and verbal support, this Méliès films clearly is concerned with foregrounding its story. The best evidence for this is that Mephistophélès's tricks, which are few and far between, all serve Faust's cause and advance his story." Abel, *The Ciné Goes to Town*, 76.

38. Méliès in fact enlisted dancers from the corps de ballet of the Paris Opéra to perform the Walpurgisnacht scene.

39. Although filmmakers of this era did not practice anything like the rapid MTV-style editing we see today, Méliès rarely produced a film with such long shots consistently filmed from the same position.

40. See, for example, Frazer, *Artificially Arranged Scenes*, 140.

41. The film departs from the Gounod mostly through the absence of several of the opera's arias, as well as the quartet in the garden. The arias that are retained are those of Mephistophélès, his rondo at the tavern, and the serenade in which he accompanies himself with mandolin, both examples of stage music, which translate easily to film. Other arias that are referred to include important stage action: Siebel's withering flower aria and Marguerite's jewel song. It is the more introspective, purely lyrical cavatines of Valentine and Faust, as well as Seibel's Act IV Romance that were not included by Méliès. The omission of the quartet may have had to do with its comic character. Méliès generally exhibits a lively sense of humor in his films, and

there are some veiled comic references to be found in *Faust et Marguerite*. The over-all tone of this film, however, is really quite serious—perhaps related to the perception of its subject as "high art." It seems as though Méliès very consciously avoided his habitually comic approach, and this may explain the omission of the quartet in the garden.

42. Documents relating to the *mise-en-scène* of the opera clearly demonstrate that Méliès use of space followed that of the opera quite faithfully.

43. Yet another similar articulation of gendered space occurs in the Walpurgisnacht sequence, where Mephistophélès, foregrounded, conjures up, from background space, history's queens and courtesans.

44. Judith Mayne, *The Woman at the Keyhole*, 138.

45. Mayne cites two such films that chronologically flank *Faust et Marguerite*: "In *Le Mélomane* (*The Melomaniac* [1903]), Méliès appears as a magical music teacher who repeatedly takes off his head and throws it on a staff to represent musical notes; in *Les Cartes vivantes* (*The Living Playing Cards* [1905]), Méliès portrays a magician who transforms playing cards into living human beings. Here, as in other of his films, Méliès looks directly at the camera, accentuating his role as solicitor of the audience's attention." Mayne, *The Woman at the Keyhole*, 138.

46. Mayne, *The Woman at the Keyhole*, 160.

47. Guy was actually one of Gaumont's secretaries.

48. There were also several post-war productions that utilized different types of more or less synchronous sound. These were generally fairly short single reel films, featuring arias or duets performed by prominent opera stars. A 1915 Biophone production, for example, presents Siegfrid Arnoldson and John Sembach singing arias from *Faust*. In 1922 Gaumont, under its English label Master, produced a series of single-reel films—"Tense Moments from Opera"—that followed a similar format. Along with *Faust*, there were "Tense Moments" from *Carmen, Don Giovanni, Marthe, Lucia di Lammermoor, Trovatore*, and *Fra Diavolo*.

49. David Robinson, *Music of the Shadows: The Use of Musical Accompaniment with Silent Films, 1896–1936* (Pordenone: Giornate del cinema muto, 1990), 17. There was also a 1911, internationally released version of 22 scenes from *Faust*, accompanied by 22 sound discs of some sort. This may have been a re-release of Guy's production, though it seems to have been directed by David Barnett rather than Guy.

50. Guy had modeled some of her earlier, less elaborate operatic scenes on those of Méliès. And like Méliès, Guy was noted for a silmilar use of ballet in many of her films. Both she and Méliès enlisted members of the corps de ballet of the Paris Opéra for their cinematic dancing scenes.

51. Film d'Art, the more successful Société cinématographique des auteurs et gens de lettres (SCAGL), Eclair's Association des compositeurs et des auteurs dar-matiques (ACAD) series, Gaumont's *Grands Films Artistiques*, Eclipse's *Série d'Art*, and also the *Séries d'Art Pathé-Frères* are the most noted of these specialized companies.

52. For example, Henri Desfontaines, a former actor for Antoine at the Odéon assumed direction in 1908 of Radios, a subsidiary of Eclipse. Emile Chautard, another former actor from the Odéon, was supervising production for Eclair's ACAD by sometime in 1909. Camille Saint-Saëns was involved in one of the first projects of Film d'Art, a new company financed in part by Pathé. He composed an original musical score for their *L'Assassinat du Duc de Guise,* a film directed by Charles le Bargy of the Comédie-Française, and premiered in 1908. A few months before the production of *L'Assassinat,* Michel Carré, son of one of the librettists of Gounod's *Faust,* had collaborated with the same company on a filmed version of his play *The Prodigal Son.* He would later join the more successful SCAGL, another Pathé subsidiary that seems to have made better use of Carré's connections to both the theater and opera. See Abel, *The Ciné Goes to Town,* 36–40.

53. These would include Marguerite praying to a shrine of the *Mater dolorosa* at the edge of town and the horseride of Méphistoélès and Faust preceding the dungeon scene. Sadoul also remarks on the Walpurgisnacht scene (not included in the fragmentary print I viewed), which takes place not within the palace of Méphistophélès, but rather among the aloe and palms of Andreani's rented villa. See Georges Sadoul, *Histoire Générale du Cinéma* (Paris: Denoël, 1973), VIII: 49–50.

54. This strategy may have been in response to Edison's recently launched series on "Grand Opera" subjects, the first of which was a *Faust,* directed by Edwin Porter, and released on Christmas Eve, 1909.

55. For example, "(Air – 'Clear the way for the Calf of Gold.')"; and "(Air – 'Jewel Song')." (Note that the print held by the Library of Congress is actually catalogued with Charles Gounod as the director of the film!) It is possible that, in some theaters, live performances of these arias may have been interpolated in the exhibition of the film.

56. The peephole shot is also used in Emile Cohl's 1910 animated version of Gounod's *Faust.* Here puppets act out the story of the opera amidst sets that reproduce in miniature those of the opera. The peephole shot occurs with the only intertitle, encircling Faust and Marguerite and providing room for the words "laisse moi, laisse moi, contempler ta frimousse." This is a play on the "laisse moi contempler ta visage" of the opera's love duet—a melody that recurs throughout the opera. ("Frimousse" translates as sweet little face, and using it is sort of like calling someone a cute little cabbage.)

57. There is of course a similar operatic practice of establishing spaces on stage, sometimes gardens, sometimes private interiors, that are marked as feminine and distinct from the more public spaces depicted in non-feminine scenes.

58. This is not to say that opera ceased to have any impact on film. Ben Brewster has shown that a specifically French impulse toward the deep staging and slow cutting we find in the early operatic adaptations continues well into the twentieth century. This style distinguishes French cinema in general from the more shallow staging and quicker cutting of the American style. Méliès *Faust et Marguerite,* indebted as it is to the operatic tableau, is often cited as a specific precursor to this French ten-

dency. For example, Brewster remarks that when Méliès provides a deep stage it is "usually for the presentation of a ballet (e.g. *La Damnation du Docteur Faust*, Tableau no. 16 [1904]). The principal aim is thus a spectacular rather than a dramatic one." Ben Brewster, "Deep Staging in French Films 1900–1914," in *Early Cinema*, 46.

59. Tom Gunning, "Enigmas, Understanding, and Further Questions: Early Cinema Research in Its Second Decade since Brighton," *Persistence of Vision* 9 (1991): 6; as quoted in Hansen, "Early Cinema, Late Cinema," 139.

60. Hansen, "Early Cinema, Late Cinema," 149.

# 2
# "There Ain't No Sanity Claus!"
## The Marx Brothers at the Opera

### Michal Grover-Friedlander

*A* *Night at the Opera* is one of, if not *the* best Marx Brothers' film, arguably because the operatic world is their natural element. The absurd medium of opera is not a far cry from the Marx Brothers' ludicrous being in the world. An excessive medium such as opera, in which words are sung performances, is akin to the Marx Brothers' distrust of meaning. Opera sides with, not against, the Marx Brothers' reinvention of the world. In *A Night at the Opera,* Groucho's, Chico's, and Harpo's act piles their insanity on top of that of opera:

*Groucho*: What's his name?

*Chico*: What do you care? I can't pronounce it. What do you want with him?

*Groucho*: I want to sign him up for the New York Opera Company. Do you know that America is waiting to hear him sing?

*Chico*: Well, he can sing loud, but he can't sing that loud.

*Groucho*: Well, I think I can get America to meet him halfway . . . But, any how, we're all set now, aren't we? Now, just you put your name right down there and then the deal is—is—uh—legal.

*Chico*: I forgot to tell you. I can't write.

*Groucho*: Well, that's all right. There's no ink in the pen, anyhow. But listen, it's a contract, isn't it?

*Chico*: Oh sure. Hey wait—wait! What does this say here? This thing here?

*Groucho*: Oh, that? Oh, that's just the usual clause. That's in every contract. That just says—uh—if any of the parties participating in this contract is shown not to be in their right mind, the entire agreement is automatically nullified.

*Chico*: Well, I don't know.

*Groucho*: It's all right. That's in every contract. That's what they call a sanity clause.

*Chico*: Ah, you fool wit me. There ain't no Sanity Claus!

*A Night at the Opera* is not the only film in which the Marx Brothers explicitly make reference to the world of opera. In *Coconuts* (1929), Harpo destroys a cash register to the music of the *Anvil Chorus* from Verdi's *Il Trovatore*. In that opera, the *Anvil Chorus* expresses the gypsies' joy at their hammering away at work. Harpo takes the chorus' text literally: the gypsies' hammering music accompanies the hammering of the cash register in the film. The piece is heard again in *Animal Crackers* (1930) where Chico plays it on the piano while Harpo accompanies him on horseshoes. In *Monkey Business* (1931), Groucho mocks an interview with a diva, and Harpo later shuts his ears while accompanying her singing. In the final scene of *Duck Soup* (1933), the Marx Brothers throw apples at Margaret Dumont's operatic rendering of Freedonia's national anthem. In *At the Circus* (1939), a short fragment from Verdi's *Aida* is heard as Margaret Dumont enters a gala dinner, followed by her attempt to give a speech. Covering her voice, a trumpeting sound of an elephant fills the room. It is a circus elephant that follows and replaces the music of *Aida*. Shortly after, an orchestra on a floating platform plays Wagner's overture to *The Flying Dutchman* as it drifts out to sea, the audience left behind on shore to enjoy the circus show that replaces the concert. In the Marx Brothers' world, "The Flying Dutchman" might well be the name of a performer on a flying trapeze in the circus. A trapeze act in fact takes place as the operatic ship sails on.[1]

Glenn Mitchell expresses the view prevalent among scholars of the relationship of the Marx Brothers to opera: "It is strange to think of the robust Marx Brothers *constantly working in parallel* with that highbrow institution, opera. *A Night at the Opera* deliberately uses it to contrast their wild spirits. . . ."[2] I would argue that opera is an essential part of their world of associations, and only superficially competes with their own musicality. Moreover, in opposition to Glenn Mitchell's view, I believe that the parody of opera in the Marx Brothers' films functions differently from their parodies of other institutions such as "the university," "democracy," "high society," serious film genres, and so on.[3] The world of opera serves to highlight—not contradict—aspects of their style, and it is for this reason that *A Night at the Opera* is unique. Their performance style is, in many ways, *analogous* to the relationship between voice and text in opera, and to opera's exaggerated and absurd constituents. The Marx Brothers's anarchism, far from merely parodying opera, inherits some of its central features.

SILENT OPERA

I would like to argue for more: the Marx Brothers' film *A Night at the Opera* is an attempt not only to think through the inheritence of opera but to think through the way *silent film* inherited opera, or to think through the transition from silent film to sound by thematizing the relation between film and opera.

Early film was marked by a special attraction to the medium of opera. One way that silent film dealt with the absence of the human voice was through appeal to the operatic voice. The appearance of the extravagant voice of opera in the context of the silent human voice might seem paradoxical, yet, as suggested by Richard Evidon, opera proliferated in early film.[4] Films of entire operas were produced, in which plot and operatic gestures were kept intact, and at times even the unrealistic settings of opera were transported into the new medium. Background music was drawn either from the opera, a number of different operas, totally unrelated music, or newly composed music.[5] The impression created was that although voices were "seen" rather than heard, the opera-turned-film was sensical and comprehensible. Opera became an example of independence from language. By virtue of the very choice to show images of voiceless opera, silent films of opera expressed a belief in the power of film to offer new ways of understanding the silence and speechlessness of the human voice.

Early cinema questioned its distance from opera not only in terms of its relation to the voice of opera, but also in relation to operatic plots. Charlie Chaplin's *A Burlesque on Carmen* (1916), for example, parodies the very act of translating an operatic plot into film. Chaplin's short film refers to Cecil B. DeMille's silent film *Carmen* (1915) featuring the famous prima donna Geraldine Farrar. In Chaplin's film, the murder of Carmen is followed by a scene in which Chaplin—cast in Don Jose's role—mimics an operatically overdramatic gesture of death. Having killed himself (Chaplin's addition to the opera's plot), he arranges and rearranges his collapse over Carmen's body in order to expose the artificiality of both deaths. Carmen and Don Jose then rise, revived and united in a big smile.[6] Chaplin's film in this way deals with two competing forms of artificiality, that of opera and cinema. In parodying the fatal ending of opera, the film exposes the visual trick available to cinema (which is irrelevant for opera), and shows cinema's artificial potential in executing an operatic ending. This ending, in which an actor is revived out of a dead character, also raises the very question of "the ending": is the ending to be accorded to the "actor of film" or to the "character of opera"?[7]

Was the attraction of silent film to opera an experimental phase later to be abandoned, a phase in which film studied its voice, gesture, plot, and theatricality in relation to opera? Or was there an affinity between film and opera beyond a confined historical period, an affinity that can be detected beyond the silent era, showing how the ideas, or thematics, of silent film persist? What happened to opera within film when film was no longer silent? What happened to the ways in which *silent film* inherited the voice of opera when cinema itself had acquired the capacity to reproduce the sound of the human voice? The issue I would like to raise with regard to *A Night at the Opera* is not whether cinema, now possessing a voice, is still attracted to opera, but whether cinema is attracted to opera in the ways in which silent film was attracted to it: whether cinema—by way of opera—wishes to remember, is nostalgic for the absent voice, or is at a loss in relation to its new voice; whether in fact it wishes to retain a sense of its silent past. I would like then to raise two interrelated issues: whether cinema, after its transformation into the talkie, looks back at its silent past, and whether the inheritance from that silent past is related in fundamental ways to the medium of opera.

It is known that Hollywood directors, producers and actors during the 1930s felt threatened by the ability of film to voice its characters. The Marx Brothers themselves were concerned about the impact of sound on their own art that owed so much to the silent period. As Groucho remarked as late as 1931: "The talkies had just intruded on the movie industry and scared the hell out of most of its members."[8] Many interpreted the advent of the talking film as a passing attraction, eventually to disappear in favor of a return to the silent film. The loss of the silent medium was felt more strongly than the gain of the human voice.[9] *A Night at the Opera* is a talking film that indeed cherishes its silent past, but only indirectly; that is, not in an actual "resilencing" of its voice, but in ways analogous to opera's problematizing of vocal emission, expression, and signification.

Opera's greatest influence on silent film lay in the attraction to the very idea of the extremity, extravagance and artificiality of the operatic voice.[10] Opera's unique representation of vocality was inscribed into the very language of cinema: not by creating an illusion of giving voice to the silent humans on screen, nor by attempting to substitute verbal for gestural language, but by causing cinematic imagery to "behave" operatically. *The Phantom of the Opera* (1925) is a paradigmatic example of this kind of influence. It portrays the relationship between silent film and the voice of opera, of what occurs when film points indirectly to its relation to the human voice through the voice of opera. Moreover, it reveals most dramatically that when the voice of opera is portrayed in silent film, that voice is itself shown to relate essentially to muteness and silence. Opera is revealed to be constantly aspiring towards the edge or extremity of song, of something beyond song, whether a cry or silence; that is, operatic singing derives its force not simply from the extravagance of the singing voice, but rather from its pointing to the limits of vocal expression, to the limits of meaning.[11] Silent film in its fascination with and anxiety about silence is uniquely suited to revealing opera's tendency to go beyond song. Introducing the voice of opera into silent film does not change the universe of silence, as voice in opera functions in the condition, or under the constant threat, of the loss of that voice, of its disintegration into the cry, or into silence.

The excessive, deformed and fragile vocality of opera is seen in the shadings, deformity, and obsessive visual style of *The Phantom of the Opera* itself. This analogy between the visual and the vocal is reinforced by a subplot in which the deformed shade of the Phantom is obsessed with the voice of the prima donna who performs in an opera within the film. The Phantom, obsessively in love with a prima donna, disables another singer so that his beloved can perform in her place. The climax of the rival prima donna's aria turns into a dreadful cry as the auditorium is darkened and the immense chandelier of the Paris opera house falls onto the audience. In the next performance, the role is sung by the Phantom's chosen prima donna. Again the auditorium is darkened, the Grand Opéra's whisperer is killed, and the singing turns into a cry as the prima donna is abducted by the Phantom. *The Phantom of the Opera* is saturated with the visualization of cries, and with the representation of failed visuality in relation to the power and force of the voice of opera. The end of the film represents a culmination of the attraction of the visual to the vocal, manifested when the Phantom dies an "operatic" death.[12]

## VISUAL OPERA

In *A Night at the Opera*, the image of silent opera is most poignantly expressed in the striking image of the mute Harpo performing opera in front of a mirror. This idea of silently enacting the voice of opera, and in that very way remaining loyal to what is essential to the operatic voice—its aspiration to silence—is precisely what I see as underlying silent film's attraction to opera. The first draft for the script of *A Night at the Opera* features Harpo as the greatest tenor in the world who fails, throughout the script, to utter a sound.[13] A trace of this abandoned idea, that is, of the centrality of silent Harpo in invoking opera, found its way into the final version: the film's first scene at the opera house is reserved for Harpo. Enacting the voice of opera, Harpo silently sings to his reflection in the mirror.[14] We are given an image of opera, or opera in a mirror, without the voice of opera. The gesture of a wide, open mouth is that of an opera singer, but Harpo, as always, is mute. The scene separates the image from its sound: with Harpo, there is no need to hear the voice in order to comprehend it as the voice of opera—it is sufficient to see Harpo miming song. The substitution of voiceless sound for sense was Harpo's underlying style and personality throughout his cinematic career and, in this scene, Harpo shows us that the sense of operatic singing can be signified in silence. Is Harpo raising an absurd question? Whether opera-within-film is essentially a wish for a visual image of a silent operatic voice?

Harpo's silent song before the mirror also evokes a central theme specific to *The Phantom of the Opera*: that of enacting the voice of opera in a *mirror*. In *The Phantom of the Opera,* the prima donna's voice, the "voice of opera," crosses over to the domain of the Phantom, located below the opera house, through a mirror. Only the Phantom's chosen prima donna is able to relate her voice and the image emanating from it, to the effect that she can go beyond her reflection in the mirror and pass through it. Harpo's singing to the mirror enacts the voice of opera as an extension of his overall muteness.

As it is not only the mirror that evokes *The Phantom of the Opera*, it is not only Harpo who enacts opera silently. In the course of the film, the Marx Brothers act out a variation on the Phantom's collapsing the chandelier, the cry, the abduction of the singer and the replacement of the "wrong" with the "right" operatic voice: the Brothers devise a plan to enable Ricardo, the tenor of their choice, to be heard at the opera house. During a performance of *Il Trovatore*, at the climax of the aria "Di quella pira," sung by the competing tenor Laspari, Chico and Harpo darken the auditorium and abduct him with the aid of the theatre's mechanics. Instead of the tenor's climactic high note, a shriek is heard and, to everyone's amazement, the tenor disappears. In place of this high note of the aria "Di quella pira," which is the most famous "high note" in the repertoire as it serves as a test for the vocal powers of any tenor attempting to reach it—the goal and climax of the aria awaited by all—there is a premature cut, a cry in the dark, and the disappearance, the silencing, of the operatic voice. Harpo visually "translates" Laspari's vocal ascent towards the high note when he (unnaturally) climbs up the operatic setting. The length of time for which Laspari holds the note is equivalent to the length of Harpo's leap. This scene dramatically positions the Marx Brothers in relation to the visualization of the operatic voice as well as the silencing of that voice and its replacement with a "better" one.[15]

Visualizing the performativity of music is a fundamental theme of the Marx Brothers' performance. It is reinforced in the opening night of the performance of *Il Trovatore*. The first music from the opera to feature in the film, the opera's orchestral prelude, is metamorphosized under the Brothers' reinterpretation of the role of the instruments. Conventionally, a Verdian orchestral prelude incorporates the opera's musical highlights without the actual vocal parts. It functions as a summary of the opera heard prior to the curtain rise. In the orchestral prelude, Harpo and Chico take over the conductor's position and abduct the music. They show us how easily operatic music can slide into a soundtrack for a ball game: the prelude music is smoothly followed by the tune "Take Me Out to the Ball Game." The gap between opera and sports is not wide. (Later the Brothers will demonstrate an even narrower gap between dying on stage and living on screen). The Brothers subvert the conductor's authority and "expose" the conductor's stick itself as a musical instrument of the orchestra. The Brothers conduct according to the orchestration, where each musical section, in their hands, acquires its own separate conductor. Although absurd from the point of view of conventional conducting, their idea of conducting visually follows the music and is visually suited to it. Harpo, joining the instrumentalists in the orchestra, sits in the string section and plays the trombone with a violin bow; the bow is then used to fence the conductor's stick, just as a violin is used as a baseball bat. What does it mean that the film slides in and out of operatic music? Is the music "visually" rather than "acoustically" determined? Do the Brothers *see* and create instruments, overriding the music produced by them?

The idea of visualizing music and emphasizing its performativity is fundamental to the Brothers' roots in silent cinema's aesthetic tradition and is reinforced in their customary musical numbers. Harpo and Chico's music solos depend on the comic/serious divide between seeing and hearing their playing. On the harp, Harpo's childlike, beastly behavior is transformed into angelic virtuoso playing. We are attracted to the new image opened up by Harpo's harp. Following the movement of his hands, and the expressions on his face, is a visual comic leftover in the otherwise acoustic comic pause. In *A Night at the Opera,* the harp solo is enhanced by an introductory piano performance: the "wrong" instrument for Harpo. This serves to delay the onset of the "right" sonority of the harp. We await the "right" instrument, as we await the "right" tenor's voice. Chico's piano performance is better known for its unique image of playing, its unschooled technique, than for its musicality. Although these are musical numbers, we depend on their visual identity for the expression of the musical.

THE SANITY CLAUSE

It is the Marx Brothers' relation to language as such that reveals the deepest affinity between their world, opera, and silent film. The Marx Brothers take the complications introduced into film by language as their main theme.[16] They relate themselves to the tradition of the burlesque silent film but do not dispense with speech; their performance does not merely depend on body gestures and the physical, just as opera does not dispense with the libretto, its text, and is not merely composed of vocal gestures. Rather, both the Marx Brothers and the medium of opera destroy words.

The Marx Brothers' performance does not depend on the unique possibilities opened up by the medium of cinema, but is rather based on their lifelong theatrical experience, mostly in vaudeville and later on Broadway. The theatrical style, the comic world of chaos and anarchy, is captured, not created, by the camera. In this style, the bodies and the personalities of the characters themselves are comic—as in vaudeville, and in the silent comedies of, for instance Chaplin and Keaton. As Gerald Mast writes: "The silent clown began with magnificent physical control. Although he usually tried to look funny, it was what he could do with his body that really counted. . . . The 'American Comedy'—the comedy of personality, died [because] as a style of physical comedy its natural medium is silence. The first decade of sound was close enough to the silent era so that the American physical comedy of personality retained much of its vitality."[17] Before filming *A Night at the Opera,* the Brothers tried out the material on tour before a live audience that allowed for improvisation. Changes were then made in the script in accordance with audience response. Silent space was added to accommodate the actual timing of laughter so that the following dialogue would not be lost. This theatricalized their act and placed the Marx Brothers' cinematic performance within its natural improvisatory setting.

The Marx Brothers' destruction of language, continues Mast, is aimed at annulling conventional modes of communication in language by revealing individual relationships to talk: from excessive vocabulary, to speech that is too literal minded, to total muteness. Groucho's speech is illogical; he talks too much and too fast, "swallowing us in a verbal maze . . . eventually we are back at the start without knowing where we have been or how we got there . . . he manipulates . . . substitutes the quantity of sound and the illusion of rational connection for the theoretical purpose of talk—logical communication . . . substitution of sound for sense. . . . Groucho is mouth."[18] Chico's comic character toys with the materiality of language; his Italian accent turns meanings upside down. Chico, elaborates Mast, "intrudes on Groucho's verbal spirals by stopping the speed with his erroneous intrusions. He makes different but similar sounds out of the key terms in Groucho's verbal web," interrupting the flow of Groucho's speech with misinterpretations, puns, and so forth. Like Groucho, he "substitutes sound for sense and appearance of meaning for meaning."[19] A third option is demonstrated by Harpo, who dispenses with words altogether although his muteness is understood, rendering language altogether dispensable.[20] This is team work in which, observes C. A. LeJeune, it is unclear "how much Harpo's dumbness owed to Groucho's gabble, or Groucho's urgency derived from Harpo's pantomime."[21] The Marx Brothers are on the edge of communication in speech, in their display of the very absurdity, materiality, sonorous movement of speech, or total dispensation with it. In all these variations on the theme of language, it is chaotic communication that creates the comedy.

The Marx Brothers' treatment of speech could be compared to the view that in opera, the purpose is voice and in the process, the libretto—the text of the opera—is seen as negligible. Opera is understood as not depending on the need to decipher words because the words in opera are redundant; they are "unnecessary" for comprehension. Meaning is supposedly conveyed by other means: synopsis, repetitive plot structures, vocal numbers (always standing for dramatic intensity) or, most importantly, the force and beauty of the voice. Opera, then, becomes an example of independence from language. Opera's image is one of vocal acrobatics: vocalization, extreme vocal ranges (high and low), melismas and cadenzas that divide the words into unrecognisable syllables, ensemble singing that conflates several texts simultaneously, and so on.[22] In this respect, the culmination of the operatic voice in song (aria, duet) is analogous to the Marx Brothers' comic numbers.

Harpo's mute performance most clearly enacts this extreme view in which opera is "comprehended" without the need, or even the wish, to understand the words sung. Furthermore, as Harpo is not silent but mute, and his muteness is deciphered and comprehended through surrogate sounds, his is the mode of communication encountered in the rendering of voiceless opera on silent film. The enactment of the voice of opera in silent film is not in an attempt to compensate for the voicelessness of silent film, but rather an extension, or complication, of the modes of silent film's communication in silence.[23]

## THE WORLD OF *IL TROVATORE*

Verdi's *Il Trovatore* (1853) is one of the most popular operas: "Few operas have enjoyed such widespread and immediate popularity, or have so solidly established themselves in the fabric of social history."[24] But it took longer for scholars to judge its quality. Indeed, over the years *Il Trovatoer* has drawn opposing responses from musicologists, considered both the "definitive melodrama . . . the ultimate challenge of Italian song," and "the most absurd and far-fetched of all."[25] In the past few decades, however, the scholarly scene has changed and the opera has secured itself in the scholars' pantheon of operatic masterworks.[26]

*A Night at the Opera*'s relation to the opera is complex. To choose an opera such as *Il Trovatore* is to choose melodrama at its extreme: burning babies, witch-hunt, gypsies burned at the stake, civil war, amorous rivalry, disguise, confused identities. It is a convoluted, illogical, and, at times, confused plot. Uncharacteristic of Verdi, the opera's motivation for the events in the opera do not occur during the opera, but rather are narrated in the opera as past events. This results in an opera with contradictory narrations, an abundance of misunderstandings, misrecognitions, and ultimately untimely deaths. It is in this sense that the Marx Brothers' reference to opera is complicated, for parody is internal to the world of opera itself and blatantl, so in the opera chosen.

Some of the most hilarious scenes in the Marx Brothers' film are those that parody opera or *Il Trovatore* specifically. Harpo, Laspari's dresser, puts on all of opera's costumes at once, each undressing reveals a costume of yet another opera. Groucho rides a horse carriage circling the opera house, he plans a late arrival so that he is sure to miss the entire performance. Groucho says, "Hey you, I told you to slow that nag down. On account of you I nearly heard the opera. Now then, once around the park and drive slowly. . . ." Groucho sells peanuts, transforming the opera into a ballgame while the orchestral prelude of *Il Trovatore* slides smoothly into baseball music. Harpo climbs up the scenery during the performance exposing the backstage. This is followed by abrupt changes of scenery from different operas, ultimately dropping in front of the singer and hiding him from the audience. In his escape from his persecutors, Harpo enters a door at midair, and falls, splitting the scenery into two. Next, with the aid of a camera trick, Harpo climbs *up* the scenery and turns off the electricity, and so on.

A closer look at these scenes reveals that parody stems from a deep understanding of the medium of opera and that, in parodying opera, the Marx Brothers are in fact parodying the medium of cinema. For instance, take the scene where Harpo changes the scenery and climbs up the operatic setting while the most famous tenor aria from *Il Trovatore*, "Di quella pira," is sung. Harpo's chaotic act points to the absurdity of unbroken song—the absurdity of a medium catering to song as opera does—and to the insignificance of the specificity of the operatic plot for the extravagant and passionate singing voice. Yet Harpo's chaotic rendering of opera also points to the way cinema simulates operatic absurdity. His gravity-defying climb, rather than using film's "realistic" illusions, shows the Marx Brothers on the verge of shattering the world in the way that opera (ridicuoulsly?) attempts to transcend it. Here, Harpo demonstrates how cinematic possibilities blend with operatic absurdity.

*Il Trovatore*'s libretto, as mentioned, displays an absurd, illogical, and mischievous progression of events. But this is also the case with the Marx Brothers' plots. On the whole, the Brothers' earlier films were built around comic scenes with little attempt to develop a progressive sensical narrative that is resolved at the end of the film. Their films were characterized by irrelevant plot twists, incongruous sight gags, inconclusive conclusions, and absurdly contrived human behavior in which mistakes were magnified, and the action was inconsistent and chaotic. These films were based on multiplicity and addition rather than unity; plots were contrived and artificial, reduced to absurdity.[27]

The structural analogy between *A Night at the Opera* and *Il Trovatore* is in fact striking. The film shares the structural concerns of number opera: how to connect and integrate the solos with the plot. In this sense, *A Night at the Opera* is a "number film." The independent comic numbers and music solos are the improvisational starting points around which a plot is constructed. They are the *raison d'être* of the film. As in opera, the plot of *A Night at the Opera* is constructed to support the occasions for song. The "production numbers," the comic numbers, and the Brothers' instrumental solos all behave as operatic numbers: they expose a new facet of the character (Harpo's change of personality in the harp solos is most pronounced).[28] There is a halt in plot development; the number develops into a climax, then cadences, and is even followed by audience applause. *Il Trovatore*'s exaggerated, excessive libretto is in fact the basis for some of the most famous operatic melodies in the canon. The most popular of them are featured within the film. The operatic numbers drawn from the opera *Il Trovatore* can therefore be seen as participating—rather than serving to create—the already operatic form of the film. The world of opera, the opera house, and the operatic performance is more than a mere "location" or "institution" to be parodied, as the film works alongside the duality of plot/music within *Il Trovatore* itself, which in turn, is paradigmatic of opera as such.

To secure the success of *A Night at the Opera*, the Marx Brothers' first film at M.G.M., the producer, Irving Thalberg attempted a more unified, coherently structured narrative. Thalberg's idea was to expand— in length and importance—the "romantic subplot," its aim being to connect the isolated comic acts, construct a clear ending, add integrated "production numbers," and integrate the harp and piano solos of Harpo and Chico.[29] All of these changes were not intended in any way to downplay the Brothers' fundamental act, but to construct a clearer narrative around their comic numbers. I would argue that the modification of the film's plot increased its dependence on the operatic plot. The plot conceived by Thalberg and his writers weaves in and out of the operatic plot. But the question, of course, is how would a clearer narrative be constructed utilizing an incoherent operatic plot? I interpret the film's dependence on *Il Trovatore*'s narrative and music in two ways: through the thematics of brothers in film and opera, and through the film's granting the troubadour an illusion of a night of song.

## BROTHERS SINGING OPERA

*Il Trovatore* revolves around the rivalry between brothers. The paradigmatically absurd opera plot is first and foremost due to the relation of the two brothers, Manrico and di Luna. The issue of brotherhood and duplication is also raised constantly at the narrative level in *A Night at the Opera*. Throughout the film, the Marx Brothers toy with the absurdities stemming from their interpretations of fraternal duplication with the understanding, of course, that everyone knows that they are indeed brothers. Such scenes include the Canadian quintuplets, the two tenors whose identities are confused by the agents, and the three beards— or the three fellows with one beard—which the Marx Brothers use to hide their identities. (In the beard scene, Ricardo acts as the fourth Marx Brother, replacing Zeppo). Does this excessive treatment of mistaken identity—in relation to brotherhood—work toward rescuing the operatic brothers from their fate?

It is the brothers in *A Night at the Opera* who reveal the possibility of avoiding the tragic operatic fate. This act of redemption is made possible through the absurdity of their actions, as if the plot of *Il Trovatore*—the horror of a fate that repeats itself—could be overcome only by that which totally destroys any remnants of meaning: that is, by comic absurdity.[30] Ricardo's attempt to take over the role of Manrico, the troubadour, also raises the threat of tragedy inherent in operatic endings as such.[31] The question raised by the film is, therefore, whether the tragic fate of opera can be subverted, whether *A Night at the Opera* can redeem *Il Trovatore* and unite Ricardo/Manrico with Rosa/Leonora despite Laspari/di Luna. This question leads us to a further level at which the relation of the opera *Il Trovatore* and the film must be addressed. The possibility of a rescue—or of a substitution that does not repeat the series of tragic substitutions that dominate the plot of *Il Trovatore*—manifests itself as the possibility of producing the right opera or the opera with the right cast.[32] I suggest that the possibility of rescuing an operatic production is an allegory for the possibility of film rescuing the fatality of opera as such. In *Il Trovatore,* it is the brothers who bring about the dreadful ending; in *A Night at the Opera* it is the (Marx) Brothers who will redeem opera.

The Marx Brothers' film is an interpretation of an ever-deeper facet of the opera. I would like to claim that *Il Trovatore* positions the quality of being a troubadour—an operatic character who is a singer—at the center of its concerns.[33] As such, the opera conveys something about the function of song in the opera. It is an opera about the *loss* of the power of singing, and how this loss brings about death. The opera is a reflection on Orpheus's incapacity to hold on to the power of song. Being a troubadour is Manrico's central attribute at the very beginning of the opera but disappears as the opera unfolds. What is at stake is the disappearance of the power of song once obtained. At the outset of the opera, all characters allude to the power of the troubadour's song, and it is this quality that wins over Leonora's love: song is emphasized in the rivalry between brothers. *A Night at the Opera* positions the rivalry over the soprano, cast in the role of

Leonora in the performance of *Il Trovatore*, as a rivalry between competing tenor voices, Laspari and Ricardo, for the role of the operatic singer, the troubadour. In the film, it is Ricardo, the tenor who tries to follow his love for Rosa and become her Manrico by singing the role in the performance at the opera house in New York. Yet Rosa is courted by a rival (the "famous" tenor Laspari), who holds the power granted to him by the world of opera.

In the opera, Leonora is won over by the beauty of the troubadour's voice. Her love depends solely on the troubadour's voice; she recognizes him by his voice. His song has the capacity to make "earth seem like heaven"; he has the power to transform the world. In this, the troubadour seems to possess the Orphic power of song. Leonora has only heard his voice and never actually seen him. This leads to a famous scene in which Leonora mistakes her lover for di Luna, his rival. Crucial to both the opera and to the Marx Brother's interpretation of it is the fact that the troubadour and di Luna do not know they are long-lost brothers, and this is precisely what may be the reason for Leonora's confusion. Leonora's error is also inscribed in the film, but unlike in the opera, the film's Leonora "corrects" her mistake when she hears her true lover's voice: Ricardo knocks on Rosa's door and hears the tone of voice intended for Laspari. He then retraces his steps and reenters, intending to hear a different tone of voice, that which knows that it is he—the lover—behind the door.

As mentioned above, the aria during which Laspari is abducted, "Di quela pira," is a crucial one for the tenor. It not only displays his vocality but also exposes the troubadour's identity and hints that his rival di Luna is his long-lost, unknown brother. This aria immediately follows "Stride la vampa," the central aria of the opera, which is also featured in the film. It is a horrible description by the gypsy, Azucena, of how she burned her own child to death. This means that the troubadour *cannot* be her son, but who is he then? The troubadour reacts to his non-identity by surrendering his voice. Because the troubadour cannot sustain his world, he becomes inexpressive; he relinquishes his power of song and turns mute for a flash.

Next follows "Di quella pira," the aria in which the troubadour reacts to his shattered identity, describing a "strange feeling" of pity for di Luna. The aria describes a duel between them in which the troubadour had the opportunity to kill di Luna yet was prevented from doing so by a strong, mysterious power. The mysterious pity the troubadour felt toward di Luna represents the eruption of the hidden knowledge of his real identity as di Luna's brother. Thus the filmic abduction of the tenor refers us to the theme of substitution and identity in *Il Trovatore* itself, with the knowledge that in opera such attempted substitutions always end in tragedy. But the abduction at the climax of "Di quella pira" will enable the true voice of opera—within the film—to sing the troubadour's role. The abduction thus allows the Marx Brothers—the filmic brothers—to intervene in the progression of fatal events occurring between the operatic brothers.

But, as I already noted, this abduction scene also evokes another world of association—that of the silent era, and in particular its treatment of the idea of opera in *The Phantom of the Opera*. (It is worth noting in this connection that both the director and the producer of *A Night at the Opera* were steeped in images of the silent era.[34]) Laspari's shriek at the climax of his aria recalls the prima donna's famous cry in *The Phantom of the Opera*. Indeed, the image of the cry representing the voice of opera, and the power of the visual in relation to the power of the vocal, are the very issues conveyed in silent film of opera.

Near the end of the film, material from near the end of the opera is performed; the *Miserere* scene is sung by Rosa and Ricardo, the tenor replaced for Laspari by the Marx Brothers. Finally the two are united both on and off stage. The film does not show the entire *Miserere* scene from the opera, but emphasizes the music for the word *farewell—addio*—a word that even those unfamiliar with the opera and its language would understand. In *A Night at the Opera*, the singing of the operatic deaths in *Il Trovatore* paradoxically serve as the climax of cinematic happiness, success, love, and marriage. (Those familiar with *Il Trovatore* would remember that the opera itself has an attempted wedding between the soprano and tenor. In the opera, however, the wedding is interrupted. The unconsummated wedding is symbolized by an extremely short love duet granted to the couple.)

In the opera, the *Miserere* conveys the troubadour's longing to die. He is accompanied by a chorus of monks singing death prayers. It is not clear to whom these prayers are addressed because there is so much death around: Leonora has just taken poison; the troubadour is awaiting his execution; and in the background are all the victims of the civil war led by the brothers on two opposing sides. We also hear the bell tolling and an accompaniment of the death topos.[35] The *Miserere* is clearly an *addio* in the sense of a death scene. In this scene in the opera, the troubadour is unaware of Leonora's presence; the farewell is not intended for her to hear, and he does not hear her. The scene in the opera, in fact, creates an "unintended" duet between two characters physically apart: the troubadour, who, as in the initial scene in which Leonora mistook him for his brother, is situated off stage, is heard yet hidden from vision. The troubadour is imprisoned in the tower while Leonora is outside singing for him, constituting a reversal of the customary troubadour role. Verdi employs "vocal space" in opera (also in the scene of the mistaken brothers) where the voices themselves are theatricalized. The film, on the other hand, uses the *Miserere* scene to unite the lovers in song and control operatic death.

Is this a similar gesture of filmic redemption with the idea of a "happy ending" for opera, with a fulfilled promise of happiness—a parody of opera's fatality, as we find, for instance, in Chaplin's *A Burlesque on Carmen*? *A Night at the Opera* only superficially revoices Chaplin's rewriting of an operatic ending. In the Marx Brothers' interpretation of opera, the power of voice is manifested in the very *disregard* for the meaning of the opera's song of death. Not only does the filmic union redeem the operatic death, but the power of the operatic voice—Ricardo's *operatic voice*, which has not been heard until this moment—provides a *filmic* expression for the power of the voice of opera. In contrast to the Phantom who is swallowed by the fatality of opera—as the vocality of opera is transcribed in his visuality—the vocality of opera in the Marx Brothers is inscribed into a *cinematic opera singer*. In contrast to Chaplin's Carmen, parodying operatic death functions to hide the Brothers' adherence to the power of the operatic voice. Ricardo is a cinematic character with vocal—not visual—powers. I would like to stress that Ricardo's vocal or operatic power is not due to the fact that we *hear* him sing (it is not the difference between a talking and a silent film), but to the fact that his singing does not signify death in the world of the Marx Brothers. By erasing the meaning of the operatic death scene, the film relies on the visual—on the literal meaning conveyed by lovers singing together: the erasure of the words carrying operatic signification restores the power of operatic voice on the filmic level. In contrast to Don Jose and Carmen in Chaplin's film who annul the deaths of opera by revealing the cinematic possibility to *undo* those deaths and revive the actors acting out their death, the Marx Brothers conflate the scene of the operatic song of death itself to signify the happy end of the cinematic characters singing this very death: the *very meaning* of singing death in opera is their revival. By claiming this as the filmic ending, *A Night at the Opera* retrieves for *Il Trovatore* the lost power of the troubadour's song.

But this is *not* the end of the Brothers' film. *A Night at the Opera* ends simultaneously (or ends once again) with a display of the Brothers' anarchic behavior, with the tearing up of every contract, with the breaking apart of every speech situation. During the *Miserere* scene's repetition in the encore, the Marx Brothers have one final say. Reinterpreting by way of repeating a previous scene in the film, the Marx Brothers once again tear up the tenor's contract so that the *Miserere* scene is not the ending of the film. This coda—a tail to the closure of the plot—stands for the tearing apart of every structure of tale, twining around the tearing up of a contract and ending with the tearing apart of a coat tail. Tearing up the contract is a return to ideas about the meaninglessness of words, to the contract's "sanity clause." Yet it would be too "ordered," too "symmetrical," to read this as the Marx Brothers' abandoning words for the sake of the power of voice. *A Night at the Opera* does not wish to "parody opera to silence," but as encountered in silent film's attraction to opera, it is drawn to the very possibilities opened up by the voice of opera in a parody of the visual sphere. The film shows the human voice in another absurd manifestation, that is, as operatic.

But then, what would be the meaning of the "right" tenor's contract being torn again at this point in the film, after he has made his way into the vocal world of opera with the help of the "happy" brothers of film? Would this represent tearing a contract between singing in opera and singing in film? "Singing death" in opera and "silencing death" in film? Between brothers in opera and

Brothers in film? If we thought at first that the end of the film bows to the power of the operatic voice, when heard or unheard, visual or acoustical, then we are disillusioned. This too—in the operatic world created by the Marx Brothers—is absurd.

NOTES

1. There is also Groucho's version of Gilbert and Sullivan's *Mikado* on television. See Allen Eyles, "A Night at the Opera," *Films and Filming* 11, no.5 (February 1965): 19.

2. Glenn Mitchell, *The Marx Brothers Encyclopedia* (London: Batsford, 1996), 189 (emphasis added).

3. For a different view, one that holds that the film retains the social assumptions of earlier films—opera as social snobbery, luxury, money, and entertainment of the rich—see Gerald Mast, *The Comic Mind* (Chicago: The University of Chicago Press, 1973/79), 285.

4. Richard Evidon, "Film," in *The New Grove Dictionary of Opera*, ed. Stanley Sadie (London: Macmillan, 1992), II: 194–200.

5. See Jeremy Tambling, "Film Aspiring to the Condition of Opera," in *Opera, Ideology and Film* (New York: St. Martin's Press, 1987), 241–67. The discussion is devoted to the advent of sound in the '30s as in *One Night of Love* and *Charlie Chan at the Opera*. Tambling mentions a few prima donnas who were lent to silent film, yet without accounting for their silent appearance. Few films in the '20s had musical scores written specifically for them. One example is Satie's musical score for *Entr'acte Cinématographique*, directed by René Clair (1924). For a thorough discussion of the music that accompanied silent film see Martin Marks, *Music and The Silent Film: Contexts and Case Studies, 1895–1924* (New York: Oxford University Press, 1997). There has been little research conducted on early films of operas. For films of operas through 1906 see *ibid.*, 258 n. 31. For special problems of compiling music for opera films see Tambling's *Opera, Ideology and Film*, 72–4. For a recent analysis see David J. Levin, *Richard Wagner, Fritz Lang, and the Niebelungen: The Dramaturgy of Disavowal* (Princeton: Princeton University Press, 1998); and Rose Theresa, "Gounod's *Faust* and the History of Early French Cinema," paper presented at the 1997 meeting of the International Musicological Society.

6. Chaplin's film, of course, is a parody directed not only towards operatic plots, but also towards the absent voices. Chaplin did not even use the opera's music for his soundtrack but composed most of the music himself.

7. For an account of the complex relationship between actor and character in film see, for instance, Stanley Cavell, *The World Viewed: Reflections on the Ontology of Film* (New York: Cambridge University Press, 1979); and Leo Braudy, *The World in a Frame: What We See in Films* (Chicago: University of Chicago Press, 1976).

8. *Groucho and Me: The Autobiography of Groucho Marx* (New York: B. Geis Associates, 1959), 166.

9. Chaplin's refusal to use synchronized dialogue in his first sound films attests to a fundamental sense of loss that accompanies the advent of sound: "[Chaplin] realiz[ed] . . . the antithesis of the comedy of physical personality and the structural demands of comedy that uses words to communicate the character's feelings and thoughts." See Mast, *The Comic Mind*, 25–6. For theoretical discussions regarding synchronization as the loss of intimacy between sound and image see Theodor Adorno and Hanns Eisler, *Composing for the Films* (London: The Athlone Press, 1994, first published by Oxford, 1947). Slavoj Žižek also renounces the notion of harmonious complementarity between sight and sound. The beginning of sound film does not alter the fundamental relationship between the visual and auditory dimensions, as voice functions as an object for the visual. The effect of the addition of the soundtrack was not a closer imitation of reality, but rather an automization of the voice. See "'I Hear you with My Eyes'; or The Invisible Master," in *Gaze and Voice as Love Objects*, eds. Renata Salecl and Slavoj Žižek (Durham: Duke University Press, 1996), 92. For other accounts of the loss inflicted on film with the achievement of synchronized speech, see Rudolf Arnheim, *Film as Art* (Berkeley: University of California Press, 1957; reprint, 1966); Sergei Eisenstein, *Film Form {and} The Film Sense*, trans. and ed. J. Leyda (New York: Meridian Books, 1957); Amy Lawrence, *Echo and Narcissus: Women's Voices in Classical Hollywood Cinema*, (Berkeley: University of California Press, 1991); Rick Altman, "Moving Lips: Cinema as Ventriloquism," *Yale French Studies*, no. 60 (1980): 67–79.

10. Michal Grover-Friedlander, *"The Phantom of the Opera*: The Lost Voice of Opera in Silent Film," *Cambridge Opera Journal* 11, no. 2 (1999): 179–92.

11. Such an interpretation of song as leading to the limit of vocal expression and of signification in language is presented, for example, in Søren Kierkegaard's discussion of Mozart's *Don Giovanni* in *Either-Or,* vols. 1 and 2, trans. Walter Lowrie (Princeton: Princeton University Press, 1944; reprint, 1971); as well as in Nietzsche's understanding of the essential Dionysian face of opera as an inheritance from Greek Tragedy in *The Birth of Tragedy*, trans. Walter Kaufmann (New York: Vintage Books, 1967). An overall view of the vicissitudes of the voice of opera, its bordering on the cry and meaninglessness, is elaborated in Michél Poizat, *The Angel's Cry: Beyond the Pleasure Principle in Opera*, trans. Arthur Denner (Ithaca: Cornell University Press, 1986; reprint, 1992).

12. See Grover-Friedlander, *"The Phantom of the Opera*: The Lost Voice of Opera in Silent Film."

13. Script by Kevin McGuinness. See Joe Adamson, *Groucho, Harpo, Chico and Sometimes Zeppo* (New York: Simon and Schuster, 1973) 251–300.

14. A similar intuition linking Harpo and the operatic voice is voiced by Kramer: "Harpo supplies his own version of the operatic voice whose absence marks his entry into the movie. . . . Garbo may talk all she likes. Harpo whistles." Lawrence Kramer, "The Singing Salami: Unsystematic Reflections on the Marx Brothers' *A Night at the Opera*," in *A Night In at the Opera: Media Representations of Opera*, ed. Jeremy Tambling (London: John Libbey, 1994) 265.

15. For the thematics of silence and the visualization of music within film see Fred Camper, "Sound and Silence in Narrative and Non-narrative Cinema" in *Film Sound: Theory and Practice* (New York: Columbia University Press, 1985) 369–81.

16. For the importance of language in the Marx Brothers' performance, see for instance Robert Benayoun, *Les Marx Brothers ont la Parole*, (Paris: èditions du Seuil, 1991).

17. Mast, *The Comic Mind*, 24–5.

18. *Ibid.* 282, 313.

19. *Ibid.* 282.

20. For a discussion of Harpo in relation to other mute characters on film, see Michel Chion, "Le Dernier mot du muet," *Cahiers du Cinéma*, no. 330 (December 1981), 4–15 and no. 331 (January 1982), 30–7.

21. C. A. LeJeune in *The Observer*, 19 November 1944, on the occasion of one of the film's reissues. Quoted in Allen Eyles, "A Night at the Opera," in *Films and Filming* 11, no. 5 (February 1965): 18.

22. For different accounts of the operatic libretti, see Arthur Groos and Roger Parker eds., *Reading Opera* (Princeton: Princeton University Press, 1988). For an extreme opinion that totally disregards the libretto see Paul Robinson, "A Deconstructive Postscript: Reading Libretti and Misreading Opera," in *Reading Opera*, 328–46. An opposite view, one in which the libretti is crucial, is voiced by Catherine Clément in *Opera, Or the Undoing of Women* (Minneapolis: University of Minnesota Press, 1979/1999).

23. Harpo's early performances were not mute: he sang with the other brothers as one of the three, then four, Nightingales. On Broadway, he transformed his act to a mute one, that is, before the Marx Brothers' move to the film industry in the late '20s. In this context, the fact that Harpo participated in a silent film from 1925 ("Too Many Kisses")—the only Marx brother to do so—is more than a mere anecdote because his acting style did not change after the silent era.

24. Marcello Conati, "Higher than the Highest, the Music Better than the Best," in *Il Trovatore* ed. Nicholas John (London: English National Opera Guide, 1983), 14.

25. Bruno Barilli, *Il paese del melodramma e altri scritti musicale*, ed. Enrico Falqui, (Vellechi, Florence, 1963); and Massimo Mila, *La giovinezza di Verdi* (Torino, 1978), both quoted in Marcello Conati's "Higher than the Highest," 7.

26. For recent scholarship see, for instance, Pierluigi Petrobelli, "Towards an Explanation of the Dramatic Structure of *Il Trovatore*," in *Music Analysis* 1/2 (1980), 129–41; William Drabkin, "Character, Key Relations and Tonal Structure in *Il Trovatore*," in *Music Analysis* 1, no. 2 (1980): 143–53; Roger Parker, "The Dramatic Structure of *Il Trovatore*," in *Music Analysis* 1, no. 2 (1980): 155–67; Martin Chusid and Thomas Kaufman, "The First Three Years of *Trovatore*," *Verdi Newsletter*, no. 15 (1987): 30–49; Elizabeth Hudson, "Performing the Past: Narrative Convention as Dramatic Content in *Il Trovatore*," in *Narrative in Verdi: Perspectives on His Musical Dramaturgy* (Ph.D. diss., Cornell University, 1993), 192–254; Scott Balthazar, "Plot

and Tonal Design as Compositional Constraints in *Il Trovatore*," *Current Musicology* 60 (1996): 51–78; James Hepokoski, "*Ottocento* Opera a Cultural Drama: Generic Mixtures in *Il Trovatore*," and Martin Chusid, "A New Source for *El Trovador* and its Implications for the Tonal Organization of *Il Trovatore*," both in *Verdi's Middle Period: Source Studies, Analysis, and Performance Practice*, ed. Martin Chusid (Chicago: University of Chicago Press, 1997), 147–96 and 207–26; Roger Parker, "Leonora's Last Act: *Il Trovatore*" in *Leonora's Last Act: Essays in Verdian Discourse* (Princeton: Princeton University Press, 1997), 168–87; Michal Grover-Friedlander, "To Die Songless: An Interpretation of a Troubadour's Death," in "Voicing Death in Verdi's Operas" (Ph.D. diss., Brandeis, 1997), 324–83.

27. Mast, *The Comic Mind*, 282–285, 3–19.

28. See Stanley Cavell, "The Acknowledgment of Silence," in *The World Viewed: Reflections on the Ontology of Film* (New York: Cambridge University Press, 1979), 159.

29. The intention was to draw in a female audience, which, according to Thalberg, was interested in films with romantic themes.

30. It is this relation between the tragic and the comic that Nietzsche discovers at the heart of ancient tragedy and which forms the basis of the possibility of an affirmation of life in the tragic. Nietzsche identifies the chorus of satyrs and its anarchic power as the remedy for the melancholy of the one who understands fate. For an elaboration of the tragic in relation to the comic within the world of opera, see Michal Grover-Friedlander, "Opera's Blind Spot," in *Motar* (Journal of the Faculty of the Arts, Tel Aviv University in Hebrew) 6 (1998): 141–46. An insight into "the power of film to achieve the happy ending" see Stanley Cavell, "Nothing Goes Without Saying," *London Review of Books*, 6 January 1994, 3; and Theodor Adorno, "Bourgeois Opera," in *Opera Through Other Eyes*, ed. David Levin (Stanford: Stanford University Press, 1993), 32.

31. On this issue see, for instance, Clément, *Opera, Or the Undoing of Woman*; Cavell, "Opera and the Lease of Voice."

32. It is unusual for the Marx Brothers' to be "involved" in their plots to the extent that they attempt to "rescue" or save the situation. Is this change due to the theme of rescue within the operatic plot of *Il Trovatore* itself?

33. For an elaboration of these ideas see Grover-Friedlander, "Voicing Death in Verdi's Operas," 324–83.

34. Sam Wood, the director, began his career in film-making as an assistant to DeMille, directing his own film in 1920, "thereafter working with Gloria Swanson, Valentino, Jackie Coogan, Norma Shearer and Marion Davies before sound came." [See Allen Eyles "A Night at the Opera," *Films and Filming* 11, no. 5 (February 1965): 18]. The producer, Irving Thalberg, produced several silent films, including *The Hunchback of Notre Dame* (1923) with Lon Chaney—the Phantom in *The Phantom of the Opera*—*He Who Gets Slapped* (1924) and *Ben Hur* (1925), prior to his collaboration with the Marx Brothers. For an entire list of Thalberg's productions, see *Groucho and Me*, 178.

35. On the death topos see Frits Noske, *The Signifier and the Signified: Studies in the Operas of Mozart and Verdi* (New York: Oxford University Press, 1990).

# 3
# *The Tales of Hoffmann*
## An Instance of Operality

*Lesley Stern*

T
HE DIVA IS DEAD.

A dead mother, moreover: memorialized in the form of a statue. Dead she may be, but the diva mother sings and her presence is conjured through her disembodied singing voice. *The Tales of Hoffmann*, based on the Offenbach opera, is full of music and singing but only two characters are actually singers: Antonia, the heroine of the third tale, is an aspiring and inspired singer, and the source of inspiration is her dead mother, a famous opera singer.

The diva lives.

In Offenbach's opera the mother is memorialized in a painting. In the film (a two-dimensional medium) she exists in the form of a three-dimensional statue: inanimate, mute, but adopting a familiar and highly legible pose: right hand on her breast, elbow at right angles to her body, and left arm held akimbo with palm facing out. During the dramatic climax of the Antonia tale, she moves from this frozen pose, becomes animated, comes alive.

I begin with the paradoxical figure of the singing dead mother, and with an instance where the intensity of the operatic oeuvre is frozen in a sculptural gesture and conjoined with a disembodied voice, to inaugurate a discussion of *The Tales of Hoffmann*, a film made by Michael Powell and Emeric Pressburger in England in 1951. Although based on Offenbach's opera of the same name, the film is not a filmed opera, but rather what Powell calls a "composed film." It deviates from the opera in a number of ways, most noticeably in the introduction of dance so that, for instance, Olympia (in the first of the three tales) is changed from a singing into a dancing doll. With the exception of Robert Rounseville (Hoffmann) and Ann Ayars (Antonia) who sang their own parts,

Powell and Pressburger cast extremely well-known dancers—Moira Shearer, Leonid Massine, Ludmilla Tcherina, and Robert Helpmann—in the main roles and recorded well-known operatic singers as the voices. In the production process, they began by making a recording of the opera with singers and then used this recording as a playback, shooting the film with dancers on a huge silent stage that had never been soundproofed. This method of playback freed up the camera in all sorts of ways: it was possible to vary the speed, run the film backwards, shoot upside down, and produce all sorts of in-camera effects (double exposure, overlap dissolves, and so on). Moreover, it meant that the music and the dance structured the film in an unusual way, imparting to it a particular rhythm.

The *Tales of Hoffmann* is full of trickery, extravagant special effects, stylized color, artificial movement, jump cuts, and magical dissolves that transform the "real" opera into a cinematic phantasmagoria. Paradoxically, however, this film, which is so specifically cinematic in its display of special effects, so far removed from the theatrical or operatic stage, generates a remarkable sense of the operatic. What emerges from this encounter between film and a particular variant of theatricality, between different modes of *mise-en-scène* or different technologies, is a kind of cinema that we might call "histrionic,"[1] characterized by certain operations that I shall call "operality."

## THE HISTRIONIC

Gilles Deleuze, in *Cinema 2: The Time-Image,* discusses the notion of a "properly cinematographic theatricality" and "a theatricality of cinema totally distinct from the theatricality of the theater (even when cinema uses it as a reference)." He is interested in what happens to various theatrical tropes, bodily postures, and modes of delivery and voicing when they are "borrowed" from the theater, but deployed differently by the cinema. He argues that the very substance of cinema, as a technology with its own potential for articulating the temporality of bodily presence (as it subsists and moves in time), produces a new theatricality with specific affects. But his interest is not circumscribed by notions of borrowing or adaptation, or by a problematic of representation:

> If we consider the relations between theatre and cinema in general, we no longer find ourselves in the classical situation where the two arts are two different ways of actualizing the same virtual image. . . . The situation is quite different: the actual image and the virtual image coexist and crystallize; they enter into a circuit which brings us constantly back from one to the other; they form one and the same 'scene' where the characters belong to the real and yet play a role. . . . It is a properly cinematographic theatricality, the 'excess of theatricality' that Bazin spoke of, and that only cinema can give to theatre.[2]

Let us give a name to this "properly cinematographic theatricality": histrionic. Taking my cue from Deleuze, I propose that histrionic cinema, while it derives much from the theater, or more specifically from a certain actorly tradition (particularly traditions of melodrama and opera, manifested most visibly in silent cinema), exceeds the actorly. Rather, we might say that in the histrionic a particular relationship exists between the actorly performance and the filmic performance: an amplification of actorly codes, registered particularly in a pronounced gesturality, triggers an ostentatious display of all the other cinematic codes. Histrionic cinema does not necessarily involve the transposition into cinema of some prior performance text, nor does the fact of transposition guarantee a histrionic dimension. Nevertheless, the histrionic is more likely to arise where there is an intersection of different regimes of performance, different systems and apparatuses. In the encounter between different performative regimes and representational systems, what is dramatized as an issue is enactment itself (and entailed in the dramatization are questions of affect and effect, questions of mediality).³ Most simply, we might say that films that adapt theater, opera, or dance are also potentially *about* the theatrical, the operatic, the dancerly, the cinematic; they are predisposed towards the histrionic.

What secures the histrionic dimension, however, is something more than "being about," something in addition to reflexivity. Histrionic cinema is at once self-conscious, ostentatious, non-naturalistic, *and* emotionally charged and affective. This dual aspect makes it somewhat paradoxical, at least within the paradigm of contemporary Western performance theory, which on the whole remains locked into an either-or approach as regards the nexus between performativity and engagement. Traditionally, engagement and illusion are ranged on one side (under the rubric of Stanislavsky) and estrangement and contemplation on the other (under the rubric of Brecht). My interest and investment in the histrionic is motivated by a desire to understand certain cinematic modalities that defy this either-or categorization, that have been neglected in contemporary theory, and for which we need to develop a critical vocabulary.

*The Tales of Hoffmann*—always providing a captivating, but also perplexing viewing experience—presents an ideal opportunity to explore the operations (or operality) of histrionic cinema. I find it to be like a magic show in that it entrances and lures me into its fictional evocations in the very process of displaying its trickery; I am exhilarated by the performativity of the film, continuously surprised by its ingenuity and virtuosity, moved in unexpected ways. I am moved somatically, my senses tickled. The film elicits an engagement (though not necessarily character identification) with, and immersion in, a sensuously gratifying and heightened fictional world.

For Deleuze, Jean Renoir is a pivotal figure; for him "theatre is inseparable—for both characters and actors—from the enterprise of experimenting with and selecting roles." He notes that often in Renoir the actor plays the role of a character in the process of himself playing a role, provoking André Bazin to speak of a kind of exaggeration in Renoir.[4] Bazin makes this point in his essay, "Theater and Cinema" in the context of discussing Pagnol, where he says the transposition of a piece of theater to cinema is possible only on the condition that it does not cause people to forget but rather to safeguard the theatricality of the oeuvre.[5] We might say that *The Tales* safeguards the operaticality of its source, but does so through subjecting the opera to certain cinematic operations that we shall name operality: operations, that is, of histrionic cinema.

The goal of this chapter is twofold, and correlatively the analytic focus oscillates between two reciprocal impulses. On the one hand, I use *The Tales* analytically, as an experimental playground, to tease out and figure out a notion of the histrionic. On the other hand, I bring the notion of histrionic to bear theoretically on the film in the hope that it will illuminate its perplexing operations.

GESTURE

"Histrionic" is now a term connoting hammy acting, and it is associated mostly with silent cinema and nineteenth-century melodrama. In adopting the term, I intend to appropriate certain connotations to do with acting but also to extend its pertinence beyond acting, and indeed to elaborate a field of operations marked by a more extensive notion of the performative. I shall focus on the gestural as that element in which the performative is crystallized (but by no means exhausted).

Roberta Pearson, in *Eloquent Gestures*, suggests that there was an histrionic acting code in early silent cinema which was later displaced by the verisimilar (between 1908 and 1913).[6] Others, such as Edgar Morin, have argued that the verisimilar, tending towards neutrality, involved a repression of the gestural quality of early acted cinema and a domestication of the actor's body; or, to put this another way, a naturalization of gesture.[7] I'm not at all convinced that one can speak of the histrionic as a code, nor that one can periodize according to a succession of codes. The argument about repression is appealing (because one can then proceed to talk about the return of the repressed, a favored activity in contemporary theory), but we should be cautious about buying it wholesale. It is somewhat like Norbert Elias's argument (or the way his argument is appropriated) in *The Civilizing Process* that early modern Europe saw an increasing inhibition of bodily impulses, a growing sense of shame about physical functions.[8] I am appreciative of attention given to silent cinema because I shall argue that a key to understanding *The Tales* and its histrionic dimension lies in a kind of genealogical link to some of the tropes of silent cinema. But I do not wish to suggest that it constitutes a return to bodily cinema, nor would I wish to flatten out the heterogeneous range of performative modalities existing in early cinema: particularly as manifested in different national cinemas, but also across genres and sometimes within single films.[9] The cinema is always (or rather, always in the case of fictional cinema involving actors) bodily, and the gestural is always important in "fleshing out" the diegetic world. I wish to focus, however, on *how* gesture is articulated, how it is performed not just by the actor but through a deployment of the cinematic apparatus. In other words, my emphasis will fall on the imbrication of acting techniques and cinematic technologies.

It is on this terrain that the histrionic can be differentiated from the quotidian, although it is not a matter of exclusive categories, but rather of tendencies. In more naturalistic cinema, the gestural tends more to the utilitarian and quotidian; in more histrionic cinema, the gestural tends more to the abstract, expressive, and stylized. In both cases, gestural inflection has the capacity to move us (viewers) in ways that involve less semantic cognition than a kind of sensory or bodily apprehension. In the case of naturalism, that apprehension is likely to be recruited to the cause of narrative or character, and in the case of the histrionic, it is more likely to be articulated according to a cinematic logic.

Although I do not think that histrionic acting in silent cinema can be considered a code (it is never as codified as seventeenth- and eighteenth-century stage acting based on rhetorical taxonomies), it is nevertheless useful to delineate some of the features of the histrionic and some of the antecedents of cinematic histrionics. Pearson points out that, in theatrical forms such as melodrama and pantomime, actors, delighting in the pretense of being another person, ostentatiously played a role:

> Disdaining to mask technique in the modern fashion, actors proudly displayed their skills, always striving to create a particular effect. . . . Audiences and critics condemned as inadequate those who did not demonstrably act: the pleasure derived not from participating in an illusion but from witnessing a virtuoso performance.[10]

This anticipates the kind of exaggeration that Bazin notices in Renoir. However, Pearson identifies a very specific mode of acting: she describes histrionic performers as using stylized conventional gestures with a limited lexicon of preestablished meanings, which were performed quickly and heavily stressed, and in making them the actors tended to utilize their arms fulsomely. Bazin's evocation of Renoir alerts us to the fact that role-playing in its gestural dimension, and the affectivity of gesture, is always articulated in a space and time delineated by a specifically cinematic momentum. (Pearson's analysis is useful for alerting us to the fact that naturalistic performance has not always been valued; there was a time when what was most appreciated in the art of acting was the quality of pretense, an evocation of fiction not anchored in the psychological. But underlying her approach is an assumption that pretense also necessarily entails a limited repertoire and restricted conventions.)

In Renoir, the cinematic momentum has to do with deep focus, long takes, and a frequently tracking camera. In European silent cinema, as discussed below, the histrionic dimension entailed very slow movements attentive to rhythm and timing "framed" by proscenium shots and relatively lengthy takes. In *The Tales,* slow motion is sometimes used to invest the facial gestures of Robert Helpmann with villainous intensity (the motion is registered in the camera speed and the close-up rather than in bodily movement).[11]

This example provides an avenue for distinguishing the histrionic from the melodramatic (even though they are related). Certainly both melodramatic and histrionic cinema are characterized by flamboyant acting and dramatically charged situations. However, whereas the dramatic element in melodrama tends to be strongly tied to plot and to the delineation of a relatively naturalistic diegetic world, in the histrionic register the dramatic situation is not necessarily grounded in a coherent diegetic world. Moments of dramatic intensity are more likely to be generated by a specifically cinematic momentum, and to be articulated in a space and time delineated according to a certain *cinematic* logic.

In the next section, I trace a slightly eccentric genealogy for *The Tales* by looking briefly at the evolution of a performative dimension in nineteenth-century opera, connecting this with both silent cinema and a certain avant-garde trajectory in the twentieth century that privileges the physical over the psychological, and the somatic over the semantic in the generation of affect.

OPERALITY

Wagner dreamed of opera as a synthesis of all the arts, as a supreme expression of metaphysics. His reaction against "normative" opera was provoked by what he saw as the ossification of both musical and dramatic conventions. He raged against the leaching of drama from the traditional opera, its refusal of the actor's presence. The actor, he believed, had been consigned to an instrumental function and performance reduced to the banal tropes of melodrama. His attention to staging as an integral element of musical composition, and the innovations there generated, sought to incorporate the actor/singer as a moving and speaking dramatic presence. He envisaged a reconceptualization of space, a spatialization of time, that would expand the range and plasticity of gestures and movements. This project of incorporation, however, was founded on an impossible vision at the heart of which is a notion of incarnation. While railing against the limits of representation Wagner extolled the principle of expressivity. If music is the soul of the world, then the actor—the actor's body—becomes an expression of that soul. The theatrical space inscribes the actor's body as a material presence in the very moment that it militates against a materialist practice of presence.

The problematic is actually played out on the stage at Bayreuth; the contradictions between epic realism and mystical mythology foreground a political and cultural impasse. Those who followed were faced with questions that demanded new directions and experimentation. In tackling the problem of staging Wagner, Adolphe Appia, the musically trained designer, collaborated with Jacques Dalcroze, who was developing the science of eurythmics. What emerges out of this context is a methodology for training actors (rather than opera singers) in movement, gesture, posture, rhythm: for work on the body as opposed to psychological incarnation. In the early part of the twentieth century, the modernist body began to emerge on the avant-garde stage, a body trained in techniques that both derived from forms of industrial labor (the Taylorism of Meyerhold) and from the array of physical culture movements and modern dance techniques that were proliferating in Europe. And indeed in Hollywood, too: "The American modern dance developed in California, just like the film."[12] Body awareness was often considered more important than a background in theater. Lillian Gish, for instance, attended the Denishawn school of dance, and Ruth St. Denis choreographed the Babylon sequences in *Intolerance*, which were copied by DeMille in *Male and Female*. Music is still central as an impetus for bodily movement, for the engendering of affect, but the synthesis of voice and body is subjected to a variety of challenges.

Meyerhold articulates the nature of this new attention to the somatic register:

> Just as Wagner employs the orchestra to convey emotions, I employ plastic movement. . . . The essence of human relationships is determined by gestures, poses, glances and silences . . . . The difference between the old theatre and the new is that in the new theatre speech and plasticity are each subordinated to their own separate rhythms and the two do not necessarily coincide. However it does not follow that the plastic has always to contradict speech; a phrase may be supported by a wholly appropriate movement, but this is no more natural than the coincidence of the logical and the poetic stress in verse.[13]

So: a dramatized body historically traversed by strains of music that now are registered as gestural resonances. We began with Wagner, with sound and fury, and find ourselves on something like a bare stage with no logical coincidence between the gestural and the voice, with actors who don't necessarily speak, and very likely don't sing. But has the operatic disappeared entirely in these new actorly techniques and theatrical technologies? I believe that this avant-garde theater owes a great deal to the operatic, but in a convoluted way, and that the influence can be identified most vividly in what may seem an odd place: silent cinema.

What Wagner hated about operatic acting is what many opera fans love, even today. Opera singers conventionally restrict their performance to a limited repertoire of grandiloquent gestures. There are, in part, practical reasons for this. As Monk Gibbons puts it, in his book on *The Tales*, "[c]ertain gestures have become traditional because a singer can make them without distressing his vocal cords or the comfort of his diaphragm."[14] The restrictive nature of the operatic acting repertoire is well illustrated in an anecdote narrated by Norman Ayrton (drama coach to Covent Garden in the 1950s) in which he details how, together with Joan Sutherland, he developed what he calls her GPE or "General Pained Expression" that she would put on in any moment of dramatic emotional tension. Her GPE and a mastery of the art of falling down served as her repertoire of acting gestures.[15] But the reasons for the nature of these gestures and their restricted range are not entirely practical; partly it is true, as Wagner pointed out, that this practice indicates an ossification. But partly this gestural modality can be understood less as a formal taxonomic system (where each gesture signifies a sentiment or a passion) and more as an announcement of the kind of fictional regime being enacted. Emotional intensity is valued over the exigencies of real time and the coherence of characterization. Bodily movement is not necessarily expressive of individualized psychological interiority. Gesture does not mirror the character's soul. Rather, these gestures, often held for an unnaturally long time, or performed hyper-emphatically, in the context of the staging and the music, serve to underline or italicize a regime of emotive fictionality in which the performers delight in role playing, in bravura and exhibitionist displays of theatricality. The spectators, who want to be moved rather than to believe, who are seeking a sensory experience (the sense of hearing and sight as well as the synaesthetic experience of touch and taste) take delight in the performative exuberance of the players and the overall staging.

## THE GRANDIOSE EPOQUE OF HYSTERICAL CINEMA

A number of film-operas were made in the so-called silent period.[16] Edwin S. Porter directed a version of *Parsifal* in 1904, in the mid-1920s King Vidor made a silent version of *La Bohème* with Lillian Gish, and Robert Wiene shot *Der Rosenkavalier* in Germany in 1926. In casting Gish, strongly associated with the histrionic style of early cinema, Vidor mobilized a correspondence between the tropes of silent histrionic acting and the affective force of operatic singing. The potentially restrictive and yet highly melodramatic inflection of the operatic acting repertoire can be made into a virtue in those modes—such as silent cinema—where the voice and body are not unified in a mimetic inflection of naturalism. In filming Wagner's *Parsifal* Syberberg took the silent cinema as his inspiration. Silent cinema is, he says, "in a quite different way from any other cinema truly filled with sound."[17] Particularly interesting is the synthetic production of the character Kundry: body and singing voice come from different sources in a way that poses notions of source and synthesis as, precisely, the impossible dilemma of theatrical representation. The bodily presence is given by the actor Edith Clever and the voice by the singer Yvonne Minton. It was necessary, he says, that "the apparition of the person should be divided in itself and in a non-psychological manner," so that the music is seen to act on her body, as that which at once "oppresses and elevates her."[18]

Silent cinema is filled with sound in a number of ways. To start, there are sound effects (usually performed by the orchestra) that interact with voice and acquire a performative dimension. There is also the ghost of music that animates the body just as the body generates musical intonation. This is the era of the great European divas, the era that Salvador Dalí refers to as "the grandiose époque of hysterical cinema." Or to recast Dalí's point, we might say it is the era that inaugurates the operality of cinema.

Dalí writes of "this cinema so marvelously, so properly close to theater. . . . There, in all its glory, an arrogant female exhibitionism."[19] He is speaking of the prewar period and just after, specifically of Italy; he mentions Bertini, Serena, Carminati, and Menichelli. We might add Lyda Borelli, and outside Italy Sarah Bernhardt, Dusa, and Asta Nielson, among others. Bernhardt is the least cinematic of the European divas, but she registers a transitional moment, when an already anachronistic theatricality acquires, through a process of delayed reaction, an afterlife in the cinema. Victoria Duckett notes that "four of Bernhardt's films—*La Tosca*, *Queen Elizabeth*, *La Dame aux Camélias* and *Adrienne Lecouvrer*— had been performed as opera and the style of her performance was more akin to the operatic stage than it was to the theater of her time."[20] Findlater recalls how she was, especially for British audiences, conceived of as "a kind of singer."[21] Looking at Bernhardt's films now (unaccompanied by music), her performances seem almost hilariously stagy, exaggerated, over-the-top—in short, caricaturedly histrionic. But the strangeness of the performative register is produced to a large degree by historical distance and the change in conventions. From the perspective of today, Bernhardt's performance seems excessive. But audiences of the time would have been much more alert to the nuances of gestural expression and more predisposed to apprehending bodily rhythms as equal in import to textual rhythms and meanings.

Bernhardt's death scenes, for which she was so famous, might seem to us today to be ridiculously drawn-out, but they are surely no more "ridiculous" (and only ridiculous from the perspective of constrained naturalism) than the drawn-out death scenes in a John Woo movie, say. Woo's death scenes are often described as "operatic" and "choreographed," and so they are—for that very reason, they can be compared to Bernhardt's death scenes. There are differences between the two, of course, having to do with temporality and rhythm, with speed and slowness. The inflationary aspect of Woo's cinema is derived from the virtuosic action of cinematic codes (particularly editing) upon actorly codes that are primarily physical (action-oriented, however, rather than gesturally inflected). By contrast, in the Bernhardt performances, the filmic conventions are more akin to the theatrical codes they borrow from: shots held for a long time in order to privilege the view—in long shot—of a highly choreographed movement set piece. Yet for all their differences, both kinds of death, like operatic deaths, are viscerally affecting; that is to say they have the capacity to move us not just sentimentally, but also sensorially. These orchestrations (of cinematic and actorly codes) are contrived to induce a mimetic rather than identificatory response among viewers. As in dance or opera, if the movement is successful, it operates kinaesthetically, entering into us, so that we encounter the sensation of moving. Both the Woo and the Bernhardt deaths are histrionic, but Bernhardt offers us a clearer example of the particular dimension of the histrionic I have called "operality," a vivid example of the propinquity of opera and silent cinema.

For contemporary audiences, delight would have been derived from watching Bernhardt's recapitulation of, and variation on, performative traits she had already thoroughly demonstrated. This dynamic of recognition and surprise, not governed by expectations of mimetic naturalism, is lucidly registered in W. B. Yeats's famous account of Bernhardt's *Phèdre* in London in 1902:

> For long periods the performers would merely stand and pose, and I once counted twenty-seven quite slowly before anybody on a fairly well-filled stage moved, as it seemed, so much as an eyelash. The periods of stillness were generally shorter, but I frequently counted seventeen, eighteen, or twenty before there was a movement. I noticed, too, that the gestures had a rhythmic progression. Sara [sic] Bernhardt would keep her hands clasped over, let us say, her right breast for some time, and then move them to the other side, perhaps, lowering her chin till it had touched her hands, and then, after another long stillness, she would unclasp them and hold one out, and so on, not lowering them till she had exhausted all the gestures of uplifted hands.[22]

The force and unexpectedness of Yeats' account is surely a function of the fact that our image of Bernhardt today is still rather than moving; she is memorialized in photographs that capture frozen histrionic gestures. Although we can recover the complex orchestration of her movements via the Yeats account of an actual stage performance and the extant films, there is a usefulness in the stills. They evoke the held pose for which she was renowned. (Her tendency to hold the pose, and thus to underline the gesture, served to put the gesture in quotation marks, to charge the body in a moment of distilled passion.) We might designate these poses as the Diva Gestures—both arms above the head with hands turned out, for instance; or one hand on breast, the other arm extended at chest level. In cinema that comes after the era of the diva, they serve as short hand to summon up not precise emotions but rather a *kind* of cinema, to indicate the histrionic register. Think of Gloria Swanson in the climax of *Sunset Boulevard*, descending the stairs, lifting her arms and holding them aloft above her head, holding the pose, holding it for an audience. Or think of the statue of the dead diva in *The Tales*, a gesture imitated by her daughter, the soprano, and also by Robert Helpmann as Dr. Miracle.

To complement this understanding of the frozen gesture, we might turn to the magnificent Italian diva, Lyda Borelli, who was much more of a film star than Bernhardt, more of a cinematic figure. She was tall and statuesque, seemingly double-jointed, using every part of her body to maximum effect and affect. In a film such as *Love Everlasting* (1913), the inexorability of fate (and attendant sensations of fear, sorrow, yearning) unravels as much through the activity of her little finger as through plot devices. Unlike Bernhardt, Borelli was never still; she tended not to hold poses, but rather to move very slowly and in a dance-like manner, albeit with a febrile intensity, from one pose into another, utilizing the technique of contrapost or recoil.

Ben Brewster and Lea Jacobs point out that Borelli's performance in *Love Everlasting* is "dependent upon and facilitated by the lengthy takes and staging in depth which are typical of European cinema [of the time] more generally."[23] *Contra-posta* or recoil was a modern technique based on a dynamic of resistance and yielding. It involved moving into a pose, finding the point of resistance and leaning out of it, thus concentrating energy. It occurs in a number of places—in the tango and its variations for instance (immortalized by another diva, Asta Nielsen, most famously in her dance in *The Abyss*),[24] and in the teachings of Meyerhold. Eisenstein, influenced by Meyerhold, and concerned with ways of generating emotion through a kind of physical performance charged by the larger context of all the cinematic codes, wrote, "I have always believed and taught that gesture (and, at a further stage, intonation) is *mise en scène* 'concentrated in the person,' and vice versa—*mise en scène* is gesture that 'explodes' into spatial sequence."[25]

In these ways, then, the cinema of the divas illustrates the intersections of dancerly, operatic, and theatrically avant-garde practices with specifically cinematic performance codes. The "grandiose époque of hysterical cinema" finds its apotheosis in *The Tales of Hoffmann*.

## THIS MEDDLE-MUDDLE OF MEDIA

On stage, in long shot, a soprano dressed in white holds out her arms in an expansive gesture. As she reaches the climax of her aria she slowly lifts them above her head; and then there is a pause, a moment of suspension as she holds the pose, before the music cuts out and her body falls, collapses back like a wave.[26] At that moment a figure in black steps forward and she subsides in his arms, dying silently. In mid-shot, framed full frontal, he lifts his black cloak with his free hand and in a slow grandiloquent gesture draws it over her inanimate body. The heavy material of his cloak becomes diaphanous like a veil (and like the music that begins again softly) as he pulls it over her: it is the veil of death. Then, in closeup, he lifts his hand to his chin and tears the skin from his face. But under this skin there is another face, and another, and another. As Dr. Miracle is stripped away to reveal the Magician Dapertutto, so the soprano Antonia is replaced in his arms—and before our very eyes—by the Venetian courtesan, Giulietta; and as the Magician is stripped away to reveal the Toymaker, Dr. Coppelius, so Giulietta is replaced by the doll, Olympia. The stage is then transformed cinematically into a dark space in which the three women dance, each alone but mirroring the others, until a fourth image materializes in a lap dissolve—Moira Shearer as Stella, the figure from the framing story of *The Tales of Hoffmann*. In turn, this image gives way to a scene of Stella dancing with her partner; the dancing pair are multiplied so that they appear as four separate images within the frame, revolving in a circle. At first it appears as a multiplication, but then you notice that the four images are all different and highly choreographed, individuated and yet interrelated in the overall composition of the frame.

Raymond Durgnat, in a piece of adjectivally demented writing, called *The Tales* (amongst other names) "this meddle-muddle of media."[27] This meddle-muddle is clearly instantiated in the sequence described above, where the force of opera and dance are demonstrably brought to bear on the cinematic *mise en scène*, and the cinematic codes are deployed to histrionic effect. Robert Helpmann's magical unmasking is less a revelation (i.e. a stripping away to reveal some core) than an exhibition of his propensity for role playing, a kind of exaggeration, and an exhibition of cinema's propensity for imbricating the performative and the transformative. In this context, actor and role, like opera and cinema, and dance and cinema, enter into a circuit of transformations. *The Tales of Hoffmann* is above all a film about performance, although not in the generic sense—of a backstage drama, say.[28]

If we think of Bernhardt and Borelli as the composite Mother of all cinematic Divas, then it is she who haunts *The Tales.* Her operatic presence returns as the disembodied voice in the scene described in the opening of this chapter, the scene in which the statue, adopting a classic histrionic gesture, comes to life. In coming alive, she animates the film with the spirit of the diva, mobilizing a systematic operation of doubling: an oscillation between animate and inanimate, character and role, opera and film (traversed by yet another medium—dance—by the ballet, *Coppelia*).

The film, like the opera, includes three tales of doomed love, but the film adds a framing device in which Hoffmann is watching the woman he loves, Stella (Moira Shearer) dancing (the ballet "The Enchanted Dragonfly"). During intermission, he retires to the inn and there begins to narrate the story of earlier loves. There is the story of Olympia the mechanical doll (also played, or danced, by Shearer), Giulietta, the Venetian courtesan (Ludmilla Tcherina), and Antonia,the singer (Ann Ayars). For all of these women, albeit in different ways, performance is a life-and-death affair. Olympia quite literally only comes "alive" when she is performing; Giulietta keeps her own soul and stays alive by stealing mens' souls, and so she performs to seduce; Antonia, a singer, is prevented from performing by illness, but being ambitious she risks the strain—and dies. In each case, it is not a matter of adopting a character, but of producing an intensity. It is a performance for an audience or for "another," and in this sense an acting, a transforming of the everyday to produce a heightened sense of the world, to invest the ordinary with the marvelous.

In each scenario, there is a figure who orchestrates the *mise en scène:* a daemonic figure played, in each instance, and always with Satanic relish, by Robert Helpmann (even when he deploys slapstick as in his Dr. Coppelius, the toymaker role).[29] In each case, he is an amanuensis figure, transforming not only other beings and elements of the world, but also himself. Most spectacularly he transforms colored candle wax into glimmering jewels (and back again), he makes figures appear and disappear (Giulietta), and brings inanimate beings to life and then renders them lifeless (Olympia, and somewhat differently, Antonia). Helpmann is supremely gestural; it is as though he is orchestrating the figures and the drama. He cues Giulietta as though she is a puppet (thus doubling motifs from the first tale), and in the duel between Hoffmann and Schlemiel (the Massine character in the Venetian tale), his hand gestures suggest he is orchestrating not just the dueling bodies but the film cuts.

He also acts out the part of filmmaker as magician, transporting us into other worlds where the logic of physics and mortality do not pertain. When Dr. Miracle pulls his cloak over Antonia, it is like the flourish of the magician: he might revive her in this move, or kill her; the magic might be beneficent or malevolent. What matters here is not the capacity of film to foster an illusion of the real, but on the contrary to transform the real. The thrill and the engagement derives from knowing that we are in a magical universe, from actually watching the magician, the tricks, the flamboyant sorcery that is cinema. The enchantment, and the terror too, derives from a region of instability, from the sometimes indiscernible difference between reality and illusion, stage and world, cinema and opera; but also between living and dead, animate and inanimate. With startling clarity *The Tales of Hoffmann*, and in particular Olympia's Tale, enacts the very uncanniness that is endemic to the kind of fictional evocation that acting, embodiment, personification, and characterization involves.

A GAUZE-ENCLOSED CIRCUS

> . . . we would build a huge cyclorama that would go two-thirds of the way around the stage and be a permanent backing. The central acting area would have circular curtain rails enclosing the whole space, and in several depths. On these rails would hang the gauze curtains—yellow, Venetian red and blue— that gave the colour tone to each of the three acts. Within this gauze-enclosed circus anything could happen.[30]

*The Tales of Hoffmann* is a lusciously synthetic world. André Bazin referred to it as the creation of "an entirely faked universe . . . a sort of stage without wings where everything is possible."[31] In this phrase, he evokes the sense of theatricality generated by the film, the very particular staginess, that nevertheless materializes as a peculiarly cinematic *mise-en-scène*. There is no set as such, built in three dimensions—but rather a series of mobile backdrops, paintings, cut outs, and miles of gauze. What we get then is the collision of virtual worlds, the screen world and the stage world, in a continuous play on depth and flatness. In some senses, the gauze substitutes for the drapes of the proscenium stage, but it is less a substitution for, than an allusion to and a multiplication of, signs of theatricality. In fact, curtain drapes do figure, at various points through the film, as an allusion to the performative, even though they do not clearly mark off the stage area from the audience's space. There is an interesting juxtapositioning, a kind of invocation of the "cinematic curtain," as the curtain comes down on the end of "The Enchanted Dragonfly" ballet, falling down the screen, heavy and impenetrable, until the image begins to break up, disintegrate, and reconfigure as the scene in the tavern.

The Tales of Hoffmann is paradoxically staged: that is to say, it is set up, synthesised, conjured into being; it is continuously creating a sense of place, a highly textured milieu, out of space. This tendency is most acutely realized in the film's appropriation of one of the oldest theatrical tricks in the book: trompe l'oeil. Trompe l'oeil is a method of painting that deceives the eye; in fact it can pertain to any sort of visual trickery, but most commonly it is a conceit for creating an illusion of three dimensionality. For trompe l'oeil to succeed, the viewer must be fooled; but—and this is crucial—also amused, and for the amusement to take effect the trick must be perceived. So it is a momentary deceit rather than a sustained illusion. And the trick shows off, displays itself, is conceited. The pleasure we take in being tricked relates to the pleasure we take in magic, in circus tricks, in the fat man singing and the soprano dying endlessly as she hits a higher and higher note;[32] it relates to a sense of wonder that we can be so transported, and simultaneously that the solid three-dimensional world, so familiar, can also be deceptive, and suddenly rendered strange. To some extent, trompe l'oeil in the theater has been tamed and put into the service of illusionism: flats painted to look like scenes in depth, but also architecture, so that theater sets are in a sense all trompe l'oeil, fake wood and marble, fake doors and windows. But it has a long association with the theater, and with theater architecture, where a particular playfulness is apparent. And in pre-nineteenth century theater, and even in some dramatic variants of non-naturalist theater and film that is nevertheless staged (such as German Expressionism), it is deployed to summon up a virtual world of chimeric surfaces.[33] A stunning example of trompe l'oeil occurs in the Olympia story where a staircase is traversed, only to be revealed as a flat carpet on which a staircase has been painted (uncannily echoed later when Giulietta walks down the staircase composed of dead men's bodies).

There is another modality of trompe l'oeil located within the conceptual space of the mise-en-scène, at the site where theatrical, cinematic, and painterly "scenes" intersect with one another and incorporate human performance. This inflection is gestural. Severo Sarduy writes about those paintings that, on the one hand, via still life demonstrate a serene illusionism while, on the other hand, disturb the stability of objects by arresting movement "at its point of maximum concentration, when the gesture reaches its zenith and definition." He gives the example of the drinker depicted amidst plates of fruit and oysters at a table whose cloths receive and reflect light. "The drinker raises his cup," he writes, "as if to offer the master painter a chance to display his technique by catching the transparency of white wine; emphatic and convivial, he 'thrusts' his hand from the painting—the grammatical denotation of the trompe-l'oeil is the quotation mark—eloquent and *bambochard*, he looks at us and 'extends' his hand: trompe l'oeil is realized in that toast, in the epiphany of that gesture."[34]

*Trompe l'oeil* is a form of conceit. There is another conceit that *The Tales of Hoffmann* dramatizes spectacularly: that is, a conceit that links opera (so defined as a genre of music, of singing, of sound) with silence, with silent cinema. This is achieved both through a debt to a particular tendency of silent cinema that can be traced via pantomime and George Méliès, and through the exploitation of an affinity, a similarity in the way that both opera and some silent films configure and dramatize the emotions, and concomitantly, work on an affective dimension.

Powell trained with Rex Ingram in the '20s and learned to edit on a silent moviola. He also learned about the affectivity of sound: how to use sound as an effect (as the orchestra would do in early days) rather than always naturalistically. In *The Tales of Hoffmann,* the sound effects are pronounced, particularly in Olympia's story (thus making all the more dramatic the moment of absolute silence when the springs leap out of her head at the end and transform into the ripples of the Venice canal in the next story). Many instances are macabre: eyes popping out of Olympia's head; the sound of screwing the eyes back in; the winding up and down of the dolls; and the terrible sounds of the dismemberment of the body (some clues as to why it might be George Romero's favorite movie).

This element of Gothic grotesquery indicates the influence of the kind of magical and spectacular cinema we associate with George Méliès. A direct forerunner to Méliès was the stage pantomime, characterized by ultrasensational pictorial effects. As realist conventions of staging came to dominate the theater, the pantomime became the last refuge of fantastic and spectacular trickery, all of which was utterly dependent upon two-dimensional staging conventions.[35] Méliès made no secret of the fact that his scenes were "fake," devised from these two-dimensional staging techniques. In addition of course he maximized the trickery by utilizing the camera's capacity for special effects to show "people disappearing magically, cut in half, flying through the air; apparitions taking horrible shapes, animals turning into human beings and human beings into animals."[36]

A common view of the relationship between cinema and stage holds that the capacity of the camera for double exposure, dissolves, and the like replaces clumsy stage apparatus, such as vampire traps, mirrors, scrims, and gauzes. But clearly in the instance of Méliès the effects are doubled, not replaced, introducing a kind of cinematic theatricality. In *The Tales of Hoffmann,* there is a similar doubling and dilation of effects, rather than replacement.

In a curious way, the absence of singing in an operatic rendering or the separation of voice and body can produce a similar doubling and uncanny sensation. In opera, the voice has a certain life of its own, an affective force that is not tied to person or to significance. The operatic voice, we might say, sings not in order to make sense, but in order to move the listener almost by moving into and inhabiting his or her body, by becoming a passionate presence.[37] In staged opera, it is often as though the voice brings into being the body (rather than the other way around). Similarly cinema brings into being bodies, that is to say, generates cinematic bodies (bodies figured out by the camera, lighting, framing, cutting, music). The operatic mode tends to exalt the emotional, frequently to summon that most romantic of states, synaesthesia, and thus to privilege the intensity of the moment over the exigencies of real time; in other words, emotional duration in the operatic often exceeds diegetic temporality.

It is this aspect that Powell and Pressburger truly exploit, and moreover, explore cinematically, prefiguring the concerns of directors like Syberburg, Losey, and Kluge, in which mediality (the meddle-muddle intersection, say, of opera, dance, film, television) does not work to achieve a grand synthesis; rather, the playback method used in *The Tales of Hoffmann* elicits an attention to the somatic register.[38] The rhythms of the body and the voice are orchestrated rather than synthesized, as in the instance where Antonia silently watches and hears her own reflection singing. By using dancers, the film mobilizes the body to demonstrate passions animated in a contrapuntal rhythm in the music and voice. Further, in its framing and conjuring of the body and bodily movement, the camera creates an operatic space in which the passions are acted out in a variety of ways. Just as, in the opera, the human voice soars, so here dancing bodies multiply, or fly through space and time, or come apart, like Olympia's dismembered leg that continues to pirouette just like a gesture in quotation marks, or the high C of a dying soprano.

*The Tales of Hoffmann* exemplifies that inflection of the histrionic that I call operality. The multiplication and doubling of operatic and cinematic performative signs produces a cinema of visceral engagement rather than of estrangement, but it is engagement tinged with terror and delight.

NOTES

1. This discussion of histrionic cinema draws on my "Acting Out of Character: *The King of Comedy* as a Histrionic Text," in *Falling for You: Essays on Cinema and Performance*, ed. Lesley Stern and George Kouvaros (Sydney: Power Press, 1999), 277–305. I elaborate the notion further in *The Scorsese Connection* (London and Bloomington: BFI and Indiana University Press, 1995), particularly chapter 6; and in "Paths that Wind Through the Thicket of Things," forthcoming in *Critical Inquiry* (fall 2001).

2. Gilles Deleuze, *Cinema 2: The Time-Image*, trans. Hugh Tomlinson and Robert Galeta (London: The Athlone Press, 1989), 83.

3. I borrow the term "mediality" from Friedrich Kittler who uses it to refer to "systems of writing down" or "notation systems." See *Discourse Networks* 1800/1900, trans. Michael Metteer and Chris Cullens (Stanford: Stanford University Press, 1990). Kittler generalizes the concept of medium, applying it to all domains of cul-

tural exchange. Media are determined by the technological possibilities of the epoch in question. Different media intersect within the realm of mediality, increasingly so in the last century, but they also engage in contestation. Since different technologies of communication occasion different ways of thinking the transposition of media is impossible. "Transpositions liquidate the medium from which they proceed," says Kittler (275). And "the transposition of media is thus an exact correlate of untranslatability" (274).

4. Deleuze, *Cinema 2*, 86.

5. André Bazin, *What is Cinema?*, vol 1, selected and translated by Hugh Gray (Berkeley: University of California Press, 1972), 117.

6. Roberta E. Pearson, *Eloquent Gestures: The Transformation of Performance Style in the Griffith Biograph Films* (Berkeley: University of California Press, 1992).

7. Morin is cited by Pascal Bonitzer, "Hitchcockian Suspense," in *Everything You Always Wanted to Know about Lacan (But Were Afraid to Ask Hitchcock)*, ed. Slavoj Žižek (London: Verso, 1992), 16–17.

8. Norbert Elias, *The Civilizing Process*, vol. 1: *The History of Manners*, trans. Edmund Jephcott (Oxford: Basil Blackwell, 1978). Elias later refines this argument, in *The Germans*, where he elaborates different gradients of formality and informalization.

9. See Ben Brewster and Lea Jacobs, *Theater to Cinema: Stage Pictorialism and the Early Feature Film* (New York: Oxford University Press, 1997).

10. Pearson, *Eloquent Gestures*, 21.

11. Scorsese writes, "When we were doing *Taxi Driver* and the close-ups of De Niro's face, I shot these faster than usual, at 36 and 49 frames per second, still under the influence of Robert Helpmann's reaction shots during the duel on the gondola." See Martin Scorsese, "Foreword" in Ian Christie, *Arrows of Desire: The Films of Michael Powell and Emeric Pressburger* (London: Faber and Faber, 1994), xvii.

12. Cecilia Olsson, "Moving Bodies," *Aura: Film Studies Journal*, 4, no. 1 (1998): 78. She continues "They were not only geographically and demographically close, but the shared interests in bodies in motion paved the way for considerable exchange."

13. *Meyerhold on Theater*, ed. and trans. Edward Braun (London: Methuen, 1969), 56.

14. Monk Gibbon, *The Tales of Hoffmann: A Study of the Film* (London: Saturn, 1951), 9.

15. *La Stupenda: A Portrait of Dame Joan Sutherland*, a 1994 Omnibus television documentary, quoted in David Meagher, "The Operatic in Film: A Thesis in Three Acts," Honors Thesis, University of New South Wales, 1995, 25, n. 20.

16. See Marcia J. Citron, *Opera on Screen* (New Haven: Yale University Press, 2000), chapter 2.

17. Hans Jürgen Syberberg, *Parsifal: Notes sur un film*, trans. Claude Porcell (Paris: Gallimard, 1982), 45. Thanks to Marion Campbell for help with reading this book.

18. Ibid., 46.

19. Salvador Dalí, "Abstract of a Critical History of the Cinema," in *The Shadow and Its Shadow: Surrealist Writings on the Cinema,* 2nd ed., ed. and intro. Paul Hammond (Edinburgh: Polygon, 1991), 71. I am grateful to Peter Wollen for drawing my attention to this writing.

20. Victoria Duckett, "Bernhardt the Bag Lady: Sarah Bernhardt, Opera, and Silent Cinema," unpublished paper, 6. Thanks to the author for making this paper available to me.

21. R. Findlater, "Bernhardt and the British Player Queens: A Venture into Comparative Theatrical Mythology," in *Bernhardt and the Theater of Her Time,* ed. E. Salmon (Westport, Conn.: Greenwood Press, 1984), 95.

22. Quoted in John Stokes, "Sarah Bernhardt," in John Stokes, Michael R. Booth, and Susan Bassnett, *Bernhardt, Terry, Duse* (Cambridge: Cambridge University Press, 1988), 59.

23. Brewster and Jacobs, *Theater to Cinema,* 111.

24. For the tango, see Yuri Tsivian, *Early Cinema in Russia and Its Cultural reception* (Chicago: the University of Chicago Press, 1988), 46–7; and "Russia, 1913: Cinema in the Cultural Landscape," in *Silent Film,* ed. Richard Abel (New Brunswick, N.J.: Rutgers University Press, 1996), 203–208. For recoil, see Alma Law and Mel Gordon, *Meyerhold, Eisenstein and Biomechanics: Actor Training in Revolutionary Russia* (Jefferson, N.C.: McFarland and Co., 1996); and Mikhail Iam polski, "Rakurs and Recoil," *Aura: Film Studies Journal,* 4, no. 1 (1998): 4–15.

25. Sergei Eisenstein, *Towards a Theory of Montage,* vol. 2, ed. Michael Glenny and Richard Taylor, trans. Michael Glenny (London: British Film Institute, 1991), 21.

26. "The expansive gesture recoils back to the body. Its collapse is like the collapse of a wave." See Theodor W. Adorno, *In Search of Wagner,* trans. Rodney Livingstone (London: NLB, 1981), 40.

27. Raymond Durgnat, *A Mirror for England: British Movies from Austerity to Affluence* (New York: Praeger, 1971), 210.

28. Yann Tobin argues that Powell and Pressburger's earlier film, *The Red Shoes,* is to a degree formulaic—a backstage drama—but *The Tales of Hoffmann* is utterly without narrative precedent or stability, and so becomes truly avant-garde. See Yann Tobin, "Le cinema retrouvé: *Les Chaussons rouges, Les Contes d'Hoffmann*," *Positif* 289 (1985): 63–66.

29. "His Toymaker, Dr. Coppelius, was the best slapstick performance I had seen since the great Ford Sterling, Captain of the Keystone Cops," writes Michael Powell in the second volume of his autobiography, *Million-Dollar Movie* (London: Mandarin, 1993), 98.

30. Powell, *Million-Dollar Movie,* 105.

31. André Bazin, *Radio-Cinéma-Télévision,* July 1951, quoted in "Les Contes d'Hoffmann," *Avant-Scène Cinema* (Special issue on Opera and Cinema), no. 360 (May 1987): 70.

32. this is marvelously parodied in the Olympia tale where the puppet-spectator's head extends inordinately as Olympia hits her high C. Marcia Citron points this out in an astute and atypical discussion (atypical in critical literature on the film) of the humor and parodic inflection in *The Tales*. See Citron, *Opera on Screen*, 137–41.

33. In the seventeenth century architects were also painters who designed sets and directed plays, masters of *trompe l'oeil*. In fact, the opera house itself is a site of shifting proportions and stability. *Trompe l'oeil* multiplies the spaces of a solid place.

34. Severo Sarduy, *Written on a Body*, trans. Carol Maier (New York: Lumen Books, 1989), 108. I am grateful to Ann Weinstone for drawing my attention to this text.

35. See Nicholas A. Vardac, *Stage to Screen: Theatrical Origin of Early Film, David Garrick to D.W. Griffith* (New York: Da Capo, 1987).

36. Lewis Jacobs, *The Rise of the American Film* (New York: Harcourt, Brace and Co., 1968), 23. Méliès made a number of Hoffmannesque fairytales: *Cinderella* in 1900, *Red Riding Hood* and *Blue Beard* in 1901.

37. The dramatized singing voice has a tendency to render all language foreign. As De Certeau notes, "The opera allows an enunciation to speak that in its most elevated moments detaches itself from statements, disturbs and interferes with syntax, and wounds or pleasures, in the audience, those places in the body that have no language either." Michel de Certeau, *The Practice of Everyday Life*, trans. Steven Rendall (Berkeley: University of California Press, 1988), 162.

38. Much of Alexander Kluge's cinema turns on the operatic, on a simultaneous fascination with opera as "the power house of emotions" and critique of the institution of opera as a series of elaborate facades for elevating the emotional and disguising the ideological impulses which underpin the emotive and passionate qualities of the operatic—"in every opera that deals with redemption, a woman gets sacrificed in Act V." *The Tales of Hoffmann* doesn't elaborate (in the way that Kluge does in *The Power of Emotions* and the series of five-minute television operas) a critique of opera, but it does put into play some similar insights, and dramatises the issues in a way that prefigures *Parsifal*. See Gertrud Koch, "Alexander Kluge's Phantom of the Opera," trans. Jeremy Gaines, *New German Critique* 49 (winter 1990): 79–88; and Miriam Hansen, "The Stubborn Discourse: History and Story-telling in the Films of Alexander Kluge," *Persistence of Vision* 2 (fall 1985): 19–29.

# 4

# The Cinematic Body in the Operatic Theater

## Philip Glass's *La Belle et la Bête*

### *Jeongwon Joe*

A s Martin Marks has noted, presenting a silent film with live music, simulating the standard practice of silent cinema, has been a growing attraction in concert halls since the 1980s.[1] Carl Dreyer's 1928 silent *The Passion of Joan of Arc* was presented at the Brooklyn Academy of Music in 1995, accompanied by the live performance of Richard Einhorn's *Voices of Light* (1994), an oratorio inspired by, and composed for, Dreyer's film. A series of cinema-concerts designed by John Goberman in 1995, called "symphonic cinema," is also an example of this type of crossover between the concert hall and the movie theater. This series included excerpts of Sergei Eisenstein's *Ivan the Terrible* and the entire film of *Alexander Nevsky*, both of which were screened with live performances of Prokofiev's original film scores.

Philip Glass's recent opera *La Belle et la Bête* (1994), an operatic adaptation of Jean Cocteau's 1946 film with the same title simulates the practice of silent cinema in an intriguing way. During the performance of Glass's *Belle*, there is no live acting. Singers perform the opera standing onstage below a film screen on which Cocteau's images are *mutely* projected. (Because Cocteau's *Belle* is a sound film, Glass had to silence its original soundtrack in order to replace it with his live music). Using Cocteau's original scenario as the libretto, Glass designed his music so as to ensure a reasonable synchronization between the singing and the projected images. Glass wanted to keep the original Cocteau scenario intact when it was converted to the libretto for his opera. A technical problem, then, was the synchronization of singing with the on-screen characters' lip movements. Glass originally planned to time the dialogue with a stopwatch and to compose music to match it. But this method was too crude, and he finally ended up using a digital time code—a black bar showing elapsed minutes, seconds, and fractions of seconds—added to a print of the film.

What distinguishes Glass's *Belle* from other "cinema-concerts" is not only its use of a sound film but also the fact that the adaptation results in an "opera": the entire narrative of the film is conveyed by singing in *Belle*. (Glass used Cocteau's screenplay as the libretto of his opera). In Goberman's symphonic cinemas, the accompanying music is mostly instrumental, producing an atmospheric support for the images rather than an operatic representation of the cinematic narrative. The Dryer-Einhorn concert includes singing, but unlike Glass's *Belle*, the vocal text does not represent the narrative content of the film: Einhorn's oratorio is a setting of some biblical texts and medieval writings mostly by female mystics, including Joan of Arc.

Glass's *Belle* reflects opera's continued attraction to cinema. Indeed, ever since the advent of the motion picture around the 1890s, opera performance has been continually exploring cinematic idioms and techniques. Franz Ludwig Hörth and Emil Pirchan used film in their Berlin production of the *Ring* for the entry of the gods into Valhalla at the end of *Das Rheingold* as early as 1928. In some operas, film screens have been included at the phase of compositional conception rather than being added at the production level. Darius Milhaud's *Christophe Colomb* (1930) and Alban Berg's *Lulu* (1937) are among the earliest examples. In *Lulu*, the premiere of which the composer did not survive to see, Berg wished to use a film screen to show all the events between the murder of Dr. Schöne and the release of his murderess, Lulu, from her sentence of one year's imprisonment.

Cinematic exploration in operatic theater has been increasingly prominent over the past few decades.[2] The attraction of cinematic techniques partly lies in the fact that they can enhance onstage actions and easily bring multiple and synchronic temporalities to the real-time theater. In *Frankenstein, The Modern Prometheus* (1990), for instance, Libby Larson employed video screens to provide flashbacks, visualize characters' unspoken inner thoughts, or show the close-ups of the onstage action.

Glass's *Belle* stands as an idiosyncratic work in the repertoire of what can be called "cinematic operas." What distinguishes Glass's *Belle* from other cinematic operas is first and foremost the absolute dominance of the cinematic screen: Cocteau's images are employed as a replacement of live acting, rather than being used as part of production devices. This radical use of cinematic images creates an intriguingly strong tension between the operatic voice and the cinematic bodies, between the live and the reproduced, between stage and screen. In spite of the century-long history of opera's attraction to cinema, transporting cinematic idioms to the operatic stage has been an ambivalent, problematic, and uneasy task. One can think of an aesthetic clash between the live, performative medium of opera and the technologically mediated apparatus of cinema. Different orientations of the two art forms in their modes of representation also render the task challenging: while cinema, at least mainstream cinema, tends to strive for realistic and naturalistic representation, opera, even *verismo* opera, is made fundamentally antirealist by the very presence of singing. Hence Siegfried Kracauer's statement: "The world of opera is built upon premises which radically defy those of the cinematic approach."[3]

This essay examines the ways in which the tension between the operatic and the cinematic is exploited in *Belle* and the ways this tension challenges and transforms the performing and viewing conventions of opera, and conversely, those of cinema as well. I also discuss how Glass's staging of *Belle* in terms of the relationships between voice and body can be situated in the discourse of post-modernism.

## COCTEAU'S ORIGINAL SOUNDTRACK VERSUS GLASS'S MUSIC

Philip Glass has shown a strong interest in the operatic exploration of cinema. Besides *La Belle et la Bête*, he produced *1000 Airplanes on the Roof* (1989), *Orfée* (1993), *Les Enfants Terribles* (1996), and most recently, *The Grace of Monsters* (1998), all employing cinematic approaches in one way or another. *Belle, Orfée,* and *Les Enfants* form the "Cocteau trilogy." Each work in Glass's trilogy adapts Cocteau's three corresponding works in different ways. *Orfée*, the first work, is a straightforward operatic setting of the film, using a condensed version of the film's screenplay as the libretto. The last work, *Les Enfants Terribles*, is a dance opera in which dance participates in the expression of the drama as an equal partner with music. Most of its characters are portrayed by one singer and one or two dancers. Lise, the heroine, for instance, is sung by a singer and also portrayed by three dancers. By doubling or tripling characters, Glass and the choreographer Susan Marshall intended to amplify single emotions or express the characters' conflicting and divided emotions.[4]

*Belle* is the most intricate and intriguing fusion of film and opera in the Cocteau trilogy. Cocteau's *Belle* was an especially good choice for an operatic adaptation because it has little dialogue. Moreover, Cocteau's dialogue is stylized rather than naturalistic without much simultaneous talking by more than one character. This is an advantage for an operatic adaptation in terms of the clarity of the text. Cocteau's film is already filled with abundant background music by George Auric, used mostly for silent scenes without spoken dialogue, and thus allowing much room for operatic reworking.[5]

Opposing most filmmakers' belief that music has a representational function, Cocteau insisted that music's power lies in the absence of signifying function and controlled his soundtrack so as to *avoid* the close association of music and image.[6] "In *Le Sang* [d'un Poète]," Cocteau said, "I shifted the musical sequences, which were too close to the images, in order to obtain accidental synchronization."[7] Accidental synchronization, often known as "chance synchronization," is a general characteristic of Cocteau's cinematic oeuvre. In *Belle*, too, Cocteau avoided a signifying intimacy between music and image, yet delineated the drama through music, whether present or absent.[8] For instance, music is used almost exclusively for the Beast's domain and the theme of love, either between Beauty and Avenant, her suitor, or between Beauty and the Beast. Background music first enters when Avenant approaches Beauty to propose, but is cut from the soundtrack when Beauty's brother, Ludovic, a realistic figure, interrupts them. After that scene, no music is heard until Beauty's father enters the domain of the Beast.[9] On the other hand, music is almost continuous throughout the first castle scene. When the father returns home released from the Beast, music is heard until the father hands Beauty a rose—a cliché for love—but music fades out from the soundtrack when Beauty's sisters, Félicie and Adélïde, enter. Diegetic noises also differentiate the real world scenes from those of the magical domain: the former are filled with diegetic noises for the details of the visuals, while diegetic noises are almost entirely avoided in the scenes at the Beast's domain.[10] When Beauty is running past the candelabra at the castle, music is the only sonic phenomenon that accompanies her movement; even Beauty's footsteps are not heard. This total absence of diegetic noises intensifies the magical atmosphere of the Beast's castle.

When Glass stripped Cocteau's film of its original soundtrack, the differentiation between the Beast's magical domain and reality could no longer depend on the presence or the absence of music or diegetic noises; music is continuous in opera and diegetic noises had disappeared when the original soundtrack was removed.[11] In Glass's opera, the difference between magic and reality is portrayed by musical characters—for instance, the use of more chromatic and colorful instrumentation for the castle scenes—and by traditional operatic means such as leitmotif. Glass used several leitmotifs: journey motif, horse motif, castle motif, love motif, and so on. In this way, Glass restored to music a signifying function that Cocteau had refused.

## BELLE AND OPERATIC CONVENTIONS

The representational function of music and its relationship to the libretto in Glass's *Belle* is not as provocative as in his earlier operas. In *Einstein on the Beach* (1976), for instance, Glass and his collaborator, Robert Wilson, adamantly avoided music's traditional function of expressing the drama of the libretto. *Einstein* is a non-narrative opera, which lacks a libretto in a traditional sense. Although called a portrait opera, it is far from a musical biography in the conventional sense because Einstein is not portrayed as a historical figure but as a poetic vision. Images replace the traditional plot and narrative development, as with the pipes and baggy pants employed as recurring images associated with Einstein.[12] In this "theater of images," vocal texts consist entirely of solfege syllables and numbers to indicate melodic and rhythmic structures, respectively. Music is wholly self-reflexive in *Einstein*; representing nothing but its own structure, it is emptied of any signifying function or psychoanalytic symbolism.

In *Belle*, the iconoclastic quality of the opera does not lie in music but in the relationship between voice and body. *Belle* opens with the overture played against the empty screen. Near the end of the overture, singers enter the stage and stand below a blue screen, casting their long shadows on it. Once the film starts to run, singers do not act but simply sing. When Cocteau's cinematic images replace the opera's visuality, the singers' bodies lose a signifying function. By simply standing on stage, fixed and immobile, impotent to act, Glass's singers refuse to use their bodies as a tool to represent the emotions and psychology of the opera's characters.[13] The immobile bodies of Glass's singers bring to mind the "non-mimetic bodies" that Andy Warhol employed in many of his films, including *Sleep* and *Kiss*. In these films, images are excruciatingly repeated, accumulated, and exaggerated through a series of close-ups of sleeping bodies and kissing couples. Warhol's cinematic body does not point to anything beyond itself: it is radically dissociated from emotive content and deprived of signifying function. As Steven Shaviro puts it, "Warhol repeats images *in order to* drain them of pathos, meaning, and memory."[14]

Both Glass and Warhol can be understood in the context of postmodern body politics, which endeavors to liberate the body from traditional constraints of emotional and psychological representation. A case in point is postmodern dance, where liberating the body from its representational function has been notable. American dance after Merce Cunningham has explored abstract movement of the body instead of its mimetic use. During the 1970s and 1980s, this postmodern deconstruction of the mimetic body became a prominent feature in performance works of the New York and West Coast avant-garde, including Robert Wilson, Richard Foreman, the Wooster Group, the San Francisco Mime Troupe, and Squat Theatre.[15] For instance, in Wilson's *the CIVIL warS*, which was shown in segments between 1983 and 1986, a highly abstract, geometrical choreography challenges traditional theater of the mimetic body. The "mathematical" disposition of slow- bodily movements used by Wilson reduces the performers' bodies to figures or signs, not unlike the singers' live bodies in Glass's *Belle*, which are reduced to musical instruments lending their dramatic function to cinematic bodies.[16]

This replacement of singers' live bodies with bodies mediated by technology radically transforms performing and viewing conventions of opera. When operatic acting is completely displaced by a cinematic screen, the aura of live performance, the cultic value of "then and there," is deeply shattered. This is because the fixity of cinematic images makes each performance of the opera cease to be unrepeatable and unique, its visual content identical at each performance. The opera is no longer performative but becomes a "mediated" entertainment, and in so doing, changes the audience's relationship to the performing bodies. Unlike traditional operatic theater, in which live bodies are an essential part of opera's spectacle, Glass's *Belle* makes singers' live bodies superfluous from the visual and representational points of view and loses the direct communication between the performers and the audience, which stands at the core of live performance.[17] Frozen on stage, impotent to act, live bodies in *Belle* no longer have an immediate phenomenal power over the audience's sight.

The phenomenal power of voice, too, wanes. Whereas in traditional operatic performance, the singer's body becomes a physical manifestation of the voice, in Glass's opera singers' voices are isolated from their bodies and re-embodied in cinematic images, destroying the traditional unity between voice and body. The disembodiment of the singers' voices in spite of the presence of their bodies on stage makes the status of voice comparable to that of recorded song: in Sam Abel's words, the singer's "voice-body" is transformed into the "voice-object."[18]

## *BELLE* AND CINEMATIC CONVENTIONS

The disembodiment of singers' voices challenges cinematic conventions as well as operatic ones. The mixture of live voice with the film images in *Belle* strongly resembles the standard practice of silent film presentations. As many film scholars have demonstrated, most of the silents were accompanied by some sort of live sound, not just live music, but also live voices.[19] There also were various attempts to accompany silent films with spoken commentaries. "The lecturer" was one such attempt, a voice that provided commentary on the images, explaining their content and meaning to the audience. What is known as "behind-the-screen-speakers" was another: actors and actresses stood behind motion picture screens and read or extemporized dialogues in synchronization with the on-screen characters. The systematic use of live speakers during silent film presentations began at least as early as 1897, explored by Lyman H. Howe. During the first decade of the twentieth century, a number of "talking picture troupes," such as Humonova, Actologue, Ta-Mo-Pic, and Dramatone, were founded to train behind-the-screen actors.[20]

The role of live singers in Glass's *Belle* is akin to that of live speakers. In silents, however, these speakers were hidden behind the screen so that the sound could most easily be assimilated to the body of the on-screen characters in order to create an illusion of unity between sound and image. But sound cinema, too, lacks such a unity. In the talkies, the unity between sound and image, between voice and body, is only technologically mediated in that image and sound are separated in the process of recording, and they are preserved on, and reproduced from, physically separated tracks. Therefore, it has been a cinematic convention not only in silents but also in sound films, at least the mainstream talkies, to reduce the distance between voice and body in order to achieve what Michel Chion calls the "impossible unity" of the two.[21] Glass's *Belle* disillusions cinema's pretended unity between voice and body by visualizing the fact that the sound source is separated from images: singers are placed not behind but in front of the cinematic screen.

The isolation of singers' voices from their bodies in *Belle* challenges another aspect of cinematic convention related to the representational quality of reproduced sound. The quality of the recorded sound's fidelity to its original has been a fundamental issue in the study of sound in the cinema. There have been two opposing arguments concerning this issue. Béla Balázs, Christian Metz, and Stanley Cavell argue that, unlike image, sound does not undergo serious, if any, loss in the process of its recording and reproduction. While sounds, considered as a volume of vibrating air waves, remain three-dimensional after mechanical mediation, photographic images projected on the two dimensional screen lack the three-dimensional flesh of the original. Balázs contends that:

> What we hear from the screen is not an image of the sound but the sound itself, which the sound camera has recorded and reproduced again. . . . There is no difference in dimension and reality between the original sound and the recorded and reproduced sound, as there is between real objects and their photographic images.[22]

Opposing this argument, Rick Altman, Alan Williams, and Thomas Levin maintain that recorded sound's fidelity to the original is an illusion. Levin refutes Metz's view that a gunshot heard in a film is not distinguishable from a gunshot heard in the street. For Levin this view is only a deception, because, strictly speaking, if recorded sound were reproduced in a different acoustic space—not in the street but the inside of the theater—it would constitute a different sound. "The fact," Levin continues, "that filmgoers take a recording of a gunshot to function within a film as a gunshot is no more or less a deception than taking a flat in a theater for the rear wall of a room." Williams furthermore demystifies the notion that recorded sound is faithful to its original by contending that every sound, whether original or reproduced, is unique since it is "spatio-temporally specific." In other words, every sound is "historical" in that every sonic event is inseparable from the time and space in which that event is made.[23] For Williams, all sound recordings are "stage representation," that is, socially constructed events. In addition to these historical and social concerns, it is true that represented sound is only partially, not perfectly, faithful to its original, because recorded sound undergoes variable degrees of transformation. Compared with photographically reproduced images, however, recorded sound is relatively more faithful to its original: at least sound reproduction undergoes no transformation in dimensional representation.

Because of the high fidelity of the reproduced sound to its original, it has been, at least in mainstream cinema, a significant function of sound to flesh out the shadowplay of flat images in favor of a more naturalistic representation of images. Various techniques have been employed to create the sense of spatial depth, for instance, through use of a camera continually moving toward or away from objects in order to articulate the space in between.[24] But as Rudolph Arnheim stresses, sound can create a stronger sense of spatiality than image.[25] Balázs contends that "We accept seen space as real, only when it contains sounds as well, for these give it the dimension of depth."[26] In *Belle*, Glass had silenced Cocteau's original soundtrack in order to re-embody the singers' voices in the cinematic bodies. When the cinematic images lose their sounds, they lose their flesh as well. Of course, Cocteau's cinematic bodies are re-envoiced with Glass's operatic music, and music in cinema does function to compensate for the lack of spatial depth in photographic images.[27] Hanns Eisler and Theodor Adorno argue that music serves, more than the speaking voice, "to breathe into the pictures some of the life that photography has taken away from them." In their view, the talkie without music is not very different from a silent movie.[28] However, the spatial function of music is only metaphorical: music creates a *general* sense of space, through its three-dimensionality, which does not necessarily correspond to the particular images on the screen. In contrast, diegetic noises articulate the very space that the shown image represents, and thus these noises more realistically, as opposed to metaphorically, corporealize the images.[29]

Glass's silencing of the original soundtrack yields another problem in creating spatial depth of cinematic images. A sense of an accurate spatial distance can be generated by creating acoustic perspective: in other words, by changing volume and reverberation levels to make sound scale match image scale. This "point-of-audition" sound improves the naturalness of image at the expense of the intelligibility of sound.[30] But it is this acoustic perspective that Glass's *Belle* undoes. In *Belle*, the space articulated by live singers does not correspond to the space shown on the screen, a discrepancy between the aural and the optical perceptions of space that yields a Brechtian alienation effect by disrupting hearing and viewing senses. This alienation effect resembles what Robert Wilson intended to create by using microphones in his live theater: "a distance between the sound and the image." Wilson compares the effect of microphones with the conditions of Greek theater:

> It's like the Greek theatre in that when the Greek actor was on stage he wore a mask, which presented an image that was different from what he was saying. It's in this way that what I'm trying to do is similar to Greek theatre—the entire stage is a mask. That's one reason I use microphones—to create a distance between the sound and the image.[31]

## *BELLE* AND POSTMODERNISM

Glass's *mise-en-scène*, which explores the tension between stage and screen, between live voice and reproduced images, can be contextualized in the discourse of postmodernism. First of all, the replacement of live performers' bodies with flat images of cinematic bodies represents a postmodern rejection of depth. Fredric Jameson brings our attention to this postmodern intellectual trend, in which "depth models," implicit in modernism, have been attacked and renounced:

. . . the dialectical model of essence and appearance: the Freudian model of latent and manifest; the existential model of authenticity and inauthenticity; and the great semiotic opposition between signifier and signified.

What replaces these various depth models, Jameson continues, is a conception of practices, discourses, and textual play that privilege a surface.[32]

Besides this "metaphorical" depthlessness in theories, Jameson discusses the literal and physical disappearance of depth. One of Jameson's examples in the area of architecture is the free-standing wall of the Crocker Bank Center in downtown Los Angeles, which is located where Raymond Chandler's Beacon Hill used to be. This wall creates the optical illusion of a structure unsupported by any volume. In Jameson's words:

This great sheet of windows, with its gravity-defying two-dimensionality, momentarily transforms the solid ground on which we climb into the contents of a stereopticon, pasteboard shapes profiling themselves here and there around us.[33]

Postmodern glorification of surface and emptiness has also been prominent in other areas of art. As already noted, Andy Warhol is greatly concerned with surfaces, literalness, and immediacy of flattened images. As The body in Warhol's works is a "flatbed" rather than a "window of the soul," to put it in Shaviro's words. His bodies are reduced to the pure look, a surface, drained of pathos, subjectivity, and any psychological depth.[34]

In *Belle*, the disappearance of depth posits the postmodern crisis of the real: instead of the singers' real bodies, flat images of Cocteau's actors constitute the visual element of the opera at the live theater. The simultaneous presentation of the live and the recorded on stage creates a disjunction between the sonic and image events in terms of their temporal and spatial relationship with the audience. In live events the audience is spatially co-present and temporally simultaneous with the events, while the recorded is characterized by the event's spatial absence and temporal anteriority with respect to the audience.[35] In *Belle*, there is a disjunction between the sonic and image events with respect to their spatio-temporal relationships with the audience: the sonic event is live, while the image event is prerecorded.

This type of disjunction characterizes the kind of live popular music concert that incorporates singers' lip-syncing to their prerecorded music. The co-presence of the live and the recorded in this type of concert, however, creates a reversed disjunction as compared to *Belle*: the sonic event is temporally anterior and spatially absent, while the image event is temporally simultaneous and spatially co-present with the audience. The representational disjunction, either between spatial co-presence and temporal anteriority or between spatial absence and temporal simultaneity, shatters the supposed "unity" of the live event, and in so doing, collapses the binary oppositions between the live and the recorded, the real and the reproduced, the immediate and the mediated. As Steve Wurtzler argues, this type of disjunction testifies to the postmodern eclipse of the real.[36] Cultural theorists such as Jean Baudrillard defined postmodernism foremost in terms of this eclipse, as a proliferation of simulacra. In postmodern culture, in which technologically reproduced images dominate, the hard-and-fast distinction between the real and its representation or simulation is effaced. "Models" take the place of the real and become "hyper-real," more real than the real.[37]

In fact, questioning the "real" has been a recurrent theme in many postmodern theatrical experiments. These works dramatize the tension between the real and technologically mediated simulations, often by confronting onstage live action with film or video projections. Squat Theatre's *Dreamland Burns* (1986) is an example. The performance of this work begins with a projection of filmed actions. At the end of the film, the screen burns up with a real fire and the live performance begins. Several actors from the film reappear as live performers, creating a tension between the real and its cinematic simulacrum. Stephen Bálint, director of the work, further heightens this tension by using four dummies that are replicas of live performers and by occasionally projecting actual actors' faces onto the faces of their inanimate replicas. *Deep Sleep* (1986), written and directed by John Jesurum for La Mama Theatre in New York, is another example of the postmodern questioning of the real. This work powerfully dramatizes the confusion between the real and the reproduced, between the stage life and the screen life, by presenting four actors trapped between two gigantic film screens suspended at opposite ends of the stage. This dialectical setting visualizes the problem of the real in our postmodern life: challenged by its technologically mediated simulation, the status of the real is no longer stable.[38]

This type of setting has become common and even regressed to banality in non-operatic theater and performance works. On the operatic stage, too, Glass's exploration of cinematic images along with live voice and body is hardly an epoch-making device. The use of filmic idioms and technology and other pop-culture icons has been increasingly popular in recent operatic production. What distinguishes Glass's *Belle* from kindred operatic works is the absolute dominance of the cinematic images in the visual realm. Yet Glass's *Belle* is not completely devoid of performative fluidity: music is performed live and singers still appear on stage, although they do not participate in acting. In this respect, Glass's *Belle* "stages" the postmodern loss of the real: the real is inscribed with the presence of live bodies and music, but at the same time is subverted by the presence of recorded images.

Given the simultaneous presence of the real and the recorded, Glass's *Belle* resembles a postmodern "parody." Linda Hutcheon contends that parody in postmodern art should not be confused with the eighteenth-century notions of parody as a witty or ridiculed imitation of the art of the past. For Hutcheon, postmodern parody is first and foremost a "double coding" that both legitimizes and subverts, foregrounds and questions, and uses and abuses what it parodies.[39]

Hutcheon discusses Maximilian Schell's *Marlene*, a documentary on Marlene Dietrich, as an example of postmodern parody. What this film questions is the much presumed authority of the documentary as a transparent record of the real. The film takes the form of interviews with Dietrich, but she appears only as a disembodied voice: during the interviews we *hear* her voice without *seeing* her, except in extensive footage of her previous concerts. Through this dualistic visual representation of her, Schell's *Marlene* addresses the problematic status of the "real" in postmodern life: the "real" can be accessed only through its mediated representations. Hutcheon describes Schell's *Marlene* as a documentary about "a willfully absent subject, one who refuses to be subjected to the discourses and representations of others."[40] The visual absence of the subject frustrates our expectations for a documentary because it destablizes the certainty of its subject, who remains elusive throughout. This in turn undermines the humanist notion of a human being as a coherent and integrated individual. And, as Hutcheon notes, the humanist-modernist concept of a coherent, continuous, and autonomous individual has been a central target of postmodern parody.[41] Similary, Glass's *Belle* problematizes a humanist-modernist concept. By disrupting the traditional unity between the voice and the body and by separating viewing from hearing, *Belle* speaks of the fragmentary and decentered subject privileged in postmodern art.

The technological dominance in the performance of *Belle* is another aspect of its postmodernist stance. In *Belle*, the visual event is technologically mediated: the cinematic screen functions not as a mere production device to support onstage actions but as *the* visual enactment of the operatic narrative. Not only at the visual level but at the musical level, *Belle* shows a positive response to technology by employing a synthesizer in the ensemble that accompanies singing. The synthesizer often creates sound effects (for example, the tolling of the clock) as well as musical sounds. Modernist movements such as *l'art pour l'art* revolted against the technological influence on art, especially photographic reproduction. Walter Benjamin has described modernists' advocacy of pure art as a "fetishistic fundamentally anti-technological notion of art."[42] Modernists adamantly resisted technological influence on art, particularly mechanical reproduction, mainly because it destroys the "aura" of an artwork. The plot of Jean-Jacques Beineix's film *Diva* (1982) unfolds around a diva who obstinately refuses to have her voice mechanically reproduced. The diva's refusal typifies the modernist fear of the loss of aura.

Unlike the modernist's refusal of, and defense against, technology, postmodern artists like Glass tend to appraise technology positively and incorporate it into their works in order to play with the depletion of aura. In *Belle*, the traditional aura of operatic performance is endangered because the live acting is replaced by technologically reproduced images. Moreover, *Belle* has shown that the operatic voice can become an isolated object even in live theater. Postmodern operatic experiments have gone far beyond what Beineix's diva feared: the stage can no longer be a sanctuary that protects the aura of her voice.

Opera is inherently a crossover form, "the third thing," to put it in Majorie Garber's words, which is too elusive to fit into binary genre definitions. Garber contends that opera performs a kind of "aesthetic transvestism," embodying one genre while wearing the aesthetic vestments of another.[43] With its postmodern transformation in cinematic attire, opera has become an even more elusive transvestite. In *Belle*, it becomes a queer hybrid between the real and the reproduced, between the operatic voice and the cinematic body, between a proscenium and a movie theater.

## NOTES

1. Martin Marks, "Music and the Silent Film," in *The Oxford History of World Cinema*, ed. Geoffrey Nowell-Smith (London: Oxford University Press, 1996), 183.

2. Examples produced from this period include Bernd Alois Zimmermann's *Die Soldaten* (1965), Robert Ashley's *Perfect Lives* (1980), Karlheinz Stockhausen's *Donnerstag aus Licht* (1981), and Steve Reich's *The Cave* (1993).

3. Siegfried Kracauer, "Opera on the Screen," *Film Culture* 1 (March-April 1955): 19.

4. Glass's attraction to cinema can be seen not only in his operatic works but also in his film scores. He scored Paul Schrader's *Mishima* (1985), a biographical film about the eccentric Japanese writer Yukio Mishima, in which the proportion of music is unprecedentedly large for a normal narrative film. In non-narrative films, *Koyaanisqatsi* [Chaos] (1983) and *Powaqqatsi* [Life in transformation] (1988), Glass and the director Godfrey Reggio explored the relationship between music and image in imaginative ways, entirely devoid of spoken dialogues. Glass also provided the score for Erroi Morris's documentary film *The Thin Blue Line* (1988), based on the true story of Randall Adams who was convicted of murdering a Dallas police officer in 1976, and *A Brief History of Time* (1991), based on Steven Hawking's book on cosmology published in 1988. The most commercially oriented films that Glass scored for include the 1992 horror *Candyman*, and more recently, Martin Scorsese's *Kundun* (1998).

5. His score brought the film the best music award at the Cannes Film Festival in 1946.

6. Ned Rorem, "Cocteau and Music," in *Jean Cocteau and the French Scene* (New York: Abbeville Press, 1984), 172.

7. Jean Cocteau, *Beauty and the Beast: Diary of a Film*, trans. Ronald Duncan (New York: Dover Publications Inc., 1972), 128.

8. Ibid. Cocteau said, "... sound and image will not run together both saying the same thing at the same time, neutralizing each other."

9. It seems that location rather than character decides the presence or absence of music. For instance, Ludovic, Belle's brother, is accompanied by music when he is in the Beast's pavilion. He was not previously accompanied by music, since he is one of

the most realistic characters in the film, along with his two sisters. But when he is in the domain of the Beast, the world of fantasy, music accompanies his actions. Conversely, there is no background music for Beauty when she is at home surrounded by realistic people.

10. Diegesis literally means a "recital of facts" in Greek. Claudia Gorbman defines diegesis as "the narratively implied spatiotemporal world of the actions and characters." Diegetic sounds are those sounds that issue from a source within the filmic narrative. See Claudia Gorbman, *Unheard Melodies: Narrative Film Music* (Bloomington: Indiana University Press, 1987), 21–2.

11. Glass preserved those noises from the original soundtrack in a few places.

12. The association of baggy pants with Einstein is rather obvious, but images of pipes need some explanation. Einstein was seriously interested in plumbing: it is known that he would have wanted to be a plumber had he not become a scientist. See Philip Glass, *Opera on the Beach* (New York: Dunvagen Music Publishers, Inc., 1987), 79.

13. There are a few moments in which singers "act" in the minimal sense of the word. For instance, when the Beast first proposes to Beauty at a dinner scene, the singer who performs the Beast moves toward the singer playing Beauty and stands behind her, imitating the movement and the position of the on-screen characters. But most of the time during the performance of the opera the singers are just standing, frozen on stage without acting.

14. Steven Shaviro, *The Cinematic Body* (Minneapolis: The University of Minnesota Press, 1993), 203.

15. Johannes Birringer, "Postmodernism and Theatrical Performance," in *International Postmodernism: Theory and Literature Practice*, ed. Hans Bertens and Douwe Fokkema (Amsterdam: John Benjamins Publishing Co., 1997), 139.

16. Johannes Birringer, *Theatre, Theory, Postmodernism* (Bloomington: Indiana University Press, 1991), 223.

17. Sam Abel, *Opera in the Flesh* (Colorado: Westview Press, Inc., 1996), 164–5.

18. Ibid., 168.

19. Among the best sources for the history of sound practice in silents are Martin Miller Marks, *Music and The Silent Film: Contexts and Case Studies, 1895–1924* (New York: Oxford University Press, 1997); Rick Altman, "The Sound of Sound: A Brief History of the Reproduction of Sound in Movie Theaters," *Cineaste* 21 (winter/sring 1995): 68–71; Rick Altman, "Introduction: Sound/History," in *Sound Theory, Sound Practice*, ed. Rick Altman (New York: Routledge, 1992), 113–25; and Raymond Fielding, "The Technological Antecedents of the Coming of Sound: An Introduction," in *Sound and the Cinema*, ed. Evan William Cameron (New York: Redgrave Publishing Company, 1980), 2–23. It has been a general notion that silent films were always accompanied by some kinds of music, at the very least by a solo piano. However, Rick Altman's recent research has shown that in presenting silent cinema, there were more diverse practices than generally regarded, which include a

totally silent performance without any accompanying sound. See Rick Altman, "The Silence of the Silents," *The Musical Quarterly*, 80 (winter 1996): 648–718.

20. Fielding, "The Technological Antecedents of the Coming of Sound," 5.

21. Michel Chion, *La Voix au Cinéma* (Paris: Cahiers du Cinema, 1982), 125.

22. Quoted in Thomas Yaron Levin, "Ciphers of Utopia: Critical Theory and the Dialectics of Technological Inscription" (Ph.D. dissertation, Yale University, 1991), 115.

23. James Lastra, "Reading, Writing, and Representing Sound," in *Sound Theory, Sound Practice*, ed. Altman, 67.

24. Lucy Fischer, "*Applause*: The Visual and Acoustic Landscape," in *Sound and the Cinema*, ed. Cameron, 185.

25. Ibid., 182.

26. Béla Balázs, *Theory of the Film: Character and Growth of a New Art* (New York: Dover Publications, 1970), 207.

27. This is why music accompanied silent cinema in addition to its function of masking noises from the projector. See Claudia Gorbman, "Narrative Film Music," *Yale French Studies*, no. 60 (1980): 186. The entire issue of this journal is devoted to the subject of cinema and sound.

28. Hanns Eisler, *Composing for the Films*, reprint ed. (New York: Books for Libraries Press, 1971), 59, 77.

29. Marcia Citron has argued that an effect of diegetic sounds is "the imposition of a frame of reality—as if the sounds are marking off events in real time and space." See Marcia J. Citron, "A Night at the Cinema: Zeffirelli's *Otello* and the Genre of Film-Opera," *Musical Quarterly* 78 (winter 1994): 719.

30. Steve Wurtzler, "'She Sang Live, But the Microphone Was Turned Off': The Live, The Recorded, and the *Subject* of Representation," in *Sound Theory, Sound Practice*, ed. Altman, 100.

31. Quoted in Birringer, *Theatre, Theory, Postmodernism*, 224.

32. Fredric Jameson, "Postmodernism or the Cultural Logic of Late Capitalism," *New Left Review*, no. 146 (Sept/Oct 1984): 62.

33. Ibid., 62.

34. Shaviro, *The Cinematic Body*, 229.

35. Wurtzler, "'She Sang Live'" 89.

36. Ibid., 93.

37. Jean Baudrillard, *Simulations*, trans. Paul Foss, Paul Patton, and Philip Beitchman (New York: Semiotext, 1983), 23.

38. Birringer, *Theatre, Theory, Postmodernism*, 120.

39. Linda Hutcheon, "An Epilogue: Postmodern Parody: History, Subjectivity, and Ideology," *Quarterly Review of Film and Video* 12, no. 1/2 (May 1990): 128–32.

40. Linda Hutcheon, *The Politics of Postmodernism* (New York: Routledge, 1989), 116.

41. Ibid., 108–9.

42. Quoted in Margot Lovejoy, *Postmodern Currents: Art and Artists in the Age of Electronic Media* (Ann Arbor: U.M.I. Research Press, 1989), 35.

43. Marjorie Garber, *Vested Interests: Cross-Dressing and Cultural Anxiety* (New York: Haper Colins, 1993), 33.

# 5
# Why Does Hollywood Like Opera?

*Marc A. Weiner*

OW MAY WE EXPLAIN THE REMARKABLY PROMINENT ROLE THAT OPERA has played in the past twenty-five years within films not intended for opera fans, but for a wide, popular audience that would otherwise evince little interest in musical dramatic art? Examples of this fairly new phenomenon (and this is simply a selection) include *Serpico*, *The Killing Fields*, *The Witches of Eastwick*, *A Room with a View*, *Godfather III*, *Pretty Woman*, *Fatal Attraction*, *Moonstruck*, *Awakenings*, *Jennifer 8*, *Heavenly Creatures*, *New York Stories*, *The Age of Innocence*, *M. Butterfly*, *Philadelphia*, *The Shawshank Redemption*, *The Fifth Element*, *Magnolia*, and *The House of Mirth*. What accounts for the fact that opera here is no longer simply atmospheric accompaniment (as in the many Puccini passages in the soundtracks of Hollywood films from the 1930s and '40s), but functions as an interpretive key, and sometimes even as the central, culminating moment in so-called blockbusters, productions that are financially dependent on success with a wide and diversified audience? This seems to be a sociologically and ideologically important feature of the relationship between opera and film that has remained relatively unexplored within the comparatively new fields of opera and film studies.[1]

If we examine how opera is employed in recent popular films—both thematically, in terms of its function within Hollywood plots, and technically, in terms of the aesthetic devices employed when opera emerges in the cinematic work—we may be able to discern their preconceptions concerning the audience, as well as the concomitant function of non-popular or elitist art. If we can understand what the assumptions concerning that diversified target audience are, we may be able to answer, if only in a provisional fashion, my titular question: "Why does Hollywood like opera?"

## PHILADELPHIA

In an effort to explore this phenomenon, I would like to examine one of the most celebrated uses of opera in recent Hollywood history: Jonathan Demme's *Philadelphia* of 1993. In this work, social and ideological issues play a particularly prominent role, and they help to account for some of the aesthetic devices employed when opera appears in numerous other films of the past twenty-five years, devices based on preconceptions of the cinematic audience.[2] The opera scene in *Philadelphia* has been singled out by both defenders and detractors as the most important of the entire film. It is generally conceded that it was this scene that earned Tom Hanks the Oscar for best performance in a leading role in 1993. (It was shown at the Oscar ceremony before Hanks received the award.)[3] Obviously, there is something about thi sscene that makes it appear both appropriate and persuasive to audiences today. But what might that be? What is the motivic and thematic context, and what are the technical devices at work in this popular film that make opera comply so seamlessly with the audience's expectations? Why is opera an important component of the plot, and how is it employed here?

*Philadelphia* relates the story of Andrew Beckett, a gay man fired from his position with a prestigious law firm because his employers discover he has AIDS, although they claim that they have let him go for other reasons. Beckett decides to take the firm to court for wrongful termination and hires Joe Miller to represent him, an attorney who, by the way, is heterosexual and, to make matters more complicated, also homophobic. The celebrated opera scene takes place in the second half of the film, well into the trial, and begins during a discussion in Beckett's apartment between the two men concerning courtroom strategy. Beckett puts on a recording of "La Mamma morta" from the 1896 opera *Andrea Chénier* by Umberto Giordano, and soon is unable to concentrate on such mundane matters as his trial. Instead, the scene portrays Beckett's attempts to narrate the dramatic details of the aria as sung by Maria Callas, a point that Wayne Koestenbaum underscored when he was interviewed about the film by National Public Radio shortly before the Oscar awards.[4]

Beckett not only narrates, he also provides a running commentary on the aesthetic details of the piece in a fashion that the musicologist Mitchell Morris describes as "somewhere between a music appreciation lecture, a translation (from the music and from the Italian), and a lip-synch."[5] As Beckett holds forth—accompanied throughout by an intravenous infusion as a constant visual reminder of his physical deterioration—his passion for the piece and his identification with the figure of Maddalena increase to such intensity that they merge into intoxication. Demme's aesthetic praxis underscores the process by slowly increasing the volume of the operatic recording, elevating the camera angle, and gradually illuminating Beckett in a rosy shimmer, a metaphor for revery that abruptly ends when the lighting becomes harshly cold and white at the conclusion to the aria. The scene thus represents a shift from the predominant realism that had characterized the film up to that point toward a different mode of presentation, one reliant on visual and acoustical metaphors suggesting interiority, unfettered passion, and perhaps a greater degree of authenticity than that allowed within the more quotidian relations depicted elsewhere in the film.

The scene reveals assumptions behind current associations attending specific kinds of art and conceptualizations of the popular. In *Philadelphia*, opera is associated with a specific set of motifs that serve to underscore the artwork's status as esoteric and exotic. The scene represents a connection between opera, the diseased body of the protagonist, homosexuality, and elevated social status, all of which make opera an emblem of everything deemed outside the norm of middle-class society. This nexus of associations is, of course, something that we have inherited from the nineteenth century, but it remains central to, though often unquestioned and thus unacknowledged in, our culture and is therefore unquestioned when it is employed as a vehicle for appealing to a wide audience. Already in his writings from the 1850s, Wagner employed these associations when he rejected foreign operatic art as aristocratic, effeminate, licentious, and diseased, all of which emphasized its status as too far removed from the "healthy," "folkish" roots of German art. These epithets would continue to emerge in discussions of opera well into the first half of the twentieth century. In *Philadelphia,* as in American culture in general, homosexuality and disease are features presented as exotic, or in any event as not belonging to mainstream cultural norms.

Throughout the film, opera is presented as the opposite of the popular. While the white and upper middle-class Beckett, until only recently a successful corporate attorney, loves *Andrea Chénier*, the African-American Joe Miller, like the beer for which he is named, is associated with sports. This point is underscored in their dialogue prior to Beckett's exegesis of the aria when Beckett asks Miller what he prays for, and Miller responds that he prays the "Phillies will win the pennant," and admits that he is "not that familiar with opera." Miller is an "ambulance chaser," the kind of injury lawyer who advertises on billboards and television, media with which he is repeatedly connected, and he is often passing out business cards or appealing to the injured public on television. It is not purely coincidental that Miller is associated with television and Beckett with opera. The polarity of the opera-loving, sick, gay man versus the aesthetically unenlightened, healthy, and straight sports fan merges with the binary opposition of high versus low culture and distinct levels of social and professional status, an opposition on which the entire film is based. I would argue that this dichotomy accounts for the film's popularity, in that the work employs aesthetic objects in such a way that they appear to reinforce audience expectations.

The remarkable thing about the opera scene—and in this it is representative of the function of opera in many films—is that it creates the impression that through opera, these social and cultural differences can be elided or temporarily broken down, despite the fact that they are actually (though covertly) reinforced and preserved throughout the film. That is, the opera scene is based on social oppositions, but these are nonetheless repressed or hidden as the scene progresses by virtue of the fact that the artform is gradually presented as universally accessible. How is this achieved? How can opera appear both elitist and at the same time as an art for everyone?

## PHANTASMAGORIA

In order to pursue this question, I would like to draw on Adorno's concept of "phantasmagoria." The points of comparison between *Philadelphia* and Adorno's *In Search of Wagner*, in which Adorno describes phantasmagoria as the key to the widespread appeal of Wagner's music dramas, are both numerous and illuminating. They have wide-ranging implications for our understanding of the role of opera in modern film, not only in Demme's work, but in virtually all of the films mentioned above that employ opera. We may recall that Adorno criticized Nietzsche for having "failed to recognize . . . [in Wagner's works for the stage] the birth of film out of the spirit of music." For Adorno, Wagner's works presaged not only the ideology of National Socialism, but something he believed was related to it, namely the aesthetic production of Hollywood as well.[6] Adorno claimed that the key to the appeal of the Wagnerian artwork was the music-drama's ability to bring about a numbing, sensual bombardment of the listening viewer, resulting purportedly in a drug-like seduction (already made note of by Wagner's contemporaries). This effaces the material dimension of the artwork and lulls the audience into perceiving the artificial construct as a natural phenomenon, into emotionally and imaginatively participating in or identifying with the aesthetically induced fantasy, and ultimately into accepting the artwork's reprehensible ideological content. He labeled this process "phantasmagoria" and opens his description of it thus:

> The occultation of production by means of the outward appearance of the product—that is the formal law governing the works of Richard Wagner. The product presents itself as self-producing. . . . In the absence of any glimpse of the underlying forces or conditions of its production, this outer appearance can lay claim to the status of being. Its perfection is at the same time the perfection of the illusion that the work of art is a reality sui generis that constitutes itself in the realm of the absolute without having to renounce its claim to image the world. Wagner's operas tend towards magic delusion, . . . in short towards phantasmagoria.[7]

If we take seriously Adorno's insights into the conflation of aesthetics and ideology in the Wagnerian work of art—which he viewed as an important precursor and cultural background to the cinema—then we must acknowledge this feature of the opera scene as well, because it evinces all of the features Adorno described as characterizing phantasmagoria. While we may certainly reject the overall nature of Adorno's film criticism as woefully undifferentiated, uninformed, and elitist, it is nonetheless remarkable just how many of his insights into the makeup of the Wagnerian artwork apply to certain features of the modern film: especially the Hollywood blockbuster. Adorno's main point here is that phantasmagoria masks the forces of its own production. In the course of *Philadelphia*'s opera scene, the status of the recording as a recording is increasingly deemphasized. Following the initial shot of the stereo equipment, when Beckett adjusts the volume, the camera never returns to this mechanical source of the sound, even though, unrealistically, the volume continues to swell as the scene nears its conclusion. In this way, the aesthetic makeup of the scene serves as a metaphor for the dissolution of objective reality and the move toward subjectivity, toward the psychological space of rapturous interiority. This feature of the Hollywood film demonstrates Adorno's insistence that film preserves the auratic nature of the Wagnerian artwork, which of course Benjamin, in his debate with Adorno on this very subject, believed was abandoned or undermined by the new artform's mechanical reproduceability.[8] Here, at least, Adorno's insights prove remarkably illuminating.

Virtually all of the phantasmagoric features that Adorno identifies in Wagner's works reemerge in the opera scene in *Philadelphia*. First, Adorno's translator, Rodney Livingston, notes that the very term "phantasmagoric" was invented for the exhibition of "optical illusions produced chiefly by means of the magic lantern," and the scene stages precisely what Adorno describes in the passage above as a "magic delusion."[9] Second, for Adorno, phantasmagoria "tends towards dream," and certainly the central theme of the cinematic scene is the intoxicating and illusory nature of the revery it stages.[10] Indeed, sound itself appears both in Adorno's *Wagner* text and in the film to function as a Fata Morgana, enticing, dangerous, and illusory.[11] Opera is not solely presented in the film as worthy of rejection owing to its status as esoteric: It is precisely its exoticism that also makes opera fascinating, and thus not only foreign and threatening, but also bewildering, seductive, and moving. It is the privileged space for the expression of fantasy, a space that is illusory within the social confines of *Philadelphia*.

Third, phantasmagoria serves to disorient the viewer by making one oblivious to temporal progression. Adorno articulates this insight thus:

> The standing-still of time and the complete occultation of nature by means of phantasmagoria are . . . brought together in the memory of a pristine age. . . . Time is the all-important element of production that phantasmagoria, the mirage of eternity, obscures. While days and months run into each other and vanish as in a moment, phantasmagoria makes up for this by representing the moment as that which endures. . . .[12]

As Beckett's revery progresses, time appears to move ever more slowly, until finally, at the conclusion to the aria, it seems to stand still. This impression is reinforced by the dramatization of interiority and by the gradual, initially unobtrusive technical shifts in lighting and camera angle, which provide the listening viewer with a set of signifiers not associated with the presentation of the flow of time depicted thus far. The opera scene essentially removes the viewer (and Miller) from the dramatic event towards which the entire film until then had been progressing: Beckett's testimony in the trial. It is significant that it is framed by the men's strategic rehearsal for this testimony prior to the scene and Miller's abrupt statement, following the aria, that such discussions are no longer necessary. (Beckett says, "I'll go over the Q and A," to which Miller replies, "No, you're ready," a surprising statement, given his previous frustration with Beckett during their rehearsal.) As the realm of the mundane is forgotten through the extravagance of the opera, the particularity of the quotidian is suspended in favor of something else: both the mode of vaulted expression scarcely contained within the quotidian as well as the timeless quality of the universal themes of love and sacrifice articulated in the aria. Because of both its extravagantly expressive ardor and the universal or timeless themes it concerns, the scene seems to stand beyond the mundane, and with it, outside the flow of normal time.

Nonetheless, there is something unmistakably nostalgic, and therefore not timeless but historically specific, about the opera scene as well. By evoking the drama of the French revolution through the nineteenth-century artwork *Andrea Chénier*, the scene serves to remove the listening viewer from the tribulations of the gay man in the modern world and to replace them with a cultural artifact, as though the film were thereby acknowledging its association with a culturally fettered realism. This would explain the film's relation to opera as one of dependence; it needs the exotic artwork to lend expression to feelings and dynamics it wishes to distance from itself. In this way, opera represents a time of more straightforward, and less cynical, expression. Instead of modern-day Philadelphia—associated with power politics, cynicism, and a mode of interpersonal exchange hardly worthy of the city of "brotherly love"—we are faced with a direct, emphatic passion that seems to have no place in the world of the listening viewer, Miller, or of the audience attending to him. The passionate, emphatic nature of the nineteenth-century opera serves as a foil to the cynicism of the modern film, and thus also not only as an emblem of the universal and the timeless, but also as a historically specific, nostalgic escape.

Finally, Adorno maintains that in the process of phantasmagoria, "sex and sexual disease become identical," a point he bases on a host of features found in Wagner's plots that would later be closely associated with the decadent movement and much of the literature of the *fin-de-siècle*, from D'Annunzio and Schnitzler to Mallarmé, Proust, Wilde, and Thomas Mann.[13] This reinforces the impression that much of the motivic vocabulary of the film constitutes a remnant from the nineteenth century, a cultural inheritance from the European tradition that continues (perhaps unconsciously or automatically) to inform the images with which our cultural material surrounds us and which reinforces the social dynamics of our world. Beckett's status as diseased is central to his function in the constellation of opera, deviant sexuality, and high social status, all of which serve to underscore his nature as different from that of the mainstream. Thus, while the phantasmagoria of the opera scene makes the artwork emerge as a natural phenomenon, enticing and seductive in the perfection of its illusory character, it also encompasses specific ideological features that make the particular appear universal and beyond question.

## PHANTASMAGORIA AND IDENTIFICATION

But my use of Adorno here is not due solely to such motivic similarities. According to Adorno, the ideological function of phantasmagoria lies in its apparent ability to suspend differences of all kinds. It is precisely this function that is discernible in the opera scene, in which the distinctions between Beckett's and Miller's social status and sexual orientations are temporarily suspended. Phantasmagoria is associated here with opera, and opera is presented as something that appears to transcend the particularity of given social conventions (that it actually reinforces them is another matter to which I will return shortly). This constitutes a central, though often unacknowledged, function of opera in a host of recent films.

The aesthetic devices of the Wagnerian music drama, according to Adorno, are the technical means through which the artwork masks its artificiality and brings the audience to view itself as reflected in the work itself: that is, to *identify* with it. This is a key to the function of opera and phantasmagoria in *Philadelphia*. The process of giving up one's individuality and entering into the collective experience of the *Gesamtkunstwerk* is, for Adorno, the key to Wagner's popularity, and the process of identification (with the artwork and with the collective) is central in this interpretation. I would argue that it also helps to account for the role of opera in this demonstrably popular Hollywood film.

The phantasmagoria of the opera scene creates identification on a host of levels, thereby creating (at least temporarily) a bridge between homosexual and heterosexual, black and white, the ill and the healthy, rich and poor, the foreign and the familiar, and even between film and audience. On one level, we have Beckett's empathic relationship with the artwork; on another, Miller—the diegetic representative of the cinematic audience—is shown to grow increasingly moved, and perhaps for the first time to understand the figure before him, as well as to appreciate the operatic material. Finally, the phantasmagoric extravagance of the all-encompassing visual and acoustical dynamic at the conclusion of the scene provides—indeed, presupposes—access on the part of the audience to Miller empathizing with Beckett, to Beckett himself, and to the operatic aria so powerfully rendered by Maria Callas. The gradual effacement of the sonic production and the expansion of the rosy vision make it easy for the audience to identify with Beckett, and with Miller's view of him. We do not, for example, observe Beckett encapsulated within a revery that remains visually or acoustically isolated from Miller or from the viewer, but are invited into the dream as well. This process of identification, so dramatically reinforced through its phantasmagoric presentation, is not unique to *Philadelphia;* it is also found in other popular films employing opera, such as *Pretty Woman, Fatal Attraction,* and *Moonstruck*, all of which concern individuals who—either ironically, humorously, or pathologically—compare themselves with figures in operas (here, by Verdi and Puccini). The process of identification in *Philadelphia* is more closely associated or rendered through phantasmagoria than is the case in these other works, but in all of them identification is a dominant phenomenon when opera appears, its diverse modes of presentation and role in the thematics of these various works notwithstanding. Identification is also available in different ways to the mass audience to which these works appeal. Thus, *Philadelphia* demonstrates a psychological and culturally determined process to which both the protagonists of many Hollywood films employing opera and the audience itself are subjected.

One way of examining how the process of identification works so effectively in *Philadelphia*, in terms of its psychological power and its cultural implications, is to interpret the scene as constructed around a metaphor that film critics have used to discuss the means by which film creates identification between its visual images, sounds, and the listening viewer. That metaphor is ventriloquism. Likening the relationship between soundtrack and image to that of the ventriloquist and his dummy, Jeremy Tambling has written that "the body of the ventriloquist speaks, and the dummy acts out the wild anarchic and libidinal impulses that are projected onto it, as though, psychoanalytically, sound is the repressed other, whose libidinal content is directed toward the image."[14] But not only sound per se, but more specifically operatic sound, signifying all of the signs of social particularity with which the artform is associated in the world of the film. Beckett's lengthy exercise in lip-synching and concomitant opera exegesis gives expression to, and momentarily makes possible identification with, the emotionally charged material that until then had appeared foreign and exotic. The libidinal energy of the (socially) repressed (both artform and sexuality, as well as the specific nature of the diseased individual) has been projected onto the visual presentation, where it becomes accessible to all: both to Miller and to the audience sympathizing with him and with Beckett. It would be wrong to suggest that opera abandons the signs of difference stigmatizing and trapping the individual in an unforgiving world. Ironically, it seems both to signify difference and to rise above the limitations of such signification. Through its accessibility toward Miller and the audience, it comes to constitute the universal, and thereby also represents the locus of freedom and of the imagination as something with which everyone can identify.

It is precisely as the signifier of freedom that opera is often employed by Hollywood, as seen, for example, in such diverse presentations of opera in prison settings as those in *M. Butterfly* and *The Shawshank Redemption.* It represents the freedom of the imagination and a longing for a society that would accept sexual freedom in other films as well, such as *Moonstruck* and especially in *Heavenly*

*Creatures* (a non-Hollywood film). When it represents particularity, opera signifies entrapment, and when it functions as a sign of the universal, it represents freedom. But perhaps it would be more accurate to say that these two significations of opera (as a sign of both the particular and the univeral) do not simply function alongside or independently of each other, but are actually equated. The art may be stigmatized and marginalized precisely *because* it signifies freedom from those very conventions that make it appear suspect. This would make sense within the all-encompassing ideology of a world that rejects difference of any kind, and would go hand-in-hand with the covert function of opera that I am suggesting.

Even as the metaphor of the dummy enacts in this quintessentially Hollywood film a liberation of the repressed through purported sympathy with the homosexual, that liberation is illusory or disingenuous. The function of the opera as a sign of the universal is ideological, disingenuous, and pernicious, and that sympathy is undermined time and again. Even as opera ostensibly comes to signify the universal in the course of the opera scene, the film emphatically associates its protagonist with the decadent trope par excellence (disease and aesthetic extravagance). Beckett's voice is replaced with that of the diva at the moment in which he lip-synchs the final high note of the aria, silently mouthing the words that Maria Callas sings. Speaking metaphorically, one could say then that the opera scene achieves the opposite of what it seems to appeal for: it silences sexuality deemed deviant and displaces it through the effacement of libidinal energy onto a foreign aesthetic material as a metaphorical corollary to the stigmatization and isolation it evinces throughout, regardless of whether that stigmatization is acknowledged or disavowed.

But why is this the case? Why would Demme wish to present opera in such a contradictory fashion? A possible (and admittedly cynical) answer would be that Demme, like other cultural producers in America, attempts not simply to underscore and to exploit the social pretensions of opera and its connection to signs of difference, but also to mask them, in part because he is dependent on a wide and diversified audience that might be alienated by such social pretensions and signs. Therefore he presents the artform as exalted—socially, aesthetically, and psychodynamically, as the locus of the imagination and of unfettered fantasy—and at the same time, he attempts to diffuse its difference, domesticate it, make it quotidian, and thus socially nonthreatening. In this way, Demme's work both reflects and contributes to a specific ideological function of opera in America as at once signifying and disavowing difference. In terms of its social and psychodynamic function, opera constitutes a labile object and institution, a locus full of contradictions within the cultural landscape in America. In *Philadelphia* and the other films mentioned above, as well as in the United States in general, social differences often accompany the artform, but they are also masked or made light of whenever it appears. As a component of a film dependent upon a large audience, this double function of opera may be attributable to specific economic strategies, but these themselves reflect more generally ideological forces.

## NON-DIEGESIS

*Philadelphia* never presents the interdependence of such interpretive possibilities (opera as the sign of the particular versus the universal) in an overt fashion. Quite the contrary; it wishes to have it both ways, to have opera manifestly appear as a vehicle for the transvaluation of particularity separating individuals even as it less emphatically continues to link the artform to their difference. This tension, between the false appearance of the message of universality and the more covert perpetuation of particularity, is presented and reinforced through a host of aesthetic devices and contexts, and not only in the celebrated opera scene. Opera also emerges, for example, as the carrier of the theme of universal (and not only "deviant") love in those few and crucial moments when the music from *Andrea Chénier* is employed non-diegetically —that is, not as music to which these figures listen, such as in the opera scene, but on the soundtrack, where it is available to the audience, but not necessarily to the film's protagonists. Divorced from the means of its production, the non-diegetic, audience-directed music can function as a commentary on the events within scenes, or as a representation of the protagonists' thoughts and auditory memories. In so doing, it invites yet further identification with the repressed material—the social particularity of the stigmatized homosexual and diseased foreign body, and the aesthetic difference of elitist culture, in this case opera.

There are two moments that, initially at least, appear to be non-diegetic that are significant for an understanding of the ideological function of opera in *Philadelphia*. The first occurs immediately after the opera scene, when Miller leaves Beckett's apartment, stops in the hallway, and considers returning to the passionate and traumatized individual, perhaps afraid that he has been too brusque in his exit. As he does so, for a moment there is an indeterminacy of sound: we hear the strains of the beginning of Maddalena's aria, but we do not know if it is being played, or if Miller only recalls it. For a moment, it is unclear whether the music is diegetic or non-diegetic, whether it is Beckett's music, or now Miller's, too. But then we realize that Beckett has begun to play the aria again on his stereo, and Miller leaves, shaking his head in amused bewilderment.

In the scene that follows, this indeterminacy manifestly moves into the realm of musical commentary, or the non-diegetic, through which we are allowed to hear what Miller may be listening to in a passage of interior auditory recollection, divorced from the explicit connection between Beckett and opera established by the diegetic production of phonograph records. Following the phantasmagoric event, during which Miller—and, I think, the audience—had come to identify with Beckett, this scene represents Miller's identification even more forcefully, and reinforces that of the audience with both Miller and Beckett. In this scene, we see Miller arrive at his house very late at night, go to his daughter and take the sleeping girl into his arms, and then get into bed where his wife has been waiting for him. Throughout, the aria from *Andrea Chénier* resounds from the soundtrack as a constant, non-diegetic accompaniment to Miller's movements on screen. We might assume that the music on the soundtrack is what Miller is thinking: the intertextual connection between the mother's love in the aria and his love for his own daughter and wife suggests that this music—and its message of love—are now applicable not only to the homosexual, but to Miller as well. We in effect are witness to Miller identifying with the very aesthetic material with which Beckett had so obviously identified. And we know that it's what the audience is listening to. It has crossed the gap separating sexual, racial, and social particularity and become a vehicle for compassion and understanding ostensibly available to all, a purportedly universal construct that overcomes difference.

But such a construct—of insight into the particular that is available to the universal—ultimately reinforces the difference it purports to transcend. It is based on the specific link between the socially circumscribed (opera, homosexuality, and disease) that it now seeks to disavow. Through that disavowal, it provides access to a wide audience schooled in the tropes of its modernist, late nineteenth-century heritage. Through gestures of inclusion, it appears to encapsulate the audience at the very moment when Miller is won over, and as he, like the listening viewer, attends to the signature of difference sounding in his memory. But that identification is shortlived. The diegetic music returns as an acoustical corollary to images of decay and marginalized sexual identity in the scene of Beckett's death. When we see him for the last time, in the hospital scene following the trial, he is shown lying in bed listening to his beloved opera recordings through earphones connected to his walkman. (This, by the way, is how we had first heard opera in the movie, while Beckett was seen receiving an intravenous transfusion.) The operatic music must return as Beckett's signature tune, because it in fact has never ceased to function as such.

Speaking charitably, one might say that the film simply presents the function of opera as a sign of the universal as ephemeral, shortlived in this world, and nothing more than a utopian moment. But a more accurate analysis would insist that the film returns the tropes linking opera to disease and marginalized sexuality in order to make the audience comfortable following its moment of empathy with the outcast. Indeed, one might argue that the return of these tropes suggests that opera was only accessible because it was filtered through the mediating link of Miller—"if he likes it, then it must be okay for me to like it, too"— and that it was Miller more than opera with which the audience had identified in the first place. Thus, its renewed connection with images of disease and difference is simply consistent, a continuation of a particularity that had informed the earlier scenes employing opera as well, both diegetically and non-diegetically.

The only time Beckett is not associated with opera, but with its social opposite, namely film, is at the conclusion of the movie, when, during a memorial celebration following his death, a home video is shown depicting Beckett as a young boy playing on a beach. I think it is simply consistent that he is presented in the film as film in the guise of a presexual, prepubescent boy. Opera remains the locus of difference, while film is the aesthetic signature of the masses. Here, Beckett's sexual difference has been subsumed by the aesthetic material. That is, when the film invokes Beckett at an age prior to the advent of sexual activity, it can associate him not with opera, but with itself, with film. Beckett is both accepted into the realm of universal love and, at the same time, the price of that acceptance is not only his demise but, more importantly, his transformation into a prepubescent being, a pre-operatic boy whose image marks a haunting absence with which the film concludes, accompanied, moreover, not by operatic music, but by the strains of a moving pop song. He gives up his particularity—recognized as different—to enter into another particularity that presents itself as universal. In a sense, this is another example of how the film "silences" him, obliterating his presence through that of another.

This tension between opera and film at the conclusion of *Philadelphia* (and thus at a privileged point) brings us back to the tensions with which the film had opened. It belies the purported universal message (the transcendence of particularity and stigmatization) of both the diegetic opera scene and its non-diegetic successor (Miller's trip home to the accompaniment of the operatic aria). And where does phantasmagoria—that engine of ideology Adorno believed so central to the popularity of the Wagnerian artwork and to the mechanisms of Hollywood—remain in *Philadelphia* within this concluding polarization? Does Demme's work suggest that phantasmagoria is cinematic, or are we left with the impression that it was an operatic phenomenon? If Adorno is right in claiming that film is the modern vessel of the Wagnerian legacy, one would expect to find phantasmagoria associated with film, and not with opera. As we have seen, this is the case in *Philadelphia*, because all of the features and motifs that Adorno identified in the *Gesamtkunstwerk* are to be found in the aesthetic makeup of the 1993 film. But in keeping with its ideology of disavowal, Demme's project attempts to mask its own connection to the device by displacing it onto the foreign artwork (the opera), thereby implicitly distancing itself from its own reliance on the Wagnerian aesthetic. By linking phantasmagoria to opera instead of to its modern-day cinematic instantiation, the film also links the device to associations of disease, sexuality, and extravagant difference. This is ironic and ideologically revealing, because this remove, or displacement of phantasmagoria from film to opera, allows for the disavowal of one of the devices through which the film itself was obviously (and moreover, successfully) calculated to effect widespread appeal. Here, too, opera's role is fraught with contradiction and tension; it is stigmatized even as it is relied on in a film incorporating tropes with which a modern audience is familiar and which it apparently finds appropriate and persuasive: that is, which helped to make it popular.

OPERA IN AMERICA

Obviously, I have been arguing that these features in *Philadelphia* are not culturally isolated, and that they point to issues within a larger social context. It would be tempting to compare the ideological function of opera in this highly successful film with that of other newer products from the Hollywood factory, such as *The Shawshank Redemption. Redemption,* another movie that concerns a relationship between a black and a white man, homosexuality, and a connection between the privileged Caucasian and the European music drama. These tensions are manifested in the scene in which the character played by Tim Robbins breaks into an office and plays a recording of *Le Nozze di Figaro* over the prison's loudspeaker system.[15] I am not suggesting that opera always and only signifies the associations I have discussed here; in this film, it clearly departs from them, even though it also emerges in a context that places the artwork not far from their concerns. Rather, comparison of *Philadelphia* with *The Shawshank Redemption* demonstrates that Demme's work reveals with particular force—and success— many of the assumptions that may function less explicitly elsewhere when opera emerges in the modern cinema, which is so dependent on, and constitutive of, our cultural universe.

But perhaps America's discomfort with European culture in general may provide one explanation for the film's (as well as its director's and audience's) need to situate opera in a realm removed from everyday experience, in the realm of privileged aesthetic fantasy and of a sexuality deemed deviant and diseased, and then to disavow that segregation. If this is true, the tensions within the film should be found throughout the American cultural landscape. And, indeed, the concomitant discomfort with and reliance on opera as foreign found in *Philadelphia* are also obviously discernible in the Metropolitan Opera's appeals to its public, which suggest a good deal of anxiety on the part of cultural producers and marketing strategists regarding the likes and dislikes of their target audience. These appeals are not straightforward, but are fraught with contradiction. On the one hand, the Metropolitan seeks to perpetuate the notion of opera as exclusive, refined, and aesthetically and socially superior; indeed, it depends on it. At the same time, it masks these associations through gestures toward a wide audience. It markets opera as high-class art for the masses, as seen in its compensatory need to package its elitist product through association with such popular cultural icons as Miss Piggy, and through the incredibly inane trivia quizzes of its broadcast intermission features so reminiscent of TV game shows.[16] The Metropolitan relies on its status as among the most prestigious (if not the most aesthetically accomplished) operatic institution in the world, and yet it disavows the exclusivity that has always accompanied opera in order to reach a wide audience. That does not mean that that audience is not also attracted to the elitist pretensions of the art; indeed, they may actually and ironically function as an unacknowledged source of its attraction today. It is precisely this double approach to opera—as exclusive and as popular—that appears to work for the Metropolitan and that emerges repeatedly when opera plays a role in modern film.

The social distinctions attending opera and film do not concern merely the income levels of their respective audiences so much as the nexus of associations, modes of self-presentation, and processes of self-identification at play in the psychodynamic interaction with specific forms of art and cultural institutions. Despite the efforts of numerous directors to merge the two artforms within film—and the recent operatic productions by such film directors as Werner Herzog and Ken Russell on numerous European stages—the media continue to function for the most part within a host of associations that serve to underscore their differences rather than their commonality. (As such, these associations represent the continuation of social and discursive traditions already discernible in the early twentieth century, when debate raged as to whether the new artform of film constituted a continuation of theatrical tradition or a radical break from it, both aesthetically and socially.[17]) These differences are ideological in nature, and that nature is both manifested and reinforced in many of the recent films employing opera, in that these social distinctions are also belied when opera emerges in the American cultural landscape. In this sense, Demme's work simply illuminates a host of associations and ideological functions attending opera that may be discerned elsewhere in American culture, most obviously, perhaps, in the public relations of its most exalted opera house.

Despite this argument, I'd like to make an important disclaimer. I am aware of the fact that the hidden, but nonetheless consistent, polar model dividing high and low culture, which I believe underlies the aesthetic of *Philadelphia*—and the marketing strategies of the Metropolitan Opera, for that matter—by no means provides an exhaustive interpretive matrix for an examination of the mass audience today, nor of the possibilities through which Demme's film could be received. Certainly there are pressures, tastes, and influences other than those I've discussed that may be involved in a host of responses to this film and to operatic performances. These, consciously or unconsciously, may compete with, take the place of, or simply accompany the responses to specific cultural codes I've been suggesting that this film draws on, and thereby presupposes on the part of the modern audience. This is one of the areas in which I would agree with those who find fault with Adorno's analysis of mass culture as too sweeping or undifferentiated.[18] The problem with such discussions, of course, is that they are based on the polar model separating, through a "great divide," high and low culture that has come to be viewed as constitutive of the modernist period, but that would subsequently be vilified in reactions to modernist theoretical thought, especially in postmodernist criticisms of the Frankfurt School as elitist and monolithic. The question, then, is whether such a polar bifurcation of culture, which may be discerned as informing the self-perception of modernism, is still useful to our current analyses of the period, as well as to analysis of its legacy in the post-modern age, or whether other, less bifurcated models may prove more useful. But the tropes in Demme's work are there for a reason, and they point to a way of viewing specific kinds of art that bypass, or simply do not take into account or address, the heterogeneity of today's audience.

The irony of the image of the audience implied by the aesthetic decisions of the makers of *Philadelphia* lies in the fact that the audience is given the opportunity to find pleasure in a foreign aesthetic material—to be able to empathize, for example, with the foreigner's love of opera—that continues to function as a sign of difference, illness, and exoticism. This contradiction or tension defines the often unacknowledged tensions within the function of opera in the American cultural landscape in general. Demme's work is a forceful representation of a set of assumptions regarding the mass audience's view of opera that informs numerous other examples of Hollywood's recent discovery and employment of opera. As long as opera both connotes difference and is made to appear to transcend particularity—that is, as long as it functions as the locus of the particular even as it is presented as the sign of the universal in the American imagination—opera will continue to have a secure place in the collective dreams of Hollywood that both reflect and reinforce those collective fantasies. It will be interesting to see what social and ideological features future meetings of film and opera reveal.

NOTES

1. Numerous investigations within the growing field of film and opera studies have been devoted to widely diversified, and yet specific or insular, examples of opera's role in cinematic history. This diversification of scholarly interest is hardly surprising, given the multiple roles opera has played in the history of cinema itself. Opera has appeared, after all, as source material for use in soundtracks, as a structural model in the makeup of Hollywood films prior to *Ben Hur*, as an intertextual, acoustical, and thematic element in works by directors as different in their aesthetic proclivities as Visconti, Wertmuller, and Russell, and as an element in the cinematic plot. (I thank Professor Erik Fischer of the Musikwissenschaftliches Institut, Universität Bonn, for bringing the structural affinity between opera and films prior to *Ben Hur* to my attention.) And some operatic scores have themselves of course incorporated a cinematic component, such as Berg's *Lulu*, Hindemith's *Hin und Zurück: eine Zeitoper*, and—as discussed in Chapter 4 of the current collection—Philip Glass's setting of Cocteau's *La Belle et la Bête*. [On the film in *Lulu* see: George Perle, *The Operas of Alban Berg*, vol. II *Lulu* (Los Angeles: University of California Press, 1985), 48–49, 149–157, esp. 152; Theodor W. Adorno, "Rede über Alban Bergs Lulu," *Gesammelte Schriften* 18 (*Musikalische Schriften* V), ed. Rolf Tiedemann and Klaus Schultz (Frankfurt a/M: Suhrkamp, 1984), 645–49.]

The heterogeneity of scholarly interests in the interconnections between cinema and opera may be attributable to the diversification of those connections itself. Examples of the heterogeneity of opera and film studies may be found in *A Night in at the Opera: Media Representations of Opera*, ed. Jeremy Tambling (London: John Libbey & Co., 1994), and in some of the material found in *The Work of Opera: Genre, Nationhood, and Sexual Difference*, ed. Richard Dellamora and Daniel Fischlin (New York: University of Columbia Press, 1997): see especially Felicia Miller, "*Farinelli's* Electronic Hermaphrodite and the Contralto Tradition," 73–92. In both of these collections of essays, different authors are concerned with such diverse phenomena as the appearance of Wagnerian music in film, with an introduction to the relatively esoteric works of Werner Schröter, with a description of operas staged and filmed outside the opera house, and with numerous investigations into specific cinematic works (for instance, the modernist and postmodernist features of such films as *Diva, Aria,* and *Farinelli*).My point is not that this diversification is regrettable, but that it is simply symptomatic of the field. In this context, see also Marcia J. Citron, *Opera on Screen* (New Haven: Yale University Press, 2000).

2. For an analysis of this work with emphasis on the discursive tradition linking sexuality, disease, and opera, see my "Opera and the Discourse of Decadence: From Wagner to AIDS," in *Perennial Decay: The Aesthetics and Politics of Decadence in the Modern Era*, ed. Liz Constable, Dennis Denhishoff, and Matthew Potolsky (Philadelphia: University of Pennsylvania Press, 1999), 119–41. I would like to thank the editors of *Perennial Decay* for permission to draw upon this earlier study, although I wish to emphasize that its focus on the discursive traditions within which Demme's film may be situated—especially the European discourse of the late nineteenth century—is quite different from the current discussion.

3. See David Denby, "Philadelphia," *New York*, 3 January 1994, 52; Roy Grundmann and Peter Sacks, "Philadelphia," *Cineaste* 20, no. 3 (summer 1993): 51; John Simon, "Philadelphia," *National Review*, 7 February 1994, 68; Andrew Sullivan, "Philadelphia," *The New Republic*, 21 February 1994, 42; James M. Wall, "Philadelphia," *The Christian Century*, 16 March 1994, 268.

4. Koestenbaum was interviewed about the scene because of his work on the homosexual cultic reverence for Callas. See Wayne Koenstenbaum, *The Queen's Throat: Opera, Homosexuality, and the Mystery of Desire* (New York: Poseidon Press, 1993).

5. I would like to thank Mitchell Morris for providing me with a copy of "Aspects of the Coming-Out Aria," a paper he presented in December 1994 at the Modern Language Association Conference in San Diego that offers a lucid and thought-provoking analysis of the opera scene in *Philadelphia*.

6. Theodor W. Adorno, *In Search of Wagner*, trans. Rodney Livingston (London: Verso, 1991). To do credit to Nietzsche, we should note that his analysis of Wagner came very close to making this very point. His formulation from 1888 reads in hindsight like a description of the music drama as film. "With Wagner at the beginning," Nietzsche writes, "there is hallucination: not of sounds, but of gestures. It is

for these that he then seeks the sound-semiotics." What Nietzsche was describing, albeit through a different terminology, was phantasmagoria, the vehicle through which Adorno believed Wagner attempted to reach a wide audience. See Friedrich Nietzsche, *Der Fall Wagner* in *Werke: Kritische Gesamtausgabe*, ed. Giorgio Colli and Mazzino Montinari (Berlin: de Gruyter, 1967–), VI. 3, 21–22.

7. Adorno, *In Search of Wagner*, 85.

8. See Walter Benjamin, "The Work of Art in the Age of Mechanical Reproduction," *Illuminations*, ed. Hannah Arendt, trans. Harry Zohn (New York: Schocken Books, 1969), 217–51.

9. Adorno, *In Search of Wagner*, 85, n.1.

10. Ibid., 91.

11. Ibid., 86.

12. Ibid., 87–88.

13. Ibid., 93–94. On the impact of these associations on the development of modernist literary strategies, see my *Undertones of Insurrection: Music, Politics, and the Social Sphere in the Modern German Narrative* (Lincoln: University of Nebraska Press, 1993). See also Erwin Koppen, *Dekadenter Wagnerismus: Studien zur europäischen Literatur des Fin de Siècle* (Berlin: de Gruyter, 1974).

14. Tambling, "Introduction," *A Night in at the Opera*, 20.

15. In her excellent analysis of this film (chapter 6 of this volume), Mary Hunter would appear to agree with my assessment of the scene's ideological baggage when she says that "the film . . . divides people by their access, or lack thereof, to this [the operatic] material; that is, by class" (p. 108), though she also claims that "the Letter Duet is the explicit reference to high culture, which is scarcely compelling as a 'source' for the opera scene" (p. 119, n.1). Obviously, I am arguing that it is precisely as a reference to the social trappings of high culture that the opera scene has a key function in the film.

16. On the Metropolitan's pandering to the modern audience, see the concluding passages in Joseph Horowitz, *Understanding Toscanini: How He Became an American Culture-God and Helped Create a New Audience for Old Music* (Minneapolis: University of Minnesota Press, 1986), 430–31.

17. See Anton Kaes, *Kino-Debatte: Texte zum Verhältnis von Literatur und Film 1909–1929* (Tübingen: Max Niemeyer; Munich: DTV, 1978).

18. This is one of the very few points in Jim Collins, *Uncommon Cultures: Popular Culture and Post-Modernism* (New York: Routledge, 1989) with which I would agree. Throughout, Collins misrepresents and, I think, misunderstands Adorno, but here at least his criticism seems valid.

# 6

# Opera *in* Film

## Sentiment and Wit, Feeling and Knowing: *The Shawshank Redemption* and *Prizzi's Honor*

### Mary Hunter

ALTHOUGH IT IS RELATIVELY COMMON TO HEAR SNATCHES OF OPERA IN THE soundtracks of Hollywood movies, Frank Darabont's *The Shawshank Redemption* (1994, score by Thomas Newman) and John Huston's *Prizzi's Honor* (1985, score by Alex North) both take the relatively unusual tack of setting a whole scene to an entire operatic number: Newman and Darabont use the Letter Duet from Mozart's *Marriage of Figaro,* and North and Huston use "O mio babbino caro" from Puccini's *Gianni Schicchi* . In both films, the music is diegetic (although this is less clear in *Prizzi's Honor* than in *Shawshank Redemption* ), and both films use opera or music more generally as a central metaphor.

To note these similarities, however, is also to reveal profound differences in what and how opera means to the characters in the films, the audiences, the relation between the audiences and the films, and the films as aesthetic and ideological wholes. These differences in part mirror the overall differences between the two films. *Shawshank Redemption* is a sentimental prison buddy story that expresses the sociopolitical values of democratic inclusivity and universal brotherhood, and the aesthetic or experiential values of engaged listening and emotional response to aesthetic phenomena. *Prizzi's Honor* is a witty spoof on a Mafia thriller; it cleverly articulates an insider culture where hierarchy outweighs individual freedom, where "knowing" is more important than "feeling," and where aesthetic phenomena like opera are semiconsciously absorbed as coded communications rather than fully attended to as emotionally fulfilling experiences. One could also add that while *Shawshank Redemption* clearly believes in its political and aesthetic vision, it also (unintentionally, I think) undercuts it. *Prizzi's Honor,* on the other hand, spoofs the culture it presents, but (or thus) at the same time presents it as seamless and coherent.

More interesting than the mere fact of these distinctions, though, is how the films marshal opera to make their points. The choice of opera rather than another genre of music, and within opera, of female numbers rather than male or mixed-gender numbers, their more or less obviously diegetic status, the coordination of the camera work with the music and with the events on screen, and the implied relation of the auditorium audience to these excerpts all contribute to *Shawshank Redemption*'s articulation of a culture of feeling and *Prizzi's Honor*'s presentation of a culture of knowing. To examine the ways in which opera conveys and embodies these specific differences, however, is also to think more broadly about how classical music can't function in relatively recent mainstream narrative Hollywood films, particularly when it is diegetic.

## THE SCENES IN QUESTION

*The Shawshank Redemption* is based on Stephen King's novella, *Rita Hayworth and Shawshank Redemption* (published 1983). It is the story of Andy Dufresne (Tim Robbins), a young banker wrongly accused of the murder of his wife. He is sent to prison for life, and the film tells the story of his generous work on behalf of the other inmates, and his deepening friendship with Red (Morgan Freeman), another lifer, in for a bad end to a petty crime. But it also tells the story of Andy's determination and cleverness. He spends years tunneling an escape passage through the crumbly prison walls; he uses his position as prison accountant (helping the wicked warden cook the books) to create a bank account in a false name, on which he can draw when he escapes, and also to publicize the administrator's corrupt dealings. In the "opera scene" in question, which occurs about halfway into the film, and which has no precedent or analogue in the book,[1] Andy has finally (after six years of weekly letters) inveigled the State into sending improved resources for the prison library. Among the second hand "sundries" that accompany the cheque for $200 is a box of LPs, including *The Marriage of Figaro*. On the spur of the moment, he decides to make the most of the opportunity, and commandeers not only the prison's record player but also its PA system to play the Letter Duet to every corner of the prison. As the gorgeous music (sung by Edith Mathis and Gundula Janowitz) issues from the rusting speakers, the prisoners—white and black, old and young, industrious and lazy, susceptible and calloused, fit and lame—are transfixed. The camera travels over the prisoners, accompanied by Red's voiceover commentary:

> I have no idea to this day what those two Italian ladies were singing about. Truth is, I don't want to know — some things are best left unsaid. I like to think they were singing about something so beautiful it can't be expressed in words and makes your heart ache because of it. I tell you, those voices soared, higher and farther than anyone in a grey place dares to dream. It was like some beautiful bird flapped into our drab little cage and made those walls dissolve away. And for the briefest of moments every last man at Shawshank felt free.

As the duet proceeds to its coda to the words "Il capirà" ("he [the Count] will understand"), the wicked prison warden, who patently and willfully does not understand Andy's motives, the opera itself, or the humanizing power of music more generally, has the glass door of the office bashed in. Andy gets two weeks in solitary confinement for his escapade.

The Letter Duet scene in *Shawshank Redemption* is the only operatic moment in the film. Indeed, it is the only classical music quoted in the movie. As we will see, a series of popular songs articulate the passing of the decades of Andy's imprisonment, but the Letter Duet forms a striking contrast to all other diegetic and quoted music. In addition, the underscore, while effective, is quite indistinct stylistically; it in no way helps to integrate the Mozart into the sound-environment of the film.

*Prizzi's Honor* is based on a novel of the same name (1982) by Richard Condon (one of several novels on the Prizzi clan). It is the story of Charley Partanna (Jack Nicholson), a rising star in the Prizzi crime family. He falls in love with, and marries, Irene Walker (Kathleen Turner), a Polish-American free-lance hit woman. This fuels the jealousy of Maerose Prizzi (Anjelica Huston), whom Charley failed to marry as expected, and whom the family has in any case spurned because of another premarital affair. Maerose's manipulations of family insecurities intersect with the family's desire to have Charley at its head, and the movie ends with Charley killing Irene and getting together with Maerose again.

The opera scene in question, which occurs about halfway through the movie, is a crucial part of Maerose's scheming. The dialogue of the scene is taken essentially verbatim from the book, but the book makes no mention of opera at this point: indeed, it makes remarkably little mention of opera throughout. In this scene, Maerose pretends to come crawling back to her father, Dominic (Lee Richardson), her principal opponent in the family, intending to revenge herself both on him and on Charley. The confrontation takes place in Dominic's home, and opens in a dressing room with Maerose darkening the shadows under and around her eyes with makeup. The ensemble right before "O mio babbino caro" from Puccini's *Gianni Schicchi* can (barely) be heard in the background. Once Maerose has walked into the dining room, served her father some food, and seated herself, "O mio babbino caro," begins. With this touching aria playing in the dining room, Maerose proceeds to punish her father and discredit Charley by describing in graphic detail how Charley forced himself upon her (although in fact she initiated the encounter). Dominic responds by clutching his already weak heart; she solicitously fetches him a glass of "water" (actually grappa), which he downs so fast he has to race out and vomit, the sound of which is clearly audible against the floating last notes of the aria. The last shot, which lingers with the last notes of the aria, shows Maerose looking maliciously triumphant.

Although "O mio babbino caro" is the tightest, most explicit, and only diegetic use of Puccini's *Gianni Schicchi*, this opera literally resonates throughout the film. Alex North's soundtrack is permeated with references to this work;

indeed, Puccini's score essentially forms the basis for Alex North's.[2] North uses the overture more or less wholesale at the beginning of the film. The descending major second motive that begins the first scene of the opera (Figure 6.1) is used throughout, both in its original form, and as the climax of a leitmotif that attaches to Charley's love for Irene (Figure 6.2). In addition to this thorough integration of *Gianni Schicchi*, Italian opera more generally also fills the film. There are several diegetic uses of opera: a grand dinner is entertained by a worse-than-mediocre band playing an arrangement of the triumphal march from *Aida*, followed by a tenor singing "Una furtiva lagrima"; later, Don Corrado, the patriarch of the clan, is shown hunched in his wing chair listening to "Questa o quella" from *Rigoletto*. In the underscore, the overture to Rossini's *Barber of Seville* makes several appearances, usually to indicate comic scurrying. Another Rossini overture (to *La gazza ladra*) is used to accompany the departure of the rival family's thugs to set fire to a Prizzi event. But the operatic masterstroke in the score is the use of the accompanimental figure to the Habañera from *Carmen* (for these purposes an honorary Italian opera) combined with a motive from the *Barber of Seville* (Figure 6.3), as Irene walks to a meeting with Dominic, who is about to hire her to kill Charley. As we will see, the integration of opera into the musical language of the film is as important to its overall meaning as the splendid isolation of the Letter Duet is to the meaning of *The Shawshank Redemption*.

Figure 6.1. Puccini, *Gianni Schicchi*, Overture, mm.6-9.

Figure 6.2. Alex North, *Prizzi's Honor*: Tune representing Carlie's love for Irene.

Figure 6.3. Alex North/Bizet/Rossini: Habañera plus *Barber of Seville* motif.

INTERPRETATIVE READINGS

*The Shawshank Redemption* and the Culture of Feeling

*The Shawshank Redemption* uses Mozart's Letter Duet to promote its sentimental vision of a society based on emotional attachments across structural boundaries. It does this in multiple and redundant ways: the excerpt develops the same theme of cross-class friendship as the film, thus doubling its significance; the character Red is shown to understand the profound meaning of the excerpt despite his general ignorance about classical music; Red's response is shown as true and universal; the act of listening is foregrounded in such a way that we, the audience, are made to empathize with the prisoners' response; the fact that the number is a female duet emphasizes the unwilled pleasure "we all" take in listening; and Mozart as an idea encapsulates the theme of music in the movie as a whole—namely that it is about memory, hope, and time—experiences that explicitly transcend boundaries.

The makers of *The Shawshank Redemption* chose both a number and an opera with specific and meaningful connections to the film.[3] Of all the numbers in the opera, this duet most touchingly embodies the sweet and socially unexpected friendship between the Countess and her maidservant, Susanna. During this number they jointly construct a letter to the Count, setting in motion a series of events intended both to restore the Count to his wife and to allow Susanna to escape his importunities and to marry her true love, Figaro. The freedom imagined by Red as the music is playing, and momentarily claimed by Andy as he appropriates the prison's communication system, is analogous to the freely loving order imagined by the women as the result of their ruse.

Although the specific plot resemblances between the opera and the film are limited to this duet and to its theme of cross-rank bonding, Wye J. Allanbrook's persuasive argument about the importance of the pastoral in *Figaro* as a whole is also borne out in *Shawshank Redemption*.[4] Allanbrook argues that the "green world" of the pastoral is the place where true friendships can be formed and exercised without concern for the normal social constraints of class and station. In the film (as in the book), Andy escapes and moves to Mexico where he starts a small hotel and boat-building business. Red is eventually paroled, finds money that Andy left for him in a field, and spends it on a trip to Mexico. The film (although not the book) ends with a view of an incredibly pristine beach, where—with no one else in sight and no other signs of "civilization"—Andy and Red are reunited. This unambiguously pastoral ending both proposes a social order based on "pure" affection, untainted by structural distinctions, and implies the real-world impossibility of such a society. For those who know the opera, the effect of this filmic echo is to double the resonance of the message.

Red, however, knows neither the opera nor the duet. He claims that he does not want to know any more about it than what he feels and imagines, and the film suggests that he is right to feel that way. Nevertheless—and this is the most powerful, explicit point of the scene—he clearly understands the point of the music. And not just the point of this particular piece, but the point of introducing beauty into the grimness of prison; namely that it serves as a momentary escape from the sordid dailiness of incarceration, and thus opens a window to the possibility of hope. Although Red is the only one who speaks, his response is clearly shared by every inmate. Much of the duet is taken up with the camera travelling throughout the prison, from the infirmary to the shop to the yard; and in every location every inmate (and guard) is standing stock still and silent, galvanized by the music, taken beyond himself into a momentary communion with all the others by the unlooked-for beauty issuing from the PA system. The obvious political points of the moment are not only that the divisions among the prisoners and between them and some guards are set aside—the capacity for emotional response to beauty being depicted as socially cohesive and well as individually enriching—but also that institutional power (vested in the uncomprehending warden and his henchmen) turns out to have no relation to moral and emotional power.

Red's (and the others') heartfelt response to this beauty raises the question of why the music chosen should be opera rather than, say, a Beethoven symphony (the other obvious choice), because of all the classical genres opera is the one with which non-initiates are typically most uncomfortable. I have no watertight answer to this question, but I would suggest that several qualities make this excerpt more dramatically effective (and perhaps even more plausible) than a Beethoven symphony. The first is meaningfulness. As eighteenth-century commentators never tired of pointing out, opera, being a texted genre, is clearly "about" something. Red starts his voiceover by saying "I have no idea what those Italian ladies were singing about," the implication being that they were in fact clearly singing about something, and that that meaningfulness (even if verbally inexpressible) is part of what obliges the listener to pay attention. The relative "meaninglessness" (in eighteenth-century terms) of a symphony would presumably not have compelled the listeners' attention in the same way, and thus would not have produced the astonished brotherhood of listeners that we see here.

The second important quality of the Letter Duet is, as Red points out, that it is sung by ladies. Astonishingly, the two singers are almost the only female voices we hear in the entire movie. The other female characters (Andy's wife, the landlady in the halfway house, the clerk in the bus station, the bank teller) are all but silent, and the popular music excerpts that punctuate the movie all use male singers.[5] Even subliminally, the sudden eruption of the female voice into the sound-world of the film highlights a centrally lacking element in the men's lives. They do, to be sure, hang pinup posters in their cells, but the film clearly demonstrates the difference between male looking, which uses its objects, and listening, where the sound of the female voice can take emotional charge of the listener. The film's use of the female voice to point to a specific absence is also related to psychoanalytic theories about the power of the "operatic voice"

(defined almost exclusively as female) to simulate the preverbal sense of bound-
ary-less unity with the mother to which we all in one way or another yearn to
return.[6] In *The Shawshank Redemption,* the filmmakers have cleverly tied the universal human yearning for boundless plenitude to the prisoners' more particular
yearning for a world with no locks. A Beethoven symphony (to return to the
obvious comparison) might have inspired a bracing hope, but an operatic excerpt
here renders the prisoners (and, by implication, the audience) both more help-
less and more emotionally fulfilled.

The fact that it is a duet intensifies this effect. Two female voices may not
double the *jouissance* of one, but their doubleness—especially in this number,
where the two voices sing the same music and neither is permanently on top or
underneath—not only increases the sensuousness of the sound, but also models
an equal companionship, similar to the relation that Andy and Red appear to
have developed. It is interesting, and perhaps not coincidental, that a more
recent prison opera scene—in *Life is Beautiful*, where Roberto Benigni comman-
deers a record player to waft the Barcarolle from Offenbach's *Tales of Hoffmann*
across the concentration camp in the hopes that his wife (also in the camp) will
hear it—is also a completely arresting (even unbearable) moment; it also uses
both the *jouissance* stimulated by the female voice and the companionship of the
duet to make its point.

To show characters absorbed in the act of listening, as both *The Shawshank
Redemption* and *Life is Beautiful* do, is to compel the auditorium audience to listen. It is also to prescribe a mode of listening: in this case, emotionally engaged
but intellectually decontextualized. This is made most obvious in Red's monologue. However, the camera work also orchestrates (or better, choreographs) our
emotional response to the music in such a way that we are not only encouraged
to identify with the prisoners as they listen, but are put in their position as willing "victims" of manipulation. The unambiguously diegetic nature of the
music—we see the record, the gramophone, the wires, the PA control system
and the speakers—reinforces the audience's need to listen along with the prisoners, but it is the camera's movements during the duet itself that instruct us
how to feel. The visual elements of the scene are set up to respond to the form
of the duet, but more strikingly, they play with and against its languorous affect,
overwhelmingly emphasizing that element of the number.

Figure 6.4 shows the camera's movements in relation to the duet as a
whole. The music of the duet is in a two-part form, with the first half divided
in the middle by a cadence in the dominant. There is, however, no significant
thematic contrast, and the second half of the form (starting in m. 37), although
it repeats the opening material, is essentially a series of closes on the tonic. The
camera does "notice" this form, to the extent that its most striking and characteristic work (the two, long travelling shots) begins with the music's most characteristic element: the (permanent) return to the tonic in the second period (m.
17). This is incidentally also the heart of Susanna's and the Countess's letter,

X=jump cut

Figure 6.4. Mozart, *The Marriage of Figaro,* "Sull'aria," camera movement and action.

Figure 6.4 (cont.). Mozart, *The Marriage of Figaro,* "Sull'aria," camera movement and action.

Figure 6.4 (cont.). Mozart, *The Marriage of Figaro,* "Sull'aria," camera movement and action.

Figure 6.4 (cont.). Mozart, *The Marriage of Figaro,* "Sull'aria," camera movement and action.

where they name the place for the assignation with the Count ("sotto i pini"). However, what really matters in this scene is the way the travelling shots capture the gentle gliding feel of the music, and the way the dissolves in the camera's second journey over the prison match the overlapping of the voices, although there is no exact coordination.

About halfway through the second section (in m. 44), just as the music becomes more languorous, the camera work starts to become busier. Rather than moving with the same quality but rhythmically out of synch with the music, as it has been, the camera now begins to contradict the feel of the music, but coordinate with its surface rhythm (even exactly in measure 49); it makes a series of regular jump cuts from the warden to Andy as the former approaches the latter with furious intent. The shock of this sudden mechanical coordination is palpable. The tension builds as the music continues its leisurely progress towards a final cadence, with the unhurried confidence of "il capirà" increasingly undercut by the camera's more agitated movements and the threats of physical violence by the warden and the chief guard. It is impossible not to notice the camera's movements in this scene, partly because so little else is "going on," and partly because they are so strikingly associated with the feel and emotional meaning of the music. And to notice them is inevitably to be drawn into the ambience of the moment, to feel with Red that, for those two minutes or so, nothing else matters. The effect of this scene—created as much by the camera's movements as by the music—is to make the feeling of freedom and hope as palpable and immediate for the audience as it is for the prisoners; paradoxically to enthrall us to the music so that we will directly experience the same lifting of the chains as those in thrall to the penal system.

The notion of universality and fraternity in the face of arbitrary social divisions is crucial to this scene. It is communicated in two ways. First, the travelling camera unites all sorts and conditions of men in a single response to the music. Second, as I mentioned above, the scene puts the auditorium audience in the same position as the prisoners, and thus includes us in the brotherhood of feeling and imagined freedom. To connect the variously disadvantaged prisoners with the variously privileged members of the audience by means of a common experience is to suggest most immediately that Mozart has a "universal" appeal, across boundaries that might otherwise seem insurmountable.

The ideology of this moment is reinforced by the way the Mozart is valued in the rest of the movie, especially in relation to the other diegetic and quoted music, none of which is classical. Andy's memories of the Mozart serve him well during his punishment for commandeering the PA system. On returning from two weeks in the hole, he announces (with a gesture strikingly reminiscent of Mozart "himself" [Tom Hulce] in Milos Forman/Peter Schaeffer's *Amadeus*) that it was the easiest time he ever did, because "Mr. Mozart" was "in here" (his head) and "in here" (his heart). The clear message is that (great) music lives in our minds and emotions as a memory that can be revived at will, reminding us that there is beauty in the world and giving us hope for the future. Mozart, then, for Andy, connects the past and the future, easing the passing of present time. The movie is full of references to the quality of time served: easy time, hard time, slow time, lost time. Time is, after all, the only thing the prisoners really have; it is also what they lose in confinement. The playing of the Letter Duet takes its listeners out of their paradoxical prison of time: when Red says " for a moment, every man felt free," he is surely thinking as much about escaping the endless weight of time on their hands as about spatial confinement.

The other quoted music in the movie also has to do with time, but it marks a series of presents. As the decades of imprisonment pass, the years are marked by timely popular songs (some diegetic, some not): Andy's car radio at the time he was supposed to have killed his wife plays Jack Lawrence's "If I Didn't Care"; the fifties are announced in the background score by Allan Roberts' and Denis Fisher's "Put the Blame on Mame"; 1963 is announced as the year of President Kennedy's assassination, but marked by Hank Williams' "Lovesick Blues," hummed enthusiastically by one of the inmates at his listening station in the newly expanded prison library, perhaps to indicate his separation from the latest trends; and the later '60s by Johnny Otis's "Willie the Hand Jive."[7] Unlike the film's popular music, which mostly stands for its decade and which is not clearly linked to the ideas of hope and memory, the Mozart transcends both its own century and the moment of its own playing.

If the film's quoted popular music marks the decades and signifies a sort of time-boundedness, the broader idea of music in the film—represented both in the deployment of the background music and in the narrative—reinforces the ideology of timelessness and universality attaching to the Mozart. The background score never literally refers to *The Marriage of Figaro*, but one of its consistent functions is to accompany Red's many voiceover narratives telling the story of Andy Dufresne's prison life. These narratives are explicitly presented as memories until the very end, which is narrated in the present tense, and which refers to Red's hopes for the future. Thus just as the Mozart connected past, present, and future for Andy, the background music of this movie suggests the same connections for Red. "Homemade" music also plays a similar role. After the opera scene, and after Andy has specifically associated the capacity to internalize music with the capacity for hope—an emotion that loosens normal temporal boundaries—Red describes how he used to play the harmonica, but quit because it was too painful (essentially raising unfulfillable hopes). Andy gives him a harmonica as a gift, but although Red puts it to his mouth he barely plays a note. However, years later, on Red's release from prison, and accompanying his decision to look for the buried money that will enable him to join Andy in Mexico, the background score accompanies this revival of hope with a snatch of harmonica music.

The operatic excerpt in *Shawshank Redemption,* then, is an integral part of its generally sentimental ideology, which is more pronounced in the film than in the book. In the book, Andy is not directly responsible for bringing down the warden, whereas that is one part of his vindication in the film. In the book, Red is Irish, the crime for which he was imprisoned was spelled out as triple murder, and his position as "the guy who can get things" is more pervasively emphasized than it is in the film. The film's casting of Morgan Freeman (an African-American) as Red increases its sentimentality, because the social distance between Andy and Red is literally and perpetually visible, and the film's message about the value of friendship and hope is commensurately more striking. I would call this shift in tone sentimental rather than simply touching or moving, because the film claims to be about larger themes than a simple accidental friendship under specific circumstances, but those larger themes rest on the demonstrably impossible foundation of a single relationship. The opera scene (again, not in the book) is crucial to this sentimentality.

As I have noted, the Letter Duet scene explicitly presents the ideal of universal brotherhood. This scene also suggests that the capacity of all fundamentally good humans to respond to (great) art is linked to the essentially human capacity for hope. The film as a whole invests heavily in the idea not only that heart and hope are available to everyone, but also that they are both humanizing and literally lifesaving. (Andy escapes because he hopes; the hope infused into Red by Andy eventually saves him from the all-too-frequent suicide of long-time prisoners suddenly released into the world.) The social order envisioned at the end is based on a fellowship of feeling and hope. Intellectual knowledge, then, may seem rather low in the film's sense of how an ideal society would work.

At the same time, however, even in the Letter Duet scene, knowledge is shown to be power. Andy (the college-educated banker, the man who never belonged in prison in the first place) is the one who knows enough about music to pick *Figaro* from the box of LPs, and then to pick the Letter Duet, which he gives to the others as a gift. He tells them later that the composer is Mozart, but, as far as we know, he never tells them the name of the opera or the situation expressed in the duet, and the particular meanings of this piece remain hidden from most of the prisoners. Thus although Red (and by extension the other prisoners) may feel that the duet is about *something*, it has for them no identifiable referent of its own, and floats in a bath of pleasurable isolation. On the one hand, not knowing about the characters or the plot gives a listener the freedom of his own imagination, and I think this is how the film intends the excerpt. On the other, however, not knowing the inherent meaning of the excerpt also limits the prisoners to the confines of their own imaginations and denies them communicative control of the music. The film never suggests that any of the prisoners might ever be in a position to replicate Andy's use of classical music. Thus while on the one hand the film shows opera as a medium of fellowship and bonding, it also divides people by their access, or lack thereof, to this material—that is, by class.[8]

This division extends out into the audience. We are shown the cover of the LP, so from the outset of the scene we know that Mozart's *Le nozze di Figaro* is what Andy plays. However, only a relatively small number of "us" will recognize the Italian title of this opera, and among us, a smaller number will know the circumstances of the duet. Some of us, then, will be simply moved, like the prisoners; others of us will know more exactly why this music is so moving at this point in the film. Perhaps without intending to, this scene creates subcultures of insiders and outsiders based on knowledge, all the while seeming to create a more idealized distinction between those who can feel (all the prisoners and some of the guards), and those who can't (the warden and his cronies). It is in part the disjunction between the realities of knowledge and the ideals of feeling that makes this moment sentimental rather than plainly moving.

### *Prizzi's Honor* and the Culture of Knowledge

Whereas the single, isolated instance of opera in *Shawshank Redemption* radiates beyond itself to make the audience feel the importance of collective emotional response, the many operatic excerpts in *Prizzi's Honor* play with and against the plot in ways that serve as communication among the characters, lending an enriching dimension to the film for audience members in the know. There are, however, few moments in the film where the characters are shown fully attending to the operatic excerpts,[9] and none where they are shown to be moved by them. Opera pervades this film, but it bears no great emotional or ideological weight, as it does in *Shawshank Redemption*. Rather, it is the common coin of this culture, and it is expected that those who truly belong will know how to use it.

Unlike the choice of opera rather than some other classical music in *The Shawshank Redemption*—not self-explanatory, but justifiable in terms of its particular effect on people—the choice of opera as the quoted and diegetic music in *Prizzi's Honor* is both obvious and in no need of special justification. As with many movies about Italian-Americans, opera is used as a conventional marker of that culture—here more than often, but the association of opera with Italians is altogether to be expected.[10] Richard Condon's novel, interestingly, makes almost no references to opera. (The tenor aria at the grand dinner is the sole reference, and it is something from *Les Vêpres Siciliennes* rather than "Una furtiva lagrima," as in the film.) However, the novel is as saturated with Italian-language references to food as the film is with opera, and in both media it is as much the sound of the references (the foods include *focaccia di Fiori di Sambuco, peperoni imbottiti, farfalline, salsiccia* ) as their content that makes the point. "Ethnic sonority," then, rather than moral, social, or symbolic meaning, is the first impression we have of the use of opera in this film.

It is, however, not surprising, either within the culture of this film or within the broader practices of operatic references in Hollywood films, that "O mio babbino caro" has direct narrative connections with the film scene in which it is used. Nor should we be surprised that *Gianni Schicchi* as a whole relates to the film's themes. *Gianni Schicchi* is about ensuring the happiness and integrity of one's family. The Donati family is furious that the patriarch Buoso's last will and testament leaves everything to a local monastery. Their neighbor Gianni Schicchi turns that greedy sense of family to his own advantage, tricks them into letting him remake Buoso's will, and transfers the most valuable assets to himself to endow his daughter Lauretta's future. At the very end of the opera, he turns to the audience and asks (rhetorically) whether the money could have been better spent: implicitly asking, in other words, what family is worth. The central issue in *Prizzi's Honor* is also the notion of "family" and the question of belonging. Charley is a Prizzi by adoption rather than birth, and his choice of Irene, a non-Italian, non-family-member to marry puts him at odds with the family leadership, who have designated him the next boss. The plot revolves around the tricks and manipulations necessary to ensure his proper marriage and his continued primary allegiance to the family. In addition, both works are comedies that hint at, but never really explore, serious issues.

The relationship between "O mio babbino caro" and the scene with Maerose Prizzi and her father is both more particular and more ironic than the global connections between the film and the opera. In this aria (the only extended lyrical moment in the opera), the ingénue Lauretta is trying to persuade her father to let her marry Rinuccio Donati. Both the aria and the film-scene involve a father and a daughter; both daughters use pathos to engage their fathers' attention; both manipulate their scheming but ultimately vulnerable fathers; and both situations turn on the daughter's choice of partner. But while Lauretta simply wants to marry, Maerose wants revenge on both her former lover and her father, and their strategies differ commensurately. Lauretta plays on her father's affection for her while Maerose uses both her father's physical weakness (his heart condition) and his prudishness about sex to punish him.     Unlike the Letter Duet scene in *The Shawshank Redemption*—where the audience is (however briefly and unintelligibly) clued in to what the opera is, and where the act of listening is foregrounded, so that even if we don't know what is playing, we do know that it is to be attended to—the "O mio babbino caro" scene in *Prizzi's Honor* gives the audience no help. The aria is never loud, and sometimes barely audible under the dialogue. There is no indication that either of the characters is listening to it, and the film as a whole includes no explicit reference either to *Gianni Schicchi* or to this number. Audience members would probably need to know the aria before really noticing that it was playing, let alone that it is diegetic.

This relationship between the auditorium audience and the operatic music holds throughout the film. We are allowed, but not invited, into the operatic world of the film; no operatic excerpts are identified, and we are never asked to pay exclusive or primary attention to the music itself, even if the characters are listening. With respect to the background score, an ignorant audience member would simply miss the references, although the music might seem unusually prominent or intrusive at times. The vocal diegetic excerpts ("Una furtiva lagrima" and "Questa o quella,") would be recognized as "opera" and thus appropriate to the culture; "O mio babbino caro" might be perceived as comic because of its affective contrast with the events in the film-scene. But even this affective contrast is not really played up because the music is so quiet and un-commented-upon. Slightly less innocent audience members might well recognize some of the excerpts, both diegetic and not: the *Barber of Seville* material is, after all, generally familiar through the Bugs Bunny version; the Habañera motive might have been especially familiar in the mid-'80s, when a rash of *Carmen* films came out; the march from *Aida* is one of the great operatic chestnuts; and "Una furtiva lagrima" is a Pavarotti favorite. Viewers might well recognize that opera forms part of the language of the movie and fits with its many other "in-jokes"; these listeners would presumably know that there was more to know about the film's music, even if they had generally no interest in pursuing that knowledge. But only the viewer as steeped in opera as the Prizzis themselves is likely to appreciate the wit of the references and the many ways in which opera is absorbed into the score.

The camera work during the "O mio babbino caro" scene is commensurate with the generally intellectual relations between film and opera. As with the scene in *The Shawshank Redemption*, the camera work is choreographed to the aria, and like that scene, this one is a striking set piece. But here the rhythm and movement of the camera is associated with the structure and dramatic pacing of the aria rather than its affect.

Figure 6.5 gives a reduced score of the aria with an indication of the camera work and dialogue as it progresses in relation to the music. Like the Letter Duet (although in a less complex manner), "O mio babbino caro" is in a lingering three-part form (in four phrases), in which the latter three phrases all serve as consequents to the opening 8–measure antecedent. Each main part begins with the same tune (measures 1, 9, 21). One obvious structural correspondence between the film-scene and the aria is that the three unequally long sections of the aria are matched (but not synchronized with) the three unequally spaced

Figure 6.5. Puccini, *Gianni Schicchi*, "O mio babbino caro," camera movement and action.

Figure 6.5 (*cont.*). Puccini, *Gianni Schicchi*, "O mio babbino caro," camera movement and action.

entries and exits to and from the dining room (she walks in with food, she walks out to get the grappa and returns; he runs out). The rhythm of the shots also links the structure of the aria with the dramatic and visual structure of the scene. Most of the shots last between one and two measures, but a couple of long shots punctuate this rhythm. The first one occurs as Maerose starts to twist the knife, having sparked her father's interest in her peaky looks, and having allowed him to attribute her pallor to Charley's abandonment of her. Starting in measure 5 of the aria, she says "He [Charley] had a use for me." As she begins mendaciously to describe how he "forced himself on" her, the camera remains quite still, but the music (in measure 9) repeats the opening tune, which emphasizes the length of the shot. This visual hanging on, even though the music seems to be starting again, effectively builds the tension of the scene, and also forms a sort of reverse rhyme with measure 24, where the music "stays still," so to speak, and the camera moves. The shortest shots in the aria occur in measures 17 and 18, at (though not with) the repeated high A-flats, as Lauretta redoubles her efforts to persuade her father, and Maerose utters the climactic "I have no honor any more."

Other effective coordinations between the camera and the aria include the long shot of Dominic clutching his heart, which occurs with the long held F in measures 19–20 (whose text is "O dio, vorrei morir"), and the moment near the end when Maerose walks into the dining room during the fermata in measure 24. Here the camera, which follows her hands as they carry the glass from the kitchen, embodies both the tension and the sense of inevitability contained in the singer's high E-flat (the dominant). The words of the aria here ("Babbo, pietà, pietà") form a particularly tight ironic comment on the film's action.

Some of these relations are audible to audience members who either know Italian or who have some knowledge of tonal music. "Vorrei morir" sung to a picture of an elderly man clutching his chest is likely to tickle the memory of even the most recalcitrant student of Italian (or Latin), and the purposeful mismatching of the camera's movements with the moments when the opening tune repeats might also be noticed, as well as the tension of the high E-flat. That is, one may not have to be a fully initiated insider to understand that the relations between the music and the visual elements of this scene have been carefully calculated. However, knowledge of both the text and the form of the aria enables one to see (and hear) the extent to which the scene plays with this number.

I would suggest that at least casual knowledge of the aria is also necessary (or at least extremely helpful) to understanding both that the music here is diegetic, and that its diegetic status is relevant to its meaning. That is, if we do not know that this is a preexistent aria, there is no way to know that it is playing in the dining room rather than simply in the background score as yet another instance of ethnic sonority. We are never shown a radio or a record player, and there is no reference to either of these sound sources in the dialogue. To fail to understand that this moment is diegetic, however, is also to fail to understand what it means.

Several things in this scene clue us in to its diegetic status. The first is that the music accompanying Maerose's secret applying of makeup before her confrontation with her father is the rowdy ensemble scene right before Lauretta's aria, whose music is inappropriate and irrelevant both atmospherically and emotionally to the scene on the screen, and which clearly starts *in media res* . To be sure, for those who know the opera there is an intellectual association between Gianni Schicchi's fatherly temper tantrum in the ensemble scene and Maerose's history with Dominic. However, despite this intellectual association, and given the norm that background soundtracks "make sense" emotionally with the narrative moment they accompany, the only reasonable interpretation of this music at this moment—given its near-inaudibility, its textural and timbral difference from "normal" background music, and its disconnection from what we see on the screen—is that it is music playing elsewhere in the house. This interpretation is bolstered by the fact that the music continues without interruption as Maerose walks into the dining room, and also that the music gets louder as she goes there. These features indicate both that the music exists in some sense independent of, and prior to, the narrative moment, and that it issues from a source within the diegesis, closer to the dining room than to Maerose's retreat. Thinking of this music as diegetic raises interesting questions of intention. Although one cannot prove this, it seems most likely that Dominic chose the music to listen to: it is, after all, his house, the sound-source[11] appears to be in or near the dining room, and he is sitting there reading the newspaper (which, in our non-musical culture may stand as a sign for listening). If Dominic did pick the piece (or choose to keep it on, if it was on the radio), we have to assume that he did so not only to wallow in the luscious expression of a properly pathetic filial attitude, but also to remind (and thus to reproach) Maerose, who must also know the opera. If Dominic chose the piece, then we can also understand Maerose as using his choice to her advantage, playing on the softening and perhaps self-satisfying effect it would have on Dominic ("Jeez, Mae, you look awful") and twisting the knife all the more viciously. If Maerose chose the aria (which is less likely, but still plausible), then Dominic becomes more of a victim, seduced by the aria into thinking that Maerose is up to sweet persuasion, and thus more vulnerable to her tactics. Whichever character chose the excerpt, though, their common knowledge of it clearly allows a lot not to be said.

However, it is also true that the diegetic status of the aria is sufficiently ambiguous that, by the end of the scene, the extra-diegetic ironic effect of the contrast between the ethereal music and the all-too-bodily result of the glass of grappa overwhelms the intra-narrative communicative effect of reproach or deception. In this way, the music functions more as underscore than as source-music. Since the diegetic status of this aria is so tenuous and unmarked, one wonders both why Huston and North made it possible to determine that it is in fact source music (with the necessary implication that the characters hear it), and why this is so hidden. I believe, as I have argued, that it is diegetic in order to be understood as a means of communication between Dominic and Maerose. As for its subtlety, that seems to me emblematic of opera's function in the film. The "background" nature of the sound suggests that opera is in the backgrounds of the characters' consciousnesses; there is no need to foreground the act of listening, either by making the music loud or more obviously diegetic, if by merely hearing and half-consciously absorbing the well-known music the characters can as effectively make their points.

It should be clear by now that *Prizzi's Honor* integrates opera into the world of the film in such a way that it both represents the characters as sharing a common web of references, and constructs the audience as insiders or outsiders based on what they *know* about opera. Neither the characters nor the audience can get very far on emotional response alone: Charley, after all, feels for Irene but in the end knows that he cannot have her, and in following the Prizzis' instructions to kill her acts on his knowledge rather than his feeling. We don't really know at the end of the movie whether Maerose, who is the real winner in the film (for better or worse), still feels for Charley, but she is more than willing to use her knowledge that he is politically the right mate for her to stimulate her feelings for him. Similarly, "outsiders" in the audience might feel that they have understood the appropriate bounciness of the Rossini excerpts or the comic pathos of "O mio babbino caro," but to those in the know it is clear that a generalized emotional response only scratches at the surface of opera's meanings and functions in this film.

This valuation of knowledge and wit over emotional response, encapsulated in the film's use of opera, is a metaphor for the way Mafia culture works (at least in the movies). A lot of the dialogue in the movie (and in others of this genre) proceeds by implication and indirection; those in the know get what's going on. Those in power choose whom to inform about what, and those out of power may lose status (or worse) without ever knowing that they were in danger. This may not be a desirable social model, but the way *Prizzi's Honor* replicates the insider/outsider distinction in the audience brings the "feel" of (movie) Mafia culture home, at least to those who can think of themselves as operatic insiders.

QUOTATION, DIEGESIS, AND UTOPIA

Neither film score has stimulated significant commentary, either in discussions of the composers, or in broader considerations of film music. Although Alex North is frequently heralded as an innovator, both for his use of jazz styles and for his modernist idiom,[12] the literature essentially ignores his work on *Prizzi's Honor*. This seems likely to be due to not only the use of literal quotations, but also to the thoroughgoing derivativeness of the score, despite its marvelous appropriateness to both the content and the tone of the film. Derivativeness is likely to be considered a flaw if the film score is viewed as an artistic creation in its own right; and more to the point here, it also contradicts the consensus about

North's virtues as a film composer.[13] The case is not so different with Thomas Newman's score to *The Shawshank Redemption*, although this composer is much younger than North and has had less of a chance to establish a fixed reputation (Newman was born in 1955; North lived from 1910 to 1991). In a recent interview, neither Newman himself nor the interviewer (Christian Lauliac) so much as mentions the score to *The Shawshank Redemption,* and *Positif* magazine's selective discography for Newman ignored this score, even though the soundtrack was released commercially.[14] In another interview, Newman himself noted that this was "a tough film to score," and the interview is filled with words like "tough," "barrel through," and "frustrating."[15] With this film the "quotedness" of the score seems less likely than Newman's apparently ambivalent feelings about his work to be a reason for the silence about it, because the quotations are a much smaller part of the whole. However, in some ways the quotations (both the *Figaro* duet and the snatches of popular music) are the most striking and interesting aspect of the score, so a certain lack of interest from the film music compositional community is perhaps not surprising.

I want to end my consideration of these little-discussed scores by considering how to place their uses of both quoted and diegetic opera excerpts within the larger context of film music theory, and by suggesting an overarching reading of such scenes. The literature on film music is generally dismissive about the use of quoted material in the background score, often because quotations are considered too intrusive and too clearly "heard" for the subliminal function of most background scores. George Burt, for example, writes, "While [quotations of national anthems] can be effective on certain occasions, they (like the "Wedding March") are usually so well known they can distract from the uniqueness of a particular dramatic situation by invoking extraneous associations."[16] And Christopher Palmer writes similarly, "Gradually [in the silent era] it was realized that scores of unoriginal material were harmful to a picture, inasmuch as they drew unwanted attention to themselves by virtue of their familiarity: the music was noticed rather than being allowed to register subliminally. This practice still persists—examples are *2001: A Space Odyssey, Elvira Madigan, 10, The Sting* and *Manhattan*—and basically the same objection holds good."[17]

However, this view does not distinguish between "super-familiar" quotations like national anthems, or the Blue Danube waltz used in *2001*, and quotations that may either be known only to a few people, or become widely recognized as "original" music only after the film score becomes well-known (both Scott Joplin's "The Entertainer," used in *The Sting*, and the Mozart concerto used in *Elvira Madigan* fall into this later category). This view also does not distinguish between a quotation that conspicuously interrupts the flow of the background score and quoted material woven subtly into the prevailing affect and texture. Nor does it take into account the purpose of a quotation or the "tone" of a film. The quotations of popular songs in the background score of *The Shawshank Redemption*, for example, are quite "intrusive," but they are clearly meant to be. That is, they are intended to convey specific and important information about the passing of time rather than to draw the audience into the action. It matters less that we recognize the particular songs than that we recognize their style in relation to the passing of the decades.

North's liberal use of *Gianni Schicchi* is different from any of the instances mentioned by Palmer, partly because of the sheer amount of musical material borrowed, and partly because the material borrowed—with the conspicuous exception of "O mio babbino caro"—already sounds like "classic" film music, so that "quotation" per se seems not quite the issue, at least not on a visceral level for most people. If one did not know *Gianni Schicchi* (and it is not the best known of Puccini's operas) nothing about it would be surprising as background music. The Rossini quotes are better known and thus perhaps potentially more intrusive. But the film as a whole does not pretend to be naturalistic (Jack Nicholson's ridiculously overdone accent alone could tell us that); it refers pervasively and conspicuously to the conventions of Mafia films, so obviously quoted material in the soundtrack is entirely appropriate.

Diegetic music is comparably ignored, if not so roughly derided, in general theories of film music. Although these theories always mention diegetic music, they usually dispose of it (typically as "setting the scene") in a paragraph or less, being more interested in the internal coherence of the integral background score, and perhaps in its status as "art," than in the complex multivalence of a score that weaves in and out of the diegesis.[18] Some of the diegetic music in *Prizzi's Honor* "sets the scene" in this way, most obviously the occasional music (at the wedding in the opening scenes, at the grand dinner, in the restaurants where Irene and Charley fall in love). Scene-setting is also the primary function of the diegetic popular songs in *The Shawshank Redemption*. But it should be clear from the discussions of the Letter Duet and "O mio babbino caro" that diegesis can serve a variety of ends beyond audible stage-prop. It is also worth mentioning that while diegesis and quotation must remain distinguishable on a theoretical level, in certain instances they blend into one another with wonderfully complex effect. ("O mio babbino caro" never stops being quoted material, but its diegetic status, as I noted above, comes increasingly into question. One might ask, then, whether our continuous awareness of its quoted status retains the music in the diegesis, even as we are also drawn into its effectiveness as soundtrack music.)

Although quotation and diegetic music have not historically been taken very seriously, writers on film music are beginning to take an interest in the pop music compilation soundtrack, not only as a commercial phenomenon that feeds into the soundtrack album business, but also as an aesthetic event, through which both contemporaneity and time-specific nostalgia can effectively and economically be invoked.[19] Writing about these soundtracks begins to address the interweaving of diegetic and non-diegetic, quoted and original music that is so important in both *The Shawshank Redemption* and *Prizzi's Honor*. However, they have not addressed the particular questions attaching to the use of classical music, or within that broad designation, the uses of opera.

Unlike quoted popular music, these quotations of classical music do not serve to stimulate nostalgia for the time of their creation,[20] and cannot, of course, lend their films a hip or up-to-date ambience. I would argue, though, that in both the movies considered here, despite their many differences, opera *does* represent a sort of nostalgia, or atavistic utopianism. Caryl Flinn has argued that the predominance of nineteenth-century classical music idioms in the background scores to classic films reinforces their escapist ideologies.[21] These uses of opera extend Flinn's thesis to quoted and diegetic uses of preexistent classical works. However, while the Letter Duet in *The Shawshank Redemption* clearly works in the way Flinn claims for the symphonic background score—by sucking the audience in to a sound world whose general stylistic manipulations we recognize and welcome—the quoted music in *Prizzi's Honor* arrives at its most meaningful results quite differently: namely by asking the audience consciously to recognize the particularity of the numbers rather than by responding viscerally to the generalities of their style.

The nostalgic or utopian aspect of *The Shawshank Redemption* is thus quite evident; its theme of fraternity is explicit, and opera's function as the emotional catalyst for this moment of inclusivity is open and uncomplicated. During the Letter Duet scene, as elsewhere in the film, the characters (and we) yearn for a sweet and lovely world where friendship conquers all, where beauty (represented both by the explicit high-art status of the Mozart and by the felt qualities of the two voices) is truth, and where both Red and Andy are (properly) recognized as good. It surely enriches the experience for some of us to *know* that the world temporarily inhabited by Susanna and the Countess is in some ways analogous to that imagined by Red and Andy, but the sense of an almost-realizable world of pure beauty and perfect friendship is accessible to all because it is primarily "felt" rather than "known." In *Prizzi's Honor*, on the other hand, the utopian element represented by opera has to do with its game-like aspect, and is explicitly not universally inclusive. Michael Walsh takes the operatic references to be a joke (played in part on film critics who didn't get it), and this general evaluation is not off the mark.[22] Socially speaking, this utopia exists for people who are already insiders: it reinforces their sense of belonging by distinguishing them from those who are not part of the group. But the in-group operatic game in this film also has another social function. In its existence as a sort of play within a play, it creates a world enclosed by the circularity of the references, in which the primary (even the only) point is to spot the connections: that is, to distance oneself from the content of the narrative to concentrate on its mechanics.

In addition, the almost exclusive use of comic opera in the soundtrack (and here I include "O mio babbino caro" as "soundtrack" music) not only lightens the tone of the whole but also suggests an analogous "shadow" world in which plot-ends are always tied up, villains always turn out to have soft hearts, and where the point is to entertain rather than to preach. This is a much simpler and less consequential world than that represented in Condon's book, where one of the points is that the boundaries between the criminals and the "good guys" are really not so clear; that legitimate businesses and racketeering are often interdependent and barely distinguishable. The movie represents this shady interface of course, but the combination of some plot-simplifications, the parodistic tone of the diegesis, and the pervasive use of comic opera distance the audience from the brute realities of the family's thuggery, and suggest a world of sheer entertainment. The appeal of this world is guaranteed not only by the fun of the game for those in the know, but also by the generally perceptible charm of the instrumental music and the workings of the female voice in "O mio babbino caro."

Thus, if the use of *The Marriage of Figaro* in *Shawshank Redemption* opens a window onto a world whose pure beauty suggests that the truth of a man's character is what matters, the use of *Gianni Schicchi* in *Prizzi's Honor* suggests a world where questions of truth, beauty, and morality are simply set aside. Both worlds are perfect of their kind, both are made desirable, both are atavistic, and neither would be so evident without opera.

NOTES

1. The only possible comparison is a dialogue (not in the movie) between Red and Andy, where the latter is describing how he set up a savings account for himself before he was sent to prison, and likens the process to an art collector protecting his Rembrandts. And the only similarity between this and the Letter Duet is the explicit reference to high culture, which is scarcely compelling as a "source" for the opera scene.

2. See Michael Walsh, "Prizzi's Opera" *Film Comment* 21, no. 5 (October 1985): 5–6, for a listing of some of the operatic references.

3. It is perfectly normal for operatic excerpts in Hollywood movies to be narratively connected to their filmic uses: the use of "Casta diva" from *Norma* in *The Bridges of Madison County*, which deals with the infidelity of a farmer's wife, of *La traviata* in *Pretty Woman*, which is the story of a low-life woman turned into a respectable creature by a rich man, or of "Addio del passato" from the same opera in *Lorenzo's Oil*, at the moment when the father discovers that his son has an incurable illness and that life will never be the same again. Nevertheless, the normalcy of the fact of narrative connection should not obscure the significance of any individual relationship between a film and an opera.

4. Wye J. Allanbrook, *Rhythmic Gesture in Mozart Le Nozze di Figaro and Don Giovanni* (Chicago: University of Chicago Press, 1983).

5. The exception is Rita Hayworth's voice, heard in an excerpt from *Gilda*.

6. See Michel Poizat, *The Angel's Cry: Beyond the Pleasure Principle in Opera*, trans. Arthur Denner (Ithaca: Cornell University Press, 1992).

7. See Mark Kermode, "Twisting the Knife," in *The Celluloid Jukebox: Popular Music and the Movies Since the 1950s*, ed. Jonathan Romney and Adrian Wooton,

(London: British Film Institute, 1995), 8–19, for a description of pop music's capacity to evoke both "now" and "then" with unparalleled immediacy.

8. Charles Nero has identified a theme of "operatic tutelage" in a number of films with opera scenes. In such scenes a person of color is represented as receiving the gift of opera from a middle or upper-middle class white man. Unpublished manuscript.

9. Don Corrado appears to be doing nothing else while "Questa o quella" is playing. The film opens with the longest sustained stretch of vocal music in the film: a performance of Schubert's "Ave Maria" during the wedding of Maerose's sister. The congregation is (mostly) still, mostly facing forward, and the music is loud on the soundtrack. But listening is really not the point. Don Corrado appears to be asleep; Charley Partanna is busy ogling Irene; and overall, the music here simply functions as background for introducing faces and the watchful atmosphere of the family.

10. *Lorenzo's Oil*, mentioned in n. 3, is one example. *Moonstruck,* in which *La bohème* features prominently, is another; most Mafia movies have at least one scene with opera or operatic singing in the background.

11. My first assumption was that the sound source is a record player; Michael Walsh, "Prizzi's Opera," assumes it is a radio. In fact the film does not show what sort of machine produces the music.

12. Christopher Palmer, *The Composer in Hollywood,* (London and New York: Marion Boyars, 1990), 295–300, discusses at length North's jazz-infused score to Elia Kazan's film of *Streetcar Named Desire*; and Royal Brown, *Overtones and Undertones,* (Berkeley: University of California Press, 1994), 344–45, puts North in his "Jazz" and "Modern" categories.

13. Christopher Palmer, *The Composer in Hollywood,* makes no mention of this score, despite devoting a section of his book to North, and North's obituaries do not dwell on this work.

14. The interview by Christian Lauliac in *Positif* 452 (October 1998): 93–4. The discography is in the same issue (101). The soundtrack was released on Epic Soundtrax in 1994.

15. The interview appeared in *Film Score Monthly* (1994). It is quoted on the website *www.filmtracks.com/titles/shawshank.html*.

16. George Burt, *The Art of Film Music* (Boston: Northeastern University Press, 1994), 57.

17. Palmer, *The Composer in Hollywood*, 13.

18. Discussions of the music in individual films, however, more often take diegetic music seriously. See, for example, Jeff Smith, "Unheard Melodies?" in *Post Theory: Reconstructing Film Studies*, ed. David Bordwell and Noel Carroll (Madison: University of Wisconsin Press, 1996), 240–5 for sensitive and detailed discussion of how both quoted and diegetic music work in *Love in the Afternoon*.

19. See especially Kermode, "Twisting the Knife."

20. The case might, of course, be different in period-piece films, where the time of the music's creation is already a "live" topic.

21. Caryl Flinn, *Strains of Utopia: Gender, Nostalgia and Hollywood Film Music* (Princeton: Princeton University Press, 1992), passim.

22. Walsh, "Prizzi's Opera."

# 7

# Is There a Text in This Libido?

## *Diva* and the Rhetoric of Contemporary Opera Criticism<sup>*</sup>

### *David J. Levin*

IN MY RECENT WORK, I HAVE BEEN THINKING ABOUT HOW WE MIGHT READ opera stagings, and read them as readings.[1] Which would not, in and of itself, merit particular mention, except that in a recent issue of *The Cambridge Opera Journal*, James Treadwell expresses some grave reservations about the project, because in his eyes, "reading," and by extension, the academic as reader, has no real place in the opera house. "Performance," he argues:

> might seem like a decisive act of interpretation—choices have to be made about how to present the given work—but, paradoxically, it also marks the point at which opera escapes the attentions of the academy in favour of a constituency which is (presumably) less grounded in theory and less committed to consciously interpretive acts.[2]

If Treadwell thinks that performance marks the point where, as he puts it, opera "escapes the attentions of the academy," he hasn't been reading the criticism I've been reading. A number of recent titles—such as *The Work of Opera* edited by Richard Dellamora and Daniel Fischlin, or *En Travesti*, edited by Patricia Juliana Smith and Corinne Blackmer— document the proliferation of academic interest in the theoretical stakes of opera in performance.[3] And yet, Treadwell may well be onto something—if inadvertently so. A number of the essays in those two volumes display an interest in opera that *has*, to use Treadwell's formulation, "escaped the attentions of the academy," not in the philological sense of operas that have gone largely unnoticed, but in a stylistic sense. Put most simply: a growing number of academics have been writing about

*This is an expanded and revised version of a paper first read at a session on Opera in Performance at the 1998 meeting of the MLA. My thanks to Linda and Michael Hutcheon, who organized the session and invited me to participate; and to Elin Diamond, who served as respondent, and whose remarks stimulated a number of the revisions I have undertaken here.

opera in explicitly lyrical, intensely personal ways—ways that are not tradition-ally "academic." They have been doing a good deal of emoting, finding ways to, as Madonna would have it, justify their love.

In this essay, I would like to think about that love and the conjunction of its conceptual and libidinal stakes. This wave of criticism—I'll refer to it here as critical Neo-Lyricism—comes at an odd moment. Just as the most staid opera houses in the U.S. are beginning to explore alternatives to rote histrionics on stage, a number of academics seem eager to fill in the gap of seemingly unmoti-vated hyperbole and proto-ritualized sentimentalization. And yet, of course, it's not that easy. Neo-Lyricism often aims for an adequation with operatic form: it emulates the object of its affections; and, perhaps more important, it seeks to render (but not necessarily to analyze) the intense affect that can suffuse the experience of opera. Thus, we might borrow a term from Herbert Lindenberger's work and describe recent opera *criticism* as the extravagant art.[4] But what are the terms of that extravagance?

The New Lyricism is not all *that* new, although it has reemerged recently with a renewed sense of vigor. Indeed, in some respects, it can count Nietzsche among its earliest and most forceful proponents. In Nietzsche's caustic view:

> Opera is the birth of the theoretical man, the critical layman, not of the artist: one of the most surprising facts in the history of all the arts. It was the demand of thoroughly unmusical hearers that before everything else the words must be understood, so that according to them a rebirth of music is to be expected only when some mode of singing has been discovered in which text-word lords it over counterpoint like master over servant. For the words, it is argued, are as much nobler than the accompanying harmonic system as the soul is nobler than the body.[5]

In Nietzsche's polemic, the hegemony of words signals opera's particular compatibility with the dreaded Alexandrian culture of cheerfulness: the culture of "empty and merely distracting diversion."[6] Absent a profound affiliation with music, opera, like tragedy, is but a shell of an artform, the stuff of intellectuals, in Nietzsche's rather alarming formulation. These days, of course, the words don't spawn diversion, but impede it; this, in a nutshell, is the observation that impels Treadwell's critique. If, in Nietzsche's view, opera lovers love the words (that lead them to meaning), in Treadwell's view, they love the music. Treadwell, I should emphasize, is not a proponent of the condition he describes, he mere-ly—and aptly—insists on its importance.

But where Treadwell treads lightly, others stomp about. Thus, for exam-ple, some ten years ago, Paul Robinson published a postscript to a book of (aca-demic) essays on operatic textuality. Robinson's rather blunt polemic, subtitled "Reading Libretti and Misreading Opera," expressed serious reservations about the project of reading opera. By way of modeling an alternative to the presum-ably staid, academic prose of his colleagues, Robinson's text took a turn toward the autobiographical. Thus, he sang the praises of immersing himself in opera, without benefit of libretto or synopsis.[7] Here is how Robinson described a characteristic episode from his *amour fou*: "I found myself listening to the performance [of Gounod's *Roméo et Juliette*] over and over. I listened without a libretto; nor did I consult a synopsis of the opera. I simply indulged myself in the thing itself."[8]

Of course, the "house" where Robinson was doing his listening was not the opera house proper: he was listening at home. Here, then, is a generically apt spin on the bourgeois fantasy of grandiloquence: in this case, a man's home is not just his castle, it is his own private *Opéra*. Needless to say, in this particular house, surtitles are not on offer. But what happens when opera enters the opera lover's psychic and physical space? It would be revealing to map the aesthetic politics of opera's deployment in the private sphere. For Brecht, who famously invokes "culinary opera" with modernist disdain, traditional opera is of the dining room (with the domestic staff hidden back in the kitchen, doing the grunge work); for Wayne Koestenbaum, opera is of the bedroom and the living room, both of which are more commodious than the closet, where it had resided in his childhood; for Wagner, opera is to be banished from the home and relocated to a newfangled church, where worshippers would set aside their quotidian concerns (having already left behind their workaday aesthetic wares) in order to rededicate themselves to an apprehension of the artwork of the future.[9] Of these positions, Koestenbaum's is the least familiar and the most symptomatic, so I propose to take a closer look at it, in order to ask what happens when opera criticism leaves the well-trodden path of textual scholarship and launches into a new world of emotive stratospherics.

The scene as it is set in Koestenbaum's writing corresponds in many ways to Robinson's account. Thus, for example, in a chapter of *The Queen's Throat* devoted to opera at home, Koestenbaum writes of "crooning, to an invisible audience, to the chest of drawers and the shut window":

> No latecomers saying "Excuse me" will mar our enjoyment. We are alone with our pleasure, and the pleasure is doubled, not diminished. Or it simply becomes a different pleasure: a mirror scene. We call such pleasures masturbatory and condemn them, as if masturbation ever harmed a soul.[10]

It is these operatic pleasures as explicitly undomesticated pleasures in the domestic sphere that catch my attention in Koestenbaum's characteristically hyperbolic prose, but, of course, not just there. Thus, for example, in his book *Opera in the Flesh: Sexuality in Operatic Performance*, Sam Abel echoes, or indeed, *amplifies* Koestenbaum's thematics and his autobiographical rhetoric: "When I go to the opera house, the performance is a physical sex act between my body and the singer's voice-body. When I listen to an opera recording, the erotic experience becomes a private masturbation fantasy."[11] How to read opera in the private sphere, and read its contemporary chroniclers? The most immediate answer, provided by Robinson, Abel, and Koestenbaum, is that opera in the private sphere induces a scene of libidinal effusion. And these snippets of lyrical criticism don't just recount that scene, they enact it. That is, lyrical criticism seems to aspire to *be* a bravura performance as much as a *record* of bravura performances.

One of the unpredictable terms of this enactment of effusion is its relationship to the specificity of the work at hand. In Abel's case, disregard is part of the program: his private masturbation fantasy is activated by listening to a recording, period—not a particular recording by a particular singer or composer or conductor. In Paul Robinson's essay, it is a particular opera—*Roméo et Juliette*—that gains him access to "the thing itself." In Terry Castle's astute and amusing essay "In Praise of Brigitte Fassbaender," it is that particular lyric soprano who does the trick.[12] Such, it would appear, are the vagaries of object choice.

And, yet, there is a marked difference between, say, Castle's essay and Koestenbaum or Abel's book. Where Koestenbaum and Abel emote unabashedly, Castle shuttles between confession, embarrassment, and analysis.[13] Of course, in saying so, I run the risk of standing in for the very academic pedantry from which all three of these authors—and with them, Neo-Lyricism more generally—clearly seek to escape. It is a real problem. Castle puts it well:

> Intellectuals, on the whole, are not used to thinking of "the capacity to admire" as a valuable human quality; indeed, so profound are our modern prejudices against anything smacking of enthusiasm or emotional excess, we are more likely to take such receptivity to others as a sign of moral and intellectual weakness. As I suggested at the outset, coming out as a fan can be an embarrassing business, especially if one wants to continue to be regarded by friends and associates as a normally functioning member of society. Being grown-up, maintaining a properly critical and self-conscious attitude toward the world—or so the ideologues teach us—requires self-control: the rooting out, the rationalization, the analyzing away of all exaggerated feeling.[14]

Castle is surely right that academic culture—especially its Teutonic wing—is unduly skeptical of enthusiasm. So let me be clear: my problem is less with Neo-Lyrical enthusiasm *per se* than with its conceptual and pragmatic terms. How so? Put most simply: I wonder what happens to textual analysis when the Neo-Lyricists get in touch with their inner diva. Of course, these particular concerns would appear to mark me as a member of Nietzsche's Alexandrian herd. But there too, I wonder about the terms of opposition: is the operatic lover's discourse necessarily logophobic?

If there is such a thing as a canonical staging of the scene I have in mind, it is in Jean-Jacques Beineix's 1981 film *Diva*.[15] In this film, the generic exoticism that accrues implicitly to opera in film is echoed in the racial exoticism of the object choice: the soprano Cynthia Hawkins, the object of a confluence of aural, carnal, and commercial desires, is a soprano of color. In this high-tech world of multinational extortion, prostitution rings, and police cover-ups—in this prototypically filmic world of action and adventure—opera in concert performance represents a distinct, static alternative. Here, opera embodies (in all senses of the word) a zone of immersion and transcendence that is inflected as antithetical to action.[16] Indeed, the diva's programmatic determination to reserve her performances for liveness (and thus, pragmatically, to resist the technological dissemination of her voice) can be understood not only as a challenge to the threat of commercialization (which is its explicit purpose) but as the film's disavowal of its own inscription on celluloid. Opera enables this disavowal, warranting a technophobic and generic presence that is as powerful as it is illusory. (The film, we might say, sings—in operatic form—the praises of a presence that it cannot redeem.[17])

In the film, the protagonist Jules (Frederic Andrei) gets into hot water for making a pirate recording of the diva Cynthia Hawkins (Wilhelmenia Wiggins Fernandez) in performance—a recording intended, he insists, for his own pleasure. In a duly portentous moment, Gorodish (Richard Bohringer)—the enigmatic, new-age, fairy-Godfather who repeatedly saves Jules and, in the end, kills the bad guy—will insist that there are no innocent pleasures.[18] Irrespective of its status as innocent or guilty (something that the film fixes on with some gusto), the film marks this particular pleasure as one that bears repeating. Thus, we will hear the same aria over and over again during the course of the film as the tape is recorded, circulated, and finally returned.

After the diva's initial performance of the aria, at the outset of the film, Jules heads backstage and manages to pilfer her satin gown. Thus, when he finally arrives at home, his hands are full: he's got the illicit recording to listen to and the gown to luxuriate with. I want to focus on this scene of Jules' homecoming, which constitutes a proto-Robinsonian (or, for that matter, proto-Koestenbaumian, proto-Abelian) scene of auditory and tactile pleasure. The multiplication of authorial references is not an idle effect: the scene of blissful auditory immersion echoes throughout contemporary—primarily, but not exclusively queer—writing on opera.[19] But what exactly transpires in the scene on film?

Jules parks his moped just outside the entrance to his living quarters, a converted garage space on an upper floor of an industrial building. Here, as in the opening of the film, the audio track is saturated with the prelude to the third act of Wagner's *Tristan und Isolde*, music that the film locates, improbably, within the diegesis, emanating from the teensy sound system balanced on the moped's handlebars. Jules, it would appear, has a thing for the operatic sounds of romantic tragedy.[20] As the music of Wally's defiant, melancholic aria swells (again) on the soundtrack, the camera shows us Jules sprawled out on a blue deck chair, the gown in his right hand, a reel-to-reel tape player cradled in his left (see Figure 7.1).

Figure 7.1 Jules, in Jean-Jaques Beineix's *Diva*, at home with his pleasure. Image courtesy of the Museum of Modern Art Stills Archive.

Although it's set at home, this scene is "about" someplace else. It shows and elicits imaginative or libidinal transport: who knows where Jules' thoughts are headed? For its part, the camera enacts a sense of Jules' abandon while figuring its technological origins: it swirls, like the music, around and about him, focusing alternately on the young hero, his reel-to-reel player, and his stereo system. W. M. Hagen's account of the scene is worth quoting at some length:

> As Jules loses himself in the taped aria of his diva, the camera both dollies and invisibly cuts farther and farther away from the subject, just as it did in the original performance. In the course of this tracking and editing, the camera incidentally discovers parts of the décor which obscure Jules. It finally "loses" him altogether as it backs through the plastic flaps that serve as a door. The glowing door becomes the center of the frame, getting smaller and smaller like the center of a vortex (like the Diva earlier), as the camera backs away. The music does not diminish in volume. The selectivity and movement of the camera create a drama of the disappearing center, while the soundtrack again asserts the primacy of the Diva's music whose point of origin, by the end of the scene, is mysterious: Is it a separation of Jules's aural point of view from his physical being or, possibly, a mindscreen memory of the film itself? In short, the film presents a visual and aural equivalent for losing oneself in music.[21]

It is clear why the diva's voice, thus introduced into the domestic space, would provoke such bliss in Jules, and unleash such an intense writerly affect in Wayne Koestenbaum or Sam Abel. "Losing oneself in music" is heady stuff, or rather, it's *bodily* stuff—and contemporary critics have been eager to chart its terms. But just what are those terms?

In this case, it seems noteworthy that the context of the aria is not just absent, but has been *absented*.[22] In part, of course, this is due to the logic of a recital, where arias are lifted from the works in which they occur. But lifted thus, the aria remains a floating signifier, allowed to drift freely—for Jules and us— in a space of simultaneous projection and immersion. And we should note that it floats in multiple registers. In *Diva*, we hear the same aria repeatedly, albeit without any dramatic anchoring. That seems to be part of the point: operatic music, here, is inflected as producing affect *an sich*, something distinct from language.[23] This only underscores the irony of the film's politics of mediation, noted earlier, because it takes mediation (in this case, the tape player) to disavow mediation (in this case, the language of the aria). The tape player, we might say, offers the means by which language is evacuated from the aria.

But what is at stake in this evacuation? Later in the film, Jules's immersion in the diva's voice will be literalized. We might say he gets into real-life hot water as he's getting into metaphorical hot water. On the morning after a romantic night spent strolling about Paris—a night whose romantic innocence the film underscores when it shows Jules and Cynthia Hawkins back in the singer's hotel room, sleeping in separate beds—the soprano allows Jules to stick around while she rehearses, and in preparation or perhaps celebration, he takes a boiling hot bath. His immersion—in the bath as in the music—is not inflected as particularly meaningful, beyond its status as an escape from meaning.[24] Not surprisingly, the film isn't interested in opera as a *variegated* signifying practice, at once bound and resistant to language. Thus, whenever the aria is performed or played back in the film, the subtitles—which otherwise grace the film in its English-language release—disappear. As a result, we don't have much of a textual entrée into Jules' bliss. Which would suggest that, much like Robinson's domestic scene, the film comprehends that bliss as separate from—if not antithetical to—a traditional sense of the aria's textual meaning.

We might say that the film shares with the Neo-Lyricists a resistance to opera's traditional textual components. But why? In order to venture an answer, I would have us return to the precise terms of Koestenbaum's claim and his pluralization of what is, essentially, a private scene. "We are alone with our pleasure," he writes, "and the pleasure is doubled, not diminished. Or it simply becomes a different pleasure: a mirror scene."[25] A mirror scene? Some of the most interesting critical writing on *Diva* has invoked the mirror stage to describe what's at stake in the film.[26] But the script of Koestenbaum's mirror scene differs markedly from that proposed in those writings or, for that matter, the scene posed in—and familiar from—Lacan's essay of the late '40s.[27]

I think we can understand Koestenbaum's "mirror" as operating discursively, less oriented around the production of an ideal ego than an *ideal-id*. In mirroring the performative hyperbole of operatic form, the writing tends to stake out alternative sites of meaning, located, for example, in the listener's private experiences rather than the diegetic situation of the aria itself. In this way, the prose presumably enacts its own order of performance, which is, in part, an academic performance of resistance to the paternal—shall we say, philological—mandate to which Castle alludes. According to that mandate, academic critics need to set aside the trappings of experience (let alone libido) in order to attend to the production and circulation of meaning. But in Koestenbaum's book, and not just there, the libidinal register *is* the meaning.[28]

This notion of "going your own way with your pleasure" is not just *suggested* by the film, it is also performed—repeatedly, in various ways—within it. On a formal level, the scene of Jules' bliss (on the beach chair, gown in one hand, reel-to-reel in the other) makes a program of the ideological stakes of "going your own way": as I noted above, the subtitles disappear when the music emerges.[29] This is all the more symptomatic because of the dramatic situation that is therewith suppressed. The aria performed, or rather, *repeated* in the scene bears more or less precisely on the performative situation of its critical reception. That is, the title character of *La Wally* is not just, as Jules will later explain, "a woman who wants to die, who sings of her broken heart."[30] Rather, the aria occurs towards the end of Act One of Catalani's opera, immediately in the wake of the title character's—that is, the diva's; or in this case, the daughter's—pronounced defiance of her father's demand that she either obey his wishes and marry a cad or pack her bags forever. True to her father's ultimatum, she is going her own way, heading for the hills.

In Catalani's work, Wally performs much the same scene that the academic Neo-Lyricists enact: a defiance of the paternal mandate. Of course, the circuit of this connection is forged by dramaturgical analysis. And dramaturgical analysis (if I may be allowed to mix metaphors) is the well-meaning baby that many of the Neo-Lyricists—and the filmmakers—tend to throw out with the soiled paternal-mandate bath water. Or, put otherwise: by dispensing with the subtitles, the film evacuates the aria of dramatic and dramaturgical reference in favor of a kind of "pure" lyricism, or perhaps, an "innocent"—because meaningless—pleasure. To the extent that they second that evacuation in the course of their defiance of a dogged academic subscription to the regime of meaning, many of the Neo-Lyricists ignore the textual sanction for their defiance of it.

This would simply be ironic, were it not for the fact that this defiant gesture tends to reproduce the very terms that it obviously abhors. In this particular instance, the unintended term is misogyny. As Jules and the film fetishize the aria qua lyricism, the apparatus is fully engaged to render Cynthia Hawkins' aria meaningless. As a result, Wally's cogent statement of defiance is rendered meaningless and, in so doing, is sentimentalized into a capitulation to the very regime that it would abandon. That is, the diva's voice—which Kaja Silverman convincingly characterizes as the maternal voice—arguably reassumes meaning in the film insofar as it emerges as meaningless. This is, of course, a very different meaning than its meaning within Catalani's work. Here, then, to be duly stentorian and Teutonic about it, is the flip side of Neo-Lyrical pleasure. I don't doubt that it's great fun to listen without a libretto, to immerse oneself in "the thing itself" (although, more than ten years later, I still don't know what "the thing itself" is). Surely we need to figure this out?

To cite the tiresome and sententious tag line from the film: there are no innocent pleasures. And while it seems silly to restrict opera to the prison house of language, it hardly seems like much of an achievement to hatch a grand escape through the familiar hatch of disavowal. Perhaps there is a modest achievement in recognizing the imbrication of words and music, texts and enthusiasm? Indeed, little is gained by purchasing the legitimation of enthusiasm at the cost of nuanced textual analysis.

## NOTES

1. "Reading a Staging/Staging a Reading," *Cambridge Opera Journal* 9, no. 1 (1997): 47–71.

2. James Treadwell, "Reading & Staging Again, " *Cambridge Opera Journal* 10, no. 2 (1998): 205. My answer to Treadwell's response appeared in *Cambridge Opera Journal* 10, no. 3 (1998): 307–11.

3. See Richard Dellamora and Daniel Fischlin, eds., *The Work of Opera: Genre, Nationhood, and Sexual Difference* (New York: Columbia University Press, 1997) as well as Patricia Juliana Smith and Corinne Blackmer, eds., *En Travesti: Women, Gender Subversion, Opera* (New York: Columbia University Press, 1995) (hereafter, Smith & Blackmer).

4. I am referring here, of course, to the subtitle of Lindenberger's *Opera: The Extravagant Art* (Ithaca: Cornell University Press, 1984).

5. See Friedrich Nietzsche, *The Birth of Tragedy,* in *The Birth of Tragedy and the Case of Wagner* (New York: Vintage, 1967), 15–144, here §19, 116.

6. Ibid., §19, 118.

7. See Paul Robinson, "A Deconstructive Postscript: Reading Libretti and Misreading Opera," in *Reading Opera*, ed. Arthur Groos and Roger Parker (Princeton: Princeton University Press, 1988), 328–46. A few years after Groos and Parker's collection appeared, I took Robinson to task for what I considered to be his program of non- or even anti-textual immersion in opera. See my Introduction to *Opera Through Other Eyes* (Stanford: Stanford University Press, 1994).

8. Robinson, 344.

9. See Bertolt Brecht, "The Modern Theater Is the Epic Theater," in *Brecht on Theater*, ed. John Willett (New York: Hill and Wang, 1964); Wayne Koestenbaum, *The Queen's Throat: Opera, Homosexuality, and the Mystery of Desire* (New York: Poseidon, 1993) [hereafter, Koestenbaum]; Richard Wagner, "The Artwork of the

Future" in *Richard Wagner's Prose Work,* vol. 1 (London: Kegan Paul, Trench, Trüber & Co., 1985), 67–213.

10. Koestenbaum, 57.

11. Sam Abel, *Opera in the Flesh: Sexuality in Operatic Performance* (Boulder, CO: Westview Press, 1996), 168.

12. See "In Praise of Brigitte Fassbaender: Reflections on Diva Worship," in Terry Castle, *The Apparitional Lesbian: Female Homosexuality and Modern Culture* (New York: Columbia University Press, 1993), 200–38; the essay also appears in Smith and Blackmer, eds., *En Travesti,* 20–58.

13. Here is how she begins her essay: "To 'come out' as the fan of a great diva is always an embarrassing proposition—as difficult in its own way, perhaps, as coming out as a homosexual. For what can be more undignified than confessing one's susceptibility to a thrilling female voice?" (Castle, 200).

14. Castle, 236.

15. *Diva,* directed by Jean-Jacques Beineix, France, 1981; released by United Artists Classics. Starring Frederic Andrei, Roland Bertin, Richard Bohringer, Gerard Darmon, Jacques Fabbri, Thuy An Luu, Dominique Pinon, Anny Romand, with the participation of Wilhelmenia Wiggins Fernandez. Produced by Irene Silberman. Director of Photography, Philippe Rousselot. Screenplay by Jean-Jacques Beineix and Jean Van Hamme.

16. Mimi White makes a similar point in her essay "They All Sing . . . :Voice, Body, and Representation in *Diva,*" *Literature and Psychology* 34, no. 4 (1988): 33–43. (Hereafter, White.) According to White, "Opera figures here [in *Diva*] as an overdetermined sign of women's romance, tragedy, demise, the voice as song foretelling death. Opera can be seen as the 'other' of contemporary popular culture, the latter finding expression in *Diva*'s thriller plot." (39)

17. See in this regard Mimi White, "They All Sing . . ." White is most interested in tracking the gender politics of the film. Thus, her reading of the diva's refusal to be recorded centers on questions of power. According to White, the diva's insistence on liveness "is utopian—a fantasy of non-division and an ideal out of step with the exigencies of a social and cultural order dominated by an international market of advanced technological development. If there is no place for the aura of the singular performance in the age of mechanical reproduction, it is merely a woman's whim to uphold the ideal of this aura in the age of digital and electronic recording technology. In *Diva* this nostalgic impossibility is figured in the female characters who think that if they sing well enough they may elude international economic networks of male domination." (35)

18. In Mimi White's rather severe account, "In the end (and this is the final scene of the film) [Jules'] 'innocent' acts of fetishizing fan-dom—taping her performance, stealing her gown—secure her capitulation to his adoring control." (White, 34)

19. Thus, we could say that the scene is variously proto-Dellamorian, -Smithian, -Reynoldsian, -Leonardi and Pope-ian—the list really does go on and on.

For Dellamora, see Richard Dellamora, "Mozart and the Politics of Intimacy: *The Marriage of Figaro* in Toronto, Paris, and New York," in Dellamora and Daniel Fischlin, eds. *The Work of Opera*, 255–75; for Smith, see the prologue to Patricia Juliana Smith, "Gli Enigmi Sono Tre: The [D]evolution of Turandot, Lesbian Monster" in Patricia Juliana Smith and Corinne E. Blackmer, eds., *En Travesti: Women, Gender Subversion, Opera*, 242–84, here, 242–5; for Margaret Reynolds, see Margaret Reynolds, "Ruggiero's Deceptions, Cherubino's Distractions," in *En Travesti*, 132–51; for Susan Leonardi and Rebecca Pope, see *The Diva's Mouth: Body, Voice, Prima Donna Politics* (New Brunswick, N.J.: Rutgers University Press, 1996).

20. Later, over breakfast, he fervently tries to convince Cynthia Hawkins to essay the role of Tosca; when he meets Alba, [Thuy An Luu] we are treated to the concluding strains of the overture to *Rigoletto* located, once again, in the sound system on his moped.

21. W. M. Hagen, "Performance Space in *Diva*," *Literature/Film Quarterly* 16, no. 3 (1988): 155–59, here 157.

22. In Robert Lang's account, this immersion is symptomatic of the regressive terms of Jules' fantasy: "to some extent, Jules' obsession with Hawkins' voice is a manifestation of a desire to return to the pre-Symbolic stage when, for the child, the mother is the source of all satisfaction, of which the sound of the mother's voice can constitute a large part." See Lang, "Carnal Stereophony: A Reading of *Diva*" *Screen* 25, no. 3, (1984): 70–79, here 71. (Hereafter, Lang.)

23. Robert Lang points out that the cinema's appeal resides, in part, in the fantasy of erasing the difference between perception and representation. The fantasmatics of music in *Diva* lands the film in the same neighborhood as much Neo-Lyrical criticism. In Lang's account, "It is a return to the pre-mirror stage where there is no perceived difference between one's body and the rest of the world that Jules craves and which is part of what draws us to the cinema. . . . It is [the] gap—between body and psyche—that the cinema (at least the kind of cinema to which *Diva* belongs) attempts to close. It is an impossible desire, but in the singing human voice, because it is the *body*, because it bears traces of what Roland Barthes calls *signifiance*, escaping the 'tyranny of meaning' one can approach it" (Lang, 76).

24. In Lang's perceptive account of the scene: "it is poetically logical, this amniotic bath that precedes her singing for him. It is the *mise-en-scène* (nativity scene) of Jules' desiring pattern." (Lang, 76)

25. Koestenbaum, 57.

26. In addition to Robert Lang's "Carnal Stereophony," see Kaja Silverman, *The Acoustic Mirror* (Bloomington: Indiana University Press, 1988), especially chapter 3: "The Fantasy of the Maternal Voice: Paranoia & Compensation," 72–100.

27. See, once again, Jacques Lacan, "The Mirror Stage as Formative of the Function of the I as Revealed in Psychoanalytic Experience," in Lacan, *Écrits*, trans. Alan Sheridan, (New York: Norton, 1977), 1–7.

28. Thus, in lieu of the traditional academic performance—a performance of successfully internalizing the paternal mandate, and ritual obedience to it—these

academics would, in a sense, go their own way, heading off in search of an account of libidinal erotics rather than philology.

29. In the French original, of course, it is not that they disappear, but that they fail to appear with the aria's onset.

30. He explains this in the course of his impromptu introductory remarks to Alba, who is about to hear the aria for the first time. See *Diva*, ca. minute 27.

# 8

# The Elusive Voice

## Absence and Presence in Jean-Pierre Ponnelle's Film *Le nozze di Figaro**

### *Marcia J. Citron*

I N *A SONG OF LOVE AND DEATH*, PETER CONRAD MAKES A PERCEPTIVE REMARK about the operatic voice: "One of the bequests of film to opera is its demonstration that song is soliloquy, not overt statement: that the voice is consciousness—or the yearning subconscious—overheard." Conrad elaborates on the soliloquy through a discussion of the love duet in Jean-Pierre Ponnelle's film *Madama Butterfly* (1974). In this rendition where characters occupy two different locations, singing lacks moving lips and the soundtrack becomes "the subliminal sounding of desire."[1]

Ponnelle deploys soliloquy imaginatively in other films for television, especially *Le nozze di Figaro* (1976), a work that drew rave notices from critics.[2] Soliloquy, or what can be described as "interior singing," occurs frequently in Ponnelle's *Figaro*, in a variety of numbers, and becomes a characteristic feature of the film. By interior singing I mean vocal music that is presented without moving lips and thus lacks an immediate and obvious visual source. We associate what we hear with a particular character because of the camera work and our recognition of the performer's voice. Yet, even though we perceive a connection with a particular character, interior singing calls into question the status and location of the voice and suggests that the voice might have a different relationship with the character—one that is more intimate than the situation in which lips move. Hence we might expect interior singing when characters reveal personal feelings, especially in arias.

In Ponnelle's *Figaro,* many arias deploy interior singing. Two numbers, the Count's "Vedrò mentr' io sospiro" and the Countess's "Porgi amor," consist entirely of interior singing. Other arias, including Cherubino's "Non so più," the Countess's "Dove sono," and Figaro's "Aprite un po' quegli occhi," offer a mixture of regular singing (exterior singing) and interior singing. Interestingly,

---

* I wish to express sincere thanks to Tim Carter, who introduced me to Ponnelle's film.

*133*

ensembles also partake of interior singing. Although no ensemble is rendered entirely as interior singing, several sections of ensembles are performed in this manner. These are generally passages in which a character expresses something personal that is at odds with the thoughts of another character or with the general tone of the number. Examples include parts of the Sextet, the finales to Acts II and IV, the trios "Cosa sento" and "Susanna, or via sortite," and the duet "Crudel! Perchè finora." Even secco recitatives, which can be considered the very opposite of fully formed song, partake of interior singing on occasion and, in so doing, open up a personal dimension that is usually absent from such numbers.

Although interior singing figures prominently in Ponnelle's film, the device still represents a departure from the usual practice of singing with moving lips in opera film. Thus Ponnelle's treatment raises important aesthetic and interpretive issues. For example, can the location of interior singing be interior if it appears in the filmic space and we hear it? And what about the fact that interior singing operates in the realm of playback? Like most opera films, *Figaro*'s music was prerecorded and then postsynchronized with the action at the time of shooting.[3] Although different from lip-synched music, interior singing also belongs to the playback system because its temporal relationship to the source is the same as that of lip-synched music. In both, prerecorded music is played back and absorbed into the final film at the time of shooting; only the absence or presence of the visual trace of the voice, the movement of lips, distinguishes the two.

In this essay, my aim is to explore complexities of interior singing in Ponnelle's *Figaro*. I am especially concerned with vocal absence and presence and their effect on hearing, agency, and filmic location: what is heard, and by whom, inside and outside the story; who initiates and who responds; and where these dynamics unfold with respect to the boundaries of the scene, the film, and the spectator. I will focus on three arias that show the power and versatility of interior singing. In Figaro's "Aprite," interior singing occurs in the opening accompanied recitative and sets the stage for the most sensational number in the film. The character literally splits into two figures during the aria. In the Count's "Vedrò," which is rendered entirely with closed mouth, time freezes as the meaning of the private sphere is reconfigured in a public space. And in Cherubino's "Non so più," shot with a lively camera and steeped in point-of-view technique, the performance drifts in and out of sonic consciousness as it limns the confused teenager. The numbers make us think about our status in relation to the audiovisual events—what do we hear of what we see, and what do we see of what we hear[4]—and the status of the operatic personas in relation to each other. What do they hear and how, and how does that tell us what they know and what they allow us to know? And how do these complexities of narrative and representation shape Ponnelle's conception of the characters and the film as a whole?

Through a study of Ponnelle's practices, I hope to open the window a bit wider on the mysterious powers of the voice. In opera film, the voice teeters at the edge of attachment to the characters because of playback; in Ponnelle's hands it becomes less tethered to a body or image through interior singing. His film *Le nozze di Figaro* provides an example of how the ideal of unified sound and image in film is an illusion.[5] In the gaps of representation—those ambiguous places that sound theorist Michel Chion calls "en creux"[6]—the possibilities for new meanings for opera in film are expanded.

## "APRITE UN PO' QUEGLI OCCHI": OPEN UP YOUR EYES (AND SEE THE VOICE)

In Act IV of Mozart's opera, Figaro sings an aria in which he castigates the fickle nature of women. They deceive, they trick, they betray men, much like witches, and the outcome is inevitable: men will be cuckolded. The diatribe, which follows a personal plaint in the accompanied recitative, is a diluted replacement for Figaro's lengthy speech against political tyranny in Beaumarchais's play. As in the poetry for the catalogue aria in *Don Giovanni*, which also includes a virtuosic display of descriptive language, the librettist gave Mozart wonderful material to set. Da Ponte's text is full of wit, rich in metaphor, and piquant in sound:

| | |
|---|---|
| Aprite un po' quegli occhi, | Just open your eyes, |
| Uomini incauti e sciocchi, | You rash and foolish men, |
| Guardate queste femmine, | And look at these women; |
| Guardate cosa son. | See them as they are, |
| | |
| Queste chiamate Dee | These goddesses, so called, |
| Dagli ingannati sensi, | By the intoxicated senses, |
| A cui tributa incensi | To whom feeble reason |
| La debole ragion. | Offers tribute. |
| | |
| Son streghe che incantano | They are witches who cast spells |
| Per farci penar, | For our torment, |
| Sirene che cantano | Sirens who sing |
| Per farci affogar; | For our confusion; |
| Civette che allettano | Night owls who fascinate |
| Per trarci le piume, | To pluck us, |
| Comete che brillano | Comets who dazzle |
| Per toglierci il lume. | To deprive us of light. |
| | |
| Son rose spinose, | They are thorned roses, |
| Son volpi vezzose, | Alluring vixens, |
| Son orse benigne, | Smiling she-bears, |
| Colombe maligne, | Malign doves, |
| Maestre d'inganni, | Masters of deceit, |
| Amiche d'affani | Friends of distress |
| Che fingono, mentono, | Who cheat and lie, |
| Ch' amore non sentono, | Who feel no love |
| Non senton pietà. | And have no pity. |
| Il resto nol dico, | The rest I need not say, |
| Già ognuno lo sa. | For everyone knows it already.[7] |

The film stages the number at night (as in the Mozart), in a clearing of an idealized woods. As the accompanied recitative begins, Figaro hovers around a bench. Gestures and facial expressions reveal his torment, but no moving lips utter the words we hear. The entire introduction proceeds in this manner. In the short pause before "Aprite," the camera presents a visual disruption as it tracks slowly to the left and reveals another Figaro. Standing and in clear focus, this Figaro—henceforth Figaro II—is dressed in the servant's clothes from the start of the film. Both figures are played by Hermann Prey, so there is a sense of doubleness or division. Figaro II sings almost all of the aria proper, and the mode returns to moving lips that parallel the heard sounds. It would be one thing for this figure to replace Figaro I, but Ponnelle gives us *both* figures in the real or implied filmic space for the rest of the number. When both figures appear in the frame, it is obvious that Figaro I is pre-filmed stock—he is fuzzier than Figaro II—and inserted at the time of shooting. During the number, the heard voice retains the same sonic signature. Definition, presence, and individual timbre are constant except for normal nuances of vocal expression.

Guided by the imperative mood of the text—"Aprite" and "Guardate" ("Open" and "Look")—Figaro II begins the aria facing the viewer squarely, in direct address. This forceful style reflects televisual practices of *reportage*, which emphasize a sense of the present as well as the viewer's co-intimacy with the message delivered on the screen.[8] Figaro II gives a cautionary lecture to men in the audience and aims other sections directly at Figaro I. A dejected figure, Figaro I contrasts with the feisty interlocutor that revives the spirited Figaro of yore. Late in the number, Figaro I responds to the taunts, at a place where Mozart rearranged the libretto so that the even-numbered lines of the third stanza—those that personalize the effects of women's deceit—are replaced by the line "Il resto nol dico" ("The rest I need not say"). The uniform response, akin to a litany, indicates the extent to which the character has capitulated to the inevitable. Figaro I utters this refrain, to Figaro II's enunciation of the crimes. The vocal dualism is reinforced by the antiphony in the music, and the pattern of each line is distinct: in register (high versus low), melodic shape, orchestral timbre (strings versus winds), and gestural function (beginning or medial versus cadential function). The differences reinforce the gulf between the figures.

A doppelgänger, a face in the mirror, arguing with itself: What does this mean for representation and narrative, and how do we interpret the status of the voice?

Before we answer these questions, we have to consider the larger frame of the scene. At the end of the preceding secco recitative, the camera settles on Figaro. Standing still, Figaro parts branches on his left as if to look at something, a gesture reminiscent of a curtain opening in a theater. The camera moves away from Figaro and traverses a path in the direction he was looking. Tracking slowly, it shows us foliage in blurred focus. The image acts as a transition to the site of the aria, in a clearing nearby. Over these idealized images, the music of the accompanied recitative begins. Soon we see a despairing Figaro, whose melodramatic gestures and expressions resemble those of silent film, and the number proceeds as described.[9]

While one's impulse is to assume that this is the same Figaro from the secco recitative, another reading is plausible and, I believe, more compelling. The mannered staging creates a gap between the outside Figaro and the action, and he becomes an objectified viewer, a voyeur, of events. His relationship to the *scena* takes the form of a projection. Although it could be interpreted as a fantasy or dream, I find it a more considered scenario, and am drawn to the idea that it plays out in his rational mind. Prior to the *scena,* Figaro represents a unified subject, but as the scene unfolds he assumes a fractured identity. Because the old Figaro is not present to our eyes, the number has a visible missing source. This suggests that the *scena* is acousmatic, lacking a visible source for the sound.[10] Not surprisingly, the workings of the *acousmêtre* in this type of film, which has prerecorded music, are more complex than in ordinary sound film.

Chion's concept of "external logic" is useful in this context. Defined as a rupture in the flow of sound, the term applies to situations in which a special narrative effect trumps normal expectations regarding the succession of sounds.[11] Jean-Luc Godard is famous for illogical juxtapositions of sound in his films, for example in *Prénom Carmen* (1983), which presents a mélange of sea-gull calls, urban traffic noises, and fragments of late Beethoven quartets.[12] In Figaro's *scena,* external logic characterizes the perceived ruptures in the sound as we are challenged to adjust our sense of the source of the sound and of the individual who is singing. This occurs because of the shifting image of Figaro. Even though the literal sound remains constant and continuous, the shifting vocal personas mean a disrupted narrative in the larger audiovisual context.

The fluid situation in the *scena* can be understood as a voice in search of a body. In the accompanied recitative, we hear a voice that lacks moving lips. Because other numbers have already been presented without moving lips, we are ready to make a connection between the seen figure and the heard voice. Soon Figaro II enters and sings the aria with moving lips, an act that threatens our certainty about the owner of the voice. A bit later, Figaro I lip-synchs in response to Figaro II's taunts. Can we really be sure about this voice? Is it a wanderer that will find its home only when the scene is over? Although a stable Figaro looks on from the side, the roaming voice that asserts a destabilized Figaro raises the spectre of the *acousmêtre* and reinforces Figaro's self-image as a fallen man. Ponnelle's sleight-of-hand changes our notion of Figaro and his identity, and the process devolves mainly through the character's own eyes. We sense that something uncanny is taking place.

### Acousmêtre

Although I have described the scene as acousmatic ("*acousmêtre*"), the situation is not clear-cut, and it is well to retrace some steps and rehearse the concept.

Brought into musicological discourse recently by Carolyn Abbate,[13] *acousmêtre* forms a linchpin of Chion's theories of sound in film. Fortunately, the voice comes under his purview, and Anglo-American scholars are blessed by the recent English-language edition (1999) of Chion's *La voix au cinéma* (1982). A later study has also been translated (*Audio-Vision: Sound on Screen* [1994]). Both books devote many pages to the *acousmêtre* and its properties. In his earlier writings, descriptions of the *acousmêtre* seem clear-cut and confident. If the source of the sound is not visible, then the sound is an *acousmêtre*, although the source must have "one foot" in the image. Acousmatic effects need not be total but can be partial. An *acousmêtre* typically moves from an acousmatic to a normal state, or vice-versa; thus a sound is acousmaticized or de-acousmaticized. In later writings, especially in an "Epilogue" to *The Voice in Cinema*, Chion admits that he had overgeneralized. What happens when a character speaks with back turned, or engages in internal musing or a review of past events, with heard voice but no moving lips? And for our purposes, what happens when the real source of the sound, the operatic music, has been emitted through lips before the shooting of the image and there is no concrete visible source for the sung music in any opera film? Are we to conclude that every opera film is acousmatic?

That would be fruitless, of course. The term was intended for departures from the norm. In *Figaro* and other opera films, however, playback constitutes the norm and hence it makes little sense to label every example of playback an *acousmêtre*. In the spirit of Chion, the term should be reserved for special situations.

Perhaps a more appropriate term for the audiovisual behavior in Figaro's *scena* is superimposition, a common technique in silent film and early sound movies. In the absence of available sound, superimposition highlighted the visual source of a sound and its apparent audition by a character, or inserted a phantom or ghostly image that became the source of arcane actions and real or imagined sounds. According to Chion, in later sound movies the literal image of the source is replaced by the *acousmêtre*. Now only the sound content inhabits the screen fiction, while its image lies beyond it, unseen. Both superimposition and the *acousmêtre* can be present, however: "one visual and the other auditory, as if mutually reinforcing one another."[14] This is the case in the Figaro scene. Figaro II approaches an apparition: a phantom reference to a persona who no longer exists. Yet Figaro II and Figaro I are driven by the vocal guidance of the unseen Figaro's voice, and hence their larger narrative existence is acousmatic. This arrangement approaches ventriloquism as master-Figaro throws his voice into two alternate bodies with different speaking mechanisms.[15] The metaphor is more interesting when we recall Figaro's assumption of mastery in his first aria, "Se vuol ballare." There he wanted to master the Count for power; here he fights for mastery of his sexual domain.

Mastery has interesting implications for the *acousmêtre* itself. With its provenance in God, who sounds his voice but remains unseen, the *acousmêtre* takes on properties of divinity and invests the unseen voice with omnipotence and omniscience. In other words, the *acousmêtre* typically assumes power over a situation and has ultimate knowledge of things seen and unseen by characters and spectators. In the "Aprite" *scena,* the ultimate master may be the outside Figaro, who is the fundamental, acousmatic vocal source. Inside the fiction something unusual occurs, however. Figaro I is acousmatic, but it is Figaro II who appears omniscient as he assumes the upper hand when he begins to sing. Thus Ponnelle inverts the typical relationship for the *acousmêtre*, as omniscience is vested in the embodied voice and not the voice with acousmatic properties. Given the ambiguities of Ponnelle's arrangement, we might be tempted to theorize the heard voice in the accompanied recitative as an instance of voice-off or voiceover rather than an *acousmêtre*. While this idea is suggestive—after all, the off-screen Figaro may be functioning as the narrator at this point—I find that the multiplicities of persona, agency, and space, which are rendered more complex by playback, throw into question the identity of the source and make voice-off/over too simplistic an interpretation. Thus I have suggested that the scene has acousmatic properties, even if this is not a clear-cut case.[16]

In any event, the ceding of the voice to Figaro II robs Figaro I of acoustic and narrative space, as the mute figure becomes object to the empowered new subject. This process of de-acousmatization collapses the power of the illusion, as it does in *The Wizard of Oz*, for example, when the God-like voice is discovered to belong to a small human whose voice has been magnified with sound machines.[17] But, unlike this example, the power of the voice in the Figaro scene increases rather than decreases because it finds an embodied home in Figaro II. As for the outside Figaro, he may not be as omniscient or omnipotent as Figaro II. What we do suspect is that he sees everything. And this, fittingly, is another trait of the *acousmêtre*.

The Double

In the scene the *acousmêtre* gives way to the notion of the double, a situation with suggestive implications. Freud's essay "The Uncanny," for example, discusses the odd effect of a figure meeting itself.[18] The person is apt to take an instant dislike to the image. Why? The double seems like a ghost and conjures up the spectre of one's own death. "Seeing oneself looking," Slavoj Žižek writes, "unmistakably stands for death. . . ."[19] And with the image of death comes denial of desire and one's very self. Figaro I undergoes a kind of death when Figaro II appears, the death of his subjectivity. The fact that he was not a fully voiced body in the opening section prepared for the change. Figaro II marks a rebirth of the old Figaro and Figaro I withers under Figaro II's intense gaze and embodied voice. Figaro I can now emerge as phantom because voice and visual clarity are denied him. His avoidance of looking at Figaro II accords with Žižek's theory that the double averts gazing directly at the original.[20]

Fearsome as he lectures and accuses his *alter ego*, Figaro II serves as super-ego and attempts to instill correct behavior in his wayward counterpart. Fully voiced (except for playback of course), he wields the power of Logos against Figaro I's lack of speech. What Ponnelle shows us through clever montage is a favorite argument of the eighteenth century: the debate between reason and feeling. Figaro II, hearkening back to the old Figaro, embodies the voice of emancipation and reason, while Figaro I capitulates to feeling and emotion. Just like the Figaro of "Se vuol ballare," Figaro II is socially progressive; bereft of reason, Figaro I is socially archaic. Figaro I's surrender to feeling also means that he has been feminized, and this is another target of the rational Figaro II. The battle comes to a head in the exchange at "Il resto nol dico," where the antiphonal music lends itself to Ponnelle's dual visual representation. The filmmaker's version of Figaro's *scena* shows how his work is informed by intimate knowledge of the music.[21]

In an essay on voice, Stanley Cavell makes perceptive comments on the opening duet of Mozart's opera that resonate with the present discussion. When contrasting Figaro's rational counting with Susanna's narcissistic involvement with her headpiece, Cavell implies that Figaro's existence as a thinking subject is altered—that he has been feminized (Mozart has Figaro accede to Susanna's music).[22] Ponnelle dramatizes a similar idea through the double in "Aprite," where manly reason is pitted against feminine emotion. A narcissistic confrontation of Figaro with himself visualizes the feminization. Thus Figaro I is not only archaic but also ripe for a feminizing look in the mirror. Figaro II does not provide a literal mirror, of course. But because of the uniformity in voice and singer-actor, the reflexiveness seems real. Of course, the notion that feeling and the feminine are false and not to be trusted will itself turn out to be false. Figaro will discover that Susanna is faithful and that his reason was deceived. With his two halves reconciled, he will emerge as a reconstituted subject and represent the truly progressive individual in his ability to embrace reason and feeling at a higher level of understanding.

"Aprite" has further implications for narcissism, specifically the subject's relationship with voice. On a variation of the Cartesian idea of "I think therefore I am," the voice has been theorized by some critics as the vehicle through which one ascertains existence. For Mladen Dolar, "s'entendre parler," hearing oneself speak, "can be seen as an elementary formula of narcissism that is needed to produce a minimal form of self. . . . For isn't the voice the first manifestation of life and, thus, isn't hearing oneself, and recognizing one's voice, an experience that precedes the recognition in the mirror?"[23] Cavell also considers awareness of one's voice a fundamental way of affirming one's existence. But unlike Dolar, who believes that singing dilutes the purity of the voice's ontology because of its aesthetic properties, Cavell accords the singing voice a role that is functionally equivalent with that of the speaking voice in its formation of the self. He sees singing as thinking: "thinking as narcissistic reflection; narcissism as capturing both the primitiveness of singing's orality and the sophistication of singing's exposure and virtuosic display."[24] Ponnelle's staging of "Aprite" with multiple agents brings thinking and narcissism to the forefront of sung expression.

Because the patterns of hearing are complex in "Aprite," their connections to identity are not always easy to determine. In the accompanied recitative, Figaro I hears his interior voice. Does a non-uttered voice count? For Dolar it probably would not, as his criteria seem to be the literal sounds and the physicalization of their utterance. If Figaro I is only thinking, then he affirms Descartes' dictum about the proof of one's existence. Because Cavell equates singing with thinking, he would be satisfied with the persona's sense of himself through the internal singing. Complicating the matter is the fact that the spectator hears a singing voice. From our point of audition—a concept of sonic perspective formulated by Chion[25]—Figaro I's existence is affirmed by the voice we understand to be his and which we think he understands as being his. The outside Figaro no doubt hears this voice. It represents a projection of an aspect of his consciousness and acts to confirm himself as well.

What about Figaro II? He is not visible in the frame when Figaro I sings and is non-existent during the accompanied recitative. But there must be a way in which he hears Figaro I because his diatribe against male folly is a response to Figaro I's words. Again, if we consider him a representative of the outside Figaro then it makes sense that he hears Figaro I. As a new figure in the visual field, Figaro II affirms his own existence through his singing voice. We never see him again in the opera, and he could seem like a fleeting vision without this marker of subjectivity. But it is important to ask whether the interaction between the two figures once the aria proper begins helps to affirm their respective selves. Figaro I, although looking away much of the time, appears to hear what Figaro II sings. He functions as narcissistic confirmation of Figaro II's existence, while Figaro I, as mentioned above, becomes increasingly phantom-like during the aria and barely utters a word. Thus his lack of existence as a thinking subject is related to an absence of self-affirming activity through singing. He lacks an "I-voice."[26]

The "I-voice" is obviously present in Figaro II, who speaks in a commanding voice to the audience and to Figaro I. Yet he began narrative life as a phantom figure in the scene. Actually he began life in Ponnelle's film of *Il barbiere di Siviglia*, made three years earlier. In that version of Rossini's "prequel" to *Figaro*, Figaro turns to the audience frequently and sings in direct address, a mode that is appropriate to an opera in which farce plays a major role. Ponnelle further affirms the connection between Figaro II and the wily barber through casting: the same singer portraying Figaro in both films. The intertextual link through Hermann Prey might come off as merely coincidental or amusing. But when Figaro II appears in "Aprite," the return of the confident manipulator from *Il barbiere* is obvious. Thus Figaro II provides narcissistic confirmation beyond the borders of the *Figaro* film and resuscitates a pre-history that affirms a reason for his existence. The outside Figaro, looking on from the side, could not have asked for a better way to affirm his existence as well.

## "VEDRÒ MENTR' IO SOSPIRO": MUST I SEE WHILE I SIGH (WHAT DOES THE COUNT SEE?)

Some forty minutes earlier in the film, we witness another defining psychological moment. It occurs near the start of Act III, a place in the story that features the Count. He undergoes a crisis in confidence as he doubts his ability to control people and events. A string of numbers plays out his conflicting emotions as new opportunities give rise to optimism but then disappoint. The sequence begins with a secco recitative in which he mulls over the confused state of affairs. Joy emerges in a duet with Susanna when she arranges to meet him later, but anger erupts in a subsequent accompanied recitative when he discovers she has tricked him. In the final segment, the aria "Vedrò," the Count vents his spleen at Figaro and plots revenge:

| | |
|---|---|
| Vedrò mentr' io sospiro, | Will I see a serf of mine made happy |
| Felice un servo mio! | While I am left to sigh, |
| E un ben, che invan desio, | And him possess a treasure |
| Ei posseder dovrà? | Which I desire in vain? |
| Vedrò per man d'amore | Will I see her, |
| Unita a un vil oggetto | Who has roused in me a passion |
| Chi in me destò un affetto, | She does not feel for me, |
| Che per me poi non ha? | United by the hand of love to a base slave? |
| | |
| Ah no, lasciarti in pace | Ah no, I will not give you |
| Non vo'questo contento! | The satisfaction of this contentment! |
| Tu non nascesti, audace! | You were not born, bold fellow, |
| Per dare a me tormento, | To cause me torment |
| E forse ancor per ridere | And indeed to laugh |
| Di mia infelicità. | At my discomfiture. |
| Già la speranza sola | Now only the hope |
| Delle vendette mie | Of taking vengeance |
| Quest' anima consola | Eases my mind |
| E giubilar mi fa.[27] | And makes me rejoice.[27] |

The entire aria is rendered as interior singing, as is a major portion of the preceding numbers, which together form an extended scene. The opening recitative of Act III is performed as soliloquy until other characters appear. With Susanna's entrance and her direct exchanges with the Count, the mode becomes exterior. The start of the duet, "Crudel! Perchè finora," continues the exterior mode as the characters agree to meet in the garden. The Count asks repeatedly whether she will come, and she says after some buffa confusion that she will. With the arrival of the main section ("Mi sento dal contento"), which turns to A major, a favorite key of seduction in Mozart,[28] the characters' reactions are expressed without moving lips. Exterior singing resumes with the return of the Count's detailed questions, but gives way to interior utterance again when the text and music of "Mi sento" reappear. Confusion breaks out afterwards. Standing at a remove in the Count's study, Susanna tells Figaro in full-voiced secco recitative that she's just won the case. The Count overhears and realizes he's been duped. He begins the accompanied recitative quoting her words, "Hai già vinta la causa." His anger is expressed in aggressive musical gestures, with moving lips; he stomps back and forth. When the music becomes lyrical, approaching an arioso style, the utterance turns interior. The Count dons judicial robe and wig, and smugly relishes the thought that Figaro will have to marry Marcellina. His demeanor is calm and rational. Except for the final line of the recitative ("il colpo è fatto" [the blow is done]), all the singing through the end of the aria is interior. At "Vedrò" the setting moves to a small courtroom. When the Count enters, the sparring characters clear a path, bow, and take up positions on opposite sides of the gallery. The Count is the featured player on a raised area in front of the assembled. They do not hear what the Count says; only we do.

Ponnelle's arrangement presents a curious situation. The use of interior singing suggests that the aria keeps to its tradition of being private, in the sense of being for the Count's ears only. Libretto and score indicate that the Count is alone during the number, in the grand tradition of *opera seria*, and most productions stage it that way. In the film, the aria is rendered in a public forum, which makes public visually and rhetorically. No one in the assembly hears it, however. Interior singing allows Ponnelle to reconfigure the private element of an aria—what it means to be airing one's thoughts, alone—and stage the number as a public spectacle that still remains private. It also means that we become privy to thoughts to which characters in the fiction do not have access. This vests us with omniscience and makes the scene more objectified and symbolic than it could otherwise be.

Symbolic meaning also attaches to the voice. Let us recall that extended interior singing begins when the Count dons the judge's robe and wig in the accompanied recitative. From that moment, the voice and regalia become players in a dynamic that is centered on power. The Count need not raise his voice to an audible level to get what he wants because his judicial authority is sufficient to intimidate Figaro and the others. He also realizes that the exterior voice leads to trouble. Full-voiced singing occurred with Susanna and led to his downfall; the audible voice does not sustain authority and will be quelled. Hence the visual trappings of power—robe, wig, and courtroom—replace the discursive effects of the exterior voice. The voice as sign of subjectivity will still be exercised, but it will operate in a private aural domain and elude entrapment by the servants.

Although my interpretation suggests that Ponnelle enacts a radical performance of "Vedrò," the idea of the courtroom comes from Beaumarchais.[29] In the play, the start of Act III takes place in the Count's throne room, and, as in the film, the Count renders a judgment before the extended household on Marcellina's claim on Figaro. Da Ponte eliminated this location and most of the dialogue, but distilled the essence of the scene into an aria for the Count, sung when he is alone in a room in his palace. In most performances, "Vedrò" is a generalized vendetta against Figaro and specific legal consequences do not occur until the secco recitative before the Sextet.[30] Ponnelle's recuperation of the courtroom underscores the menace of the Count and the fear of the other characters. The physical layout also follows the directions in the play, with the antagonists positioned in opposite places: Marcellina, Bartolo, and Antonio on one side of the court; Figaro and Susanna on the other in front of a horde of peasants. We recognize the peasant group as a thematic image from elsewhere in the film, as in their appearance in the recapitulation of Figaro's "Se vuol ballare."[31]

The Gaze

The gaze in "Vedrò" forms another key element in the visual apparatus that replaces the heard voice. For characters inside the fiction, the gaze assumes the rhetorical and discursive force of the voice; it takes over many of the functions of normal operatic music in opera film. For spectators outside the fiction—namely the television viewing audience, for whom the heard voice is real—the gaze views the workings of the fictional gaze and its relation to the interior voice. As for the Count, the voice he hears in his mind's ear interacts with his powers of looking and seeing. The camera is often centered on his looking and what he sees, situating the Count's visual signature in cinematic point-of-view. In Ponnelle's hands, the technique exaggerates the subjectivity of the Count and visualizes his obsession with power over Figaro. Figaro's inability to hear the Count's voice robs him of some of the Count's knowledge, but it also raises the stakes in the eye-to-eye contact. In several places in the aria, especially near the end, extreme close-ups of the eyes of each figure show their relationship as a battle of wills.

    This manly combat is not set on an equal footing, of course, because the Count enjoys a clear advantage through his social position. His august appearance on a raised throne asserts his dominance over the others, and he invokes a controlling gaze throughout the number. When the Count enters the court, he stares long and hard at Figaro, who bows to his superior. The visual pun is striking: uttering "Vedrò" ("Will I see"), the Count measures the object of contempt in his eyes: as if mere looking could dispel the outcome he fears he will witness. The ironic coupling becomes a major trope in the number. At the next mention of "Vedrò," we see Figaro and Susanna from the Count's sharply focused gaze. The last pair of lines in the stanza are rendered in an exaggerated visual pose: a sharp-angled, full-body shot of the Count from below. We assume this is what Figaro and Susanna see, but they are too far from the platform to create such an angle. It depicts what the Count represents to them or what he hopes to represent to them: a towering figure of awe who must be obeyed.[32] During the second occurrence of this stanza, the subjective tension increases through gazes that hone in more keenly on details. Besides the close-ups of eyes, the Count fixates on the clasped hands of the couple and we see it through his eyes. Not coincidentally, the Count has just sung text about having to see the servants united by the hand of love ("Vedrò per man d'amore/Unita a un vil oggetto . . ."). Next his circle of vision (through a zoom out by the camera) expands to their faces and bodies. The accelerated images and the expectant timpani rolls tell us that something is about to happen.

Part two of the aria brings change. With a faster tempo comes the first decisive visual gesture, as the Count crisply takes a seat on the throne. From this point the text is also different, because it addresses Figaro directly. At "Tu non nascesti, audace!" ("You were not born, bold fellow"), a line characterized by Wye Allanbrook as "the centerpiece of the aria,"[33] the Count interrupts his gaze with a snap of the head that visualizes the snapped rhythm of "audace." Gestural rhythm accelerates further. The faceoff between the Count and Figaro intensifies through shot and countershot in which eyes fill frame. The culminating coloratura is done with a sustained tight shot of the Count's eyes, as if the vocal virtuosity crowns his mastery over his servant. Ponnelle may be suggesting that Figaro is so intimidated that this is what his fevered mind sees. I see it more as the camera's gaze into what the Count believes he is accomplishing over Figaro: dominating him with his power. It shows the voice's message rather than its effect on its object.

The voice in "Vedrò" could be considered a lawless voice because it operates outside the usual constraints of vocal representation.[34] Yet, in this scene, the Law is invoked in the story. The Count uses legal power to reassert social control in the Almaviva household. He does this by suppressing the heard or lawful voice, which becomes a tool of manipulation by others, and supplanting it by other lawful measures. For the remainder of the opera, the Count's exterior voice continues to betray him: in the revelations of the Sextet, the run-ins with Figaro before the wedding, and the romantic assignations in Act IV. "Vedrò" marks the apex of his power in the film. Interior singing, or an absent voice, may be all that is possible for an outmoded figure, and if so he is a functional mute. But our omniscient point-of-audition reveals that his power is still a force to be reckoned with.

Time

In the opera, the archaic nature of the Count renders him frozen in time. The music of "Vedrò" brings out this quality, with its Baroque mannerisms, abrupt changes, harmonic retrogressions, and curious coloratura.[35] His social discomfort is conveyed in an inability to find a workable musical language. Suspended, he cannot move forward or back. In the film, the interior voice attenuates the feeling of suspension and arrests time by extending the psychology of one or two moments. The voice effectively freezes image and plot, and the freed-up dramatic time is available for an intense interplay of subjectivities. Figaro is mute and motionless and the Count functionally silent, but by the end of the scene we know much more about their relationship.

Arias in general tend to arrest time; they interrupt the forward progress of the drama so that a character, usually alone, can express emotion. An interior voice is suited to this situation, as Ponnelle shows in the Countess's "Dove sono," where the interior "I-voice" reminisces back to early courtship over sepia-tinted images of the past.[36] But how does an interior voice affect time in a public setting, as in "Vedrò?" As we know, in the film, ensembles are rendered as interior singing in several places. Mostly these are passages that humanize or texturalize the drama through asides or personal reactions amid group interaction, and that counteract the linear motion of Mozart's dramaturgy. Thus a persuasive interpretation of Ponnelle's "Vedrò" is that the aria is made to function like an ensemble in voice and time because it resembles an extended aside: one long reaction to prior events, expressed amid others. Although silent, other characters in the courtroom are players in the drama. Linked to the Count by the camera, they participate in a group interaction that is not very different from that of the ensemble.

The scene generates great tension, a palpable *frisson* that is missing from the usual performance of "Vedrò." One reason is that many markers of normal narrative are missing. Besides the absence of moving lips, there is no outside noise. There are no reactions from other characters to the music and their deafness cuts them off from the Count's rhetorical world. They merely stare at him and do not move, frozen in time, space, and emotion. The Count does not move or gesture much, although he is more active than his audience; his sense of time is also attenuated. The interior voice acts as a divider between them: the Count is animated by it and responds to it, while the others have no awareness of it and appear inanimate. Once again, external logic in sound creates an interesting dissonance as the Count and the others function at different speeds. This confuses the sense of time in the scene.

Although the interior voice creates those differences, it also mediates between them. This is because the interior voice is closely allied with the gaze, and the Count's interactions with Figaro are visualized by a strong reciprocal gaze. The rhythm and structure of this pattern of images becomes mannered, because the figures are filmed using exaggerated camera angles. Time becomes erased in the obsession on eyes, hands, and the trappings of power, neutralizing the impact of the voice and its associated powers on the two men. In other words, the camera forms a bridge between static images and the moving voice, and in this way lessens the gap between the audiovisual makeup of the Count and Figaro.

Small physical gestures take on great import in "Vedrò": hands clasping a bit more tightly, the Count craning his neck or snapping his head. For the courtroom spectators, the spectacle is mime in suspended time. The Count's few gestures are exaggerated and melodramatic. For Ponnelle, the effect marks another return to the theater and the venue of the opera's source. The scene comes off as thoroughly cinematic, however, and it is the interior voice that provides the link between the two art forms. This is ironic, because operatic music is thought to work against the needs of cinema in opera film.[37] Yet, as we have seen, the interior voice is much more than mere operatic music. It packs a lot of "added value" and exposes narrative and representation to novel combinations of music and image.[38] In "Vedrò," the interior voice allows a redefinition of the meanings of public and private, and of the ways in which time and image limn character, persona, and agency.

## "NON SO PIÙ COSA SON": I NO LONGER KNOW WHAT I AM (AND WHAT MY VOICE MEANS)

As we have discussed, "Aprite" and "Vedrò" center around seeing: "Aprite" with a command to look, "Vedrò" a question about the need to look. Cherubino's "Non so più" operates at a more basic level as it wonders about the fundamental question of identity: Who am I? The text is reflexive, holding up a mirror to the emitter of the words. Much has been written about the mirror-like nature of Cherubino in relation to other characters, including their sexual foibles, and in relation to his description in the libretto.[39] In "Non più andrai," for example, Figaro calls him "Narcisetto, Adoncino d'amor" ("Little Narcissus, little Adonis of love"). An amorous butterfly ("farfallone amoroso") reminiscent of Puck, he also sets romantic imbroglios into motion but manages to escape unscathed. Sexually, Cherubino embodies the androgyny of the trousers role—a woman's voice in a male character's body—and yet stirs up strong desires in others.[40] Kierkegaard, for one, recognized the subversive quality of the teenager and labeled him a "Don Giovanni *in potentia*," the representative of the first stage in a progression toward realization of the erotic.[41] He is also a young Count, and hence the Count's fears of him are fully justified.[42]

Cherubino airs strong desires of his own in "Non so più." Unlike Figaro and the Count, Cherubino is experiencing sexual awakening and is very confused. In Ponnelle's hands, the aria recalls Conrad's idea (cited at the start of this essay) on the operatic soliloquy in film as consciousness overheard. Here Cherubino dips in and out of consciousness as interior singing alternates with exterior singing. Echoing her behavior in the Mozart-Da Ponte version, Susanna appears with him in the scene, but in the film she hears only the exterior voice. The use of two types of singing accords with Cherubino's confusion and his inability to sustain a coherent thought. It also picks up on the formal structure of the music, which is a modified rondo. While the disposition of interior and exterior modes does not stick slavishly to the form, it offers a new way of expressing the idea of alternation that underlies a rondo.

Cherubino's consciousness through voice is enacted as a circle dance with camera and space. Unlike "Aprite" and "Vedrò," this aria is shaped by spatial movement and has few static points of origin in the camera. In fact, during a substantial portion of the number, the camera is hand-held and imparts a nervous quality to the character. Sometimes it shoots from Cherubino's eyes, sometimes it peers into them. As in "Vedrò," point-of-view technique exaggerates subject positioning and means that the gaze is working closely with the voice. Unlike "Vedrò," however, there is no truly sustained gaze at work; looking becomes jumpy or unfocused, or shifts to another object.

Susanna behaves differently from the observer (Figaro) in "Vedrò," because she reacts to what she hears and sees. When we see Cherubino from her vantage point, we sense that the image represents a projection of what he is thinking instead of a view of what she really sees. The camera records the psychology of Cherubino's consciousness more than Susanna's reactions. As for Cherubino, his anguished looks and fearful body movements suggest a persona imprisoned behind the bars of body and voice. The voice occasionally escapes beyond the barrier of the body—when his singing is explicit—but it seems squelched much of the time. Near the end of the number, when Cherubino utters haltingly "E se non ho chi m'oda, Parlo d'amor con me" ("And if no one hears me, I speak of love to myself"), the voice surfaces but the character ends up more imprisoned. Pinned at the far end of the room, Cherubino cowers against a stone wall as the camera moves away from him in a slow zoom. He is isolated and the voice is trapped within him: appropriately, we might say, because he imagines "speaking of love to himself" (code words for masturbation?) if no one is around to listen.

Cherubino's resistance to the exterior voice revolves around Susanna and Figaro's bed.[43] As the aria begins, he is face down in the pillow. Soon he looks at the camera, but the voice is still interior. Eventually he lands on his feet and begins the circling motion with Susanna and the camera. What does Cherubino hear of what he sings? He hears it all, with little distinction between interior and exterior voice as he slips easily from one to the other. The aria resembles a fevered dream—a sexual dream perhaps—and the conscious-unconscious voice reflects an irrational core. Cherubino's voice roams, within his persona, in search of a secure subjective anchor. It desires, but its object is not to be found: a familiar notion because it echoes Kierkegaard's ideas about the elusiveness of desire.[44] Thus Ponnelle's deployment of cinematic voice reinscribes Kierkegaard's Romantic views about Cherubino and his relation to the erotic.[45] More generally it challenges the operatic voice as sign of an integral subjectivity.

A NOVEL EFFECT

The three arias we have explored are concerned with identity. In Figaro's "Aprite," the disruptive object-voice forces the character to face himself. In "Vedrò," the Count rejects the exterior voice because it leads to his downfall. And in "Non so più," Cherubino is in search of the object-voice and through it an identity. The success of the interior voice in its narrative work in the film is due largely to Ponnelle's dependence on point-of-view technique in the camera.

With its strong articulation of observer status, inside and outside the fiction and filmic space, and dynamic zooms that exaggerate presence and emotion, point-of-view as deployed by Ponnelle creates a visual interplay of persona and character that fills out the multiple agencies implied by the use of the interior voice. The interior voice would be little more than a cute gimmick without this expressive visual device.

The interior voice establishes a strong object-voice that, although tied to a character, is quite independent. Unlike most objects, which are fixed, this object has great flexibility and mobility: it can recede and reappear, rearrange time, and redefine venue and agency. Hence the interior voice wields considerable power for narrative and representation, and for the way we view them.

This power has a larger role in the film, and it concerns another element in the way sound is structured. A striking aspect of the film is the difference in sound in the secco recitatives. Recorded live at the time of shooting, these recitatives have a resonant presence that forms a sharp contrast with the "canned" quality of the prerecorded numbers, which include everything else. As a result, the film seems to be divided into two levels: one of real-time, embodied drama in the secco recitatives, and the other of unfocused and disembodied wash in the full musical numbers. Ponnelle's use of interior singing, which occurs in many numbers, adjusts the differences by reinforcing subjectivity in prerecorded numbers. This creates greater dramatic presence in the canned numbers so that they are not overpowered by the secco recitatives.

Another means of understanding Ponnelle's strategy comes by way of a different medium, the novel. Ponnelle draws on the rich narrative potential of the novel to multiply voices in the film and create personas who are capable of expression at varied levels of consciousness, from varied subject positions. The rhetorical stance he invokes can shift with agility from first-person to third-person to direct interaction. The solution eases tensions between film and theater—film with its impetus toward speed, theater its predilection for character—by allowing for an enlivened dramatic pace in moments that are focused on character. The novelistic mode also overcomes dramatic limitations of playback and postsynchronization by reveling in the dissonance between what is seen and what is heard, and moving us beyond the visual text to a dramatic realm that exists "en creux," in the gaps. These gaps are not the normal places of film, opera, or theater, but they establish new realms of normalcy in this film.

During the overture, Ponnelle hints at literary intentions when he shows us books by Voltaire and Montesquieu: the written word as key to this filmic interpretation. Thus Ponnelle restores the literary roots of *Figaro*. Even though they are not its literal roots in a play, the enriched narrative potential in Ponnelle's treatment approaches that of Beaumarchais's talkative play, *Le mariage de Figaro*. This does not mean that Ponnelle slights music in favor of literature. It means that a literary sensibility becomes a feasible way of enacting this opera as film. And this, as we know, is no mean feat given the divergent tendencies of opera and film.

NOTES

1. Peter Conrad, *A Song of Love and Death: The Meaning of Opera* (St. Paul: Graywolf Press, 1996), 273, in chapter "New Theaters."

2. Favorable reviews include Martin Bernheimer, "Ponnelle's Figaro Will Wed on 28," *Los Angeles Times*, 5 October 1977, Part IV, 10; Lon Tuck, "A Million-Dollar TV 'Figaro' That Improves on the Original," *Washington Post*, 5 October 1977, 1 (D) and 11 (D); David Hurwitz, *Ovation* 9, no. 12 (January 1989): 47; Peter G. Davis, "Surprise Packages," *New York*, 10 April 1989, 108–10; Harvey E. Phillips, "The Basics," *Opera News* 56, no. 2 (August 1991): 45; and William Albright, *Opera Quarterly* 8, no. 3 (autumn 1991), 129. On the negative side is Harold Rosenthal, who criticizes the use of soliloquy, in *Opera* 32 (1981): 537–38.

Major sources for Ponnelle and the film include his interview with Heinz Oppen, trans. Mary Whittall, that is enclosed in the video package for British distribution: DGG 072 403–1; the book of interviews, *Imre Fabian im Gespräch mit Jean-Pierre Ponnelle* (Zürich: Orell Füssli, 1983), especially 50–5; *Jean-Pierre Ponnelle: Arbeiten für Salzburg* (Salzburg: Salzburg Festspiele,1989), which contains articles, interviews, photos and facts on productions, and a complete list of his films; Frederick J. and Lise-Lone Marker, "Retheatricalizing Opera: A Conversation with Jean-Pierre Ponnelle," *Opera Quarterly* 3, no. 2 (summer 1985): 25–44; and Sanda Chiriacescu-Lüling, *Herrschaft und Revolte in Figaros Hochzeit: Untersuchung zu szenischen Realisationsmöglichkeiten des sozialkritischen Aspekts in W. A. Mozarts Die Hochzeit des Figaro anhand von sechs videogezeichneten Inszenierungen* (Erlangen: Lüling, 1991).

3. Except for secco recitatives, most of which were recorded live at the time of shooting; see the concluding section, below.

4. Questions posed by Michel Chion in "Introduction to Audiovisual Analysis," in *Audio-Vision: Sound on Screen*, trans. Claudia Gorbman (New York: Columbia University Press, 1994), 192.

5. For other examples, see the study of individual films in Marcia J. Citron, *Opera on Screen* (New Haven: Yale University Press, 2000); my essay "A Night at the Cinema: Zeffirelli's *Otello* and the Genre of Film-Opera," *The Musical Quarterly* 78, no. 4 (winter 1994): 700–41; H. Marshall Leicester, "Discourse and the Film Text: Four Readings of *Carmen*," *Cambridge Opera Journal* 6, no. 3 (November 1994): 245–82; Jeongwon Joe, "Hans Jürgen Syberberg's *Parsifal*: The Staging of Dissonance in the Fusion of Opera and Film," *The Music Research Forum* 13 (July 1998): 1–21; Jeremy Tambling, *Opera, Ideology and Film* (New York: St. Martin's Press, 1987); and portions of Tambling's edited volume, *A Night in at the Opera: Media Representations of Opera* (London: John Libbey, 1994).

6. Chion, *Audio-Vision*, xvii.

7. English translation by Lionel Salter (1968) from the booklet accompanying the CD recording of the opera, *Le Nozze di Figaro*, DGG 431619–2 (1991), 294, 296.

8. For more on direct address in televised opera see Citron, *Opera on Screen*, 234–37, which discusses the device in Peter Sellars's telecast productions of Mozart's *Così fan tutte* and Handel's *Giulio Cesare*. Further exploration of direct address appears in Citron, "The Performance of Vision in Peter Sellars's Television Production of *Così fan tutte*," in *Music, Sensation, and Sensuality*, ed. Linda Austern (New York: Garland Press, forthcoming). Richard Dellamora discusses stagings of *Figaro* in which Figaro points directly at the audience or camera in "Aprite," in "Mozart and the Politics of Intimacy: *The Marriage of Figaro* in Toronto, Paris, and New York," in *The Work of Opera: Genre, Nationhood, and Sexual Difference*, ed. Richard Dellamora and Daniel Fischlin (New York: Columbia University Press, 1997), 262.

9. The similarity to silent film was pointed out by Deanna Shemek at my presentation on this *scena*, at "In and Out of Opera: A Conference on the Media and Spaces of the Operatic," University of California, Santa Cruz, 29 October 2000.

10. Chion explores the *acousmêtre* at length in "Part I: Mabuse: The Magic and Power of the Acousmêtre," in *The Voice in Cinema*, trans. Claudia Gorbman (New York: Columbia University Press, 1999), 17–57. See also the section "The Acousmêtre" in *Audio-Vision*, 129–30.

11. Chion, *Audio-Vision*, 46–48.

12. For an incisive discussion of *Prénom Carmen* see Chion, *Le Son au Cinéma* (Paris: Éditions de l' Étoile, 1992), 188–89. Godard's music practices in the context of the New Wave and other movements of the 1960s are explored by Royal Brown, "Modern Film Music," in *The Oxford History of World Cinema* (Oxford: Oxford University Press, 1996), 564.

13. Especially in Abbate's "Debussy's Phantom Sounds," *Cambridge Opera Journal* 10, no. 1 (1998): 67–96.

14. Chion, *The Voice in Cinema*, 136.

15. Abbate explores ventriloquism in her work on agency in opera and film. See especially her "Ventriloquism," *Meaning in the Visual Arts: Views from the Outside*, ed. Irving Lavin (Princeton: Princeton University Press, 1995), 305–12. Gary Tomlinson's philosophical discussion of vocal possession is also pertinent, in *Metaphysical Song: An Essay on Opera* (Princeton: Princeton University Press, 1999), 112–15.

16. Perceptive remarks on these aspects of the voice-space relationship in the *scena* were offered by Mary Ann Smart and Kaja Silverman at my presentation at the conference "In and Out of Opera."

17. See Chion, *The Voice in Cinema*, 28–29.

18. Freud's essay appears in *Art and Literature*, ed. James Strachey and Albert Dickson (Hammondsworth: Penguin, 1985), 335–76. Lawrence Kramer discusses Freud's views on the double, in " 'As If a Voice Were in Them': Music, Narrative, and Deconstruction," in *Music as Cultural Practice, 1800–1900* (Berkeley: University of California Press, 1990), 176–214.

19. Žižek, " 'I Hear You with My Eyes'; or the Invisible Master," in *Gaze and Voice as Love Objects*, ed. Renata Salecl and Slavoj Žižek (Durham: Duke University Press, 1996), 94.

20. Žižek, " 'I Hear You with My Eyes'," 94.

21. Ponnelle considers the camera an additional musical language that contributes to the vertical and horizontal dimension of the score; see the video booklet (DGG 072 403–1), and *Imre Fabian im Gespräch*, 50–55. For his familiarity with music generally in opera see James Levine, "Jean-Pierre Ponnelle (1932–1988): An Appreciation," *Opera* 39 (1988): 1284–86; and Christopher Alden, "Beyond the Particular," *Opera Cues (Houston Grand Opera)* 39, no. 2 (winter 1999): 17. For personal insights on Ponnelle and music I am indebted to Vera Calabria, a production assistant to Ponnelle in the 1970s and 1980s, who kindly shared her thoughts in a phone interview in January 1999.

22. Stanley Cavell, "Opera and the Lease of Voice," in *A Pitch of Philosophy: Autobiographical Exercises* (Cambridge, MA: Harvard University Press, 1994), 151–52.

23. Mladen Dolar, "The Object Voice," in *Gaze and Voice as Love Objects*, 13.

24. Cavell, "Opera and the Lease of Voice," 136, 138.

25. Chion, *Audio-Vision*, 89–92.

26. For this concept see Chion, *The Voice in Cinema*, 49–51.

27. Translation by Lionel Salter in *Le Nozze di Figaro*, 231–32, except for my English rendition of "Vedrò" (Salter has "Must I see").

28. For a comparative study see Richard Stiefel, "Mozart's Seductions," *Current Musicology*, no. 36 (1983): 151–66.

29. Tim Carter observes that many productions of the opera in the 1960s and 1970s, which would include this film (1976), emphasize the political aspects and hence the Beaumarchais; see his *W. A. Mozart: Le Nozze di Figaro* (Cambridge: Cambridge University Press, 1987), 140–42.

30. Depending on the version one hears, that recitative will come directly after "Vedrò" or the Countess's "Dove sono." For advocacy of Ponnelle's arrangement, which places "Dove sono" before the Sextet, see Robert Moberly and C. Raeburn, "Mozart's 'Figaro:' The Plan of Act III," *Music and Letters* 46 (1965): 134–36. Alan Tyson rejects this view in "Le Nozze di Figaro: Lessons from the Autograph Score," *The Musical Times* 122 (1981): 456–61. Julian Rushton discusses the two positions in his entry on the opera in *The New Grove Dictionary of Opera*, ed. Stanley Sadie (London: Macmillan, 1992), III: 634.

31. For a descriptive analysis see Chiriascescu-Lüling, *Herrschaft und Revolte*, 145–46.

32. A similar exaggeration through an extremely low angle at close range occurs in Ponnelle's film *Madama Butterfly*. As Pinkerton sings to Sharpless in Act I of the pleasures of American life, a bottle of whiskey shot from below fills the frame as a symbol of American culture. Here the aim is a critique of American capitalism and imperialism.

33. Allanbrook, *Rhythmic Gesture in Mozart*: *Le Nozze di Figaro and Don Giovanni* (Chicago: University of Chicago Press, 1983), 141. See also Brigid Brophy, *Mozart the Dramatist* (New York: Da Capo, 1988), 111.

34. See Dolar, "The Object Voice," 18–28, for a discussion of the lawless voice.

35. For a fuller discussion of these traits see Allanbrook, *Rhythmic Gesture in Mozart*, 140–45.

36. Chion's discussion of the "I-voice" associates it mainly with flashback (*The Voice in Cinema*, 49–51).

37. For the aesthetic challenges in opera film see chapter 1 of Citron, *Opera on Screen*. See also my essay, "A Night at the Cinema."

38. A term coined by Chion to describe what sound does to image to give it expressive meaning; see his *Audio-Vision*, 8–9.

39. For example Brophy, in the chapter "Seduction in Mozart's Operas," *Mozart the Dramatist*, 105–08; and Allanbrook, *Rhythmic Gesture in Mozart*, 96–99.

40. Margaret Reynolds explores the sexual aspects of Cherubino in "Ruggiero's Deceptions, Cherubino's Distractions," in *En Travesti: Women, Gender Subversion, Opera*, ed. Corinne E. Blackmer and Patricia Juliana Smith (New York: Columbia University Press, 1995), 132–51.

41. In his famous essay "The Immediate Erotic Stages or the Musical-Erotic," in *Either/Or*, part 1, ed. and trans. Howard V. Hong and Edna H. Hong (Princeton: Princeton University Press, 1987), 45–136.

42. One sign of the link is that Figaro also refers to the Count as Narcissus, for example near the end of Act III ("Il Narciso or la cerca"), when Figaro sees the Count reading a note of romantic assignation.

43. It is interesting that other numbers in Act I are shot with a circling motion around the bed. One expects it in numbers with Susanna and Figaro, as in the first two duets of the opera, but it forms a major motif in other situations too. See, for example, the duet between Marcellina and Susanna, a contest of sexual superiority for Figaro's hand; and Figaro's aria "Non più andrai," which plays not only to Cherubino but to others, including the Count and Basilio.

44. Kierkegaard, "The Immediate Erotic Stages," for example 75–76.

45. Another opera film that picks up on ideas from Kierkegaard's essay is Losey's *Don Giovanni*; for a discussion of similarities see Citron, *Opera on Screen*, 172, 178–79.

# 9
# Verdi in Postwar Italian Cinema

*Deborah Crisp* and *Roger Hillman*

T O THE ITALIAN PUBLIC OF THE MID-NINETEENTH CENTURY, VERDI'S significance as a musical and political figure was multifaceted. As a composer of operas he was immensely popular, achieving the rare distinction among composers of both immediate and lasting recognition. Over the previous hundred or so years, Italy's primacy in instrumental music had been challenged by Germany and Austria, and even opera had come under threat from the burgeoning traditions of national opera. As an Italian composer of international repute, Verdi played a large part in regaining for Italy some of the status it had lost as a musical leader. Verdi the musician was therefore lauded by the Italian public not only for his operas, but also for his role as an international representative of their musical culture, returning Italy to its rightful place in the operatic hierarchy.

As a composer of operas, Verdi was well positioned to become a political figure. The opera was a center of social life in nineteenth-century Italy. The opera house provided a meeting place, and although they didn't mix, all classes of society were theoretically able to participate in the social interaction it afforded. At times of political unrest, the authorities became very conscious of the potential for the opera house to become a forum for revolutionary tendencies. A diverse crowd with diverse opinions exposed to powerful music and drama: this combination fostered the development of Verdi's political reputation.

Recent research by Roger Parker has called into question the extent of Verdi's political involvement during the early years of his career.[1] Parker claims that there is little evidence to support the popular notion that Verdi's operas of the 1840s, such as *Nabucco* (1842), *I Lombardi* (1843), *Ernani* (1844), and *Attila* (1846), were politically motivated, and recognized as such by audiences of that decade. He suggests that these works emerged only later as the representative music of the Risorgimento. By the 1860s, however, Verdi's direct involvement in politics suggests that his reputation as a "political" composer was well established. In 1859, he was elected to represent his hometown of Bussetto in the assembly of the Parma provinces; the same year, his name became a patriotic slogan (Viva V.E.R.D.I: fortuitously, Vittorio Emanuele Re D'Italia). In 1861, he was elected as a deputy to the first Italian Parliament, a position he held (though with increasing disinclination) until September 1865.

From the 1840s through the 1870s, Verdi produced a succession of popular works. Regardless of the extent of political intent in the early operas, and despite the fact that not one of Verdi's operas is set in contemporary Italy, audiences of the later Risorgimento period responded to perceived parallels with their own situation. Verdi's status as *the* composer of the Risorgimento was established, and remains to the present day. In 1965, Dallapiccola summarized the prevailing view: "The phenomenon that is Verdi is unimaginable without the Risorgimento. Whether or not he played an active part in it is unimportant; he absorbed its air and its tone [and in words and music] formulated a style through which the Italian people found a key to their dramatic plight and vibrated in unison with it."[2]

Performances of Verdi's operas declined in the first two decades of the twentieth century, his reputation eclipsed for a time by that of Wagner, whose music was receiving international acclaim.[3] With the rise of Italian fascism in the early 1920s through World War II, Verdi was resurrected as an icon of Italian culture and patriotism by members of the Resistance as well as the Fascists. In the postwar years of soul-searching and reconstruction, Verdi remained a political and cultural reference point, and as such he figured prominently in Italian cinema of the time.

As part of the process of coming to terms with the prewar Fascist era and its ongoing presence in postwar politics, both the Left and the Center-Right of Italian politics mythologized the Resistance as "a Second Risorgimento."[4] Film directors such as Luchino Visconti, Marco Leto, Bernardo Bertolucci, Franco Zeffirelli, and Paolo and Vittorio Taviani used references to Verdi and his music to recall the years of the Risorgimento. Many of these films adopt a critical stance towards Verdi, whose relocation into a contemporary context inevitably raises questions. In Leto's *La villeggiatura,* for instance, references to Verdi seem to represent the too comfortable acceptance by the bourgeoisie of the myths of past history. Thus, the very nature of Verdi's relevance to postwar Italian society and the appropriateness of the widely adopted Risorgimento analogy become suspect.

Visconti's *Senso,* on the other hand, is one of few films of this era actually set in the mid-nineteenth century, and references to Verdi are more transparent and less problematic. A performance of *Il trovatore* provides a rich cultural backdrop for this film; it also ignites the political and personal narratives of the film.

## VISCONTI'S *SENSO* (1954)

The film is set in the Veneto region of Italy in the spring of 1866 during the Austrian occupation. Livia, wife of Count Serpieri, finds her allegiance torn between loyalty to the Italian patriots and her love for Franz Mahler, an Austrian soldier. Mahler exploits Livia's affections, and persuades her to give him the patriots' money that Livia was holding, telling her that the only way he can survive the war is to purchase a false medical certificate, and implying that they will be together afterwards. Mahler travels to Verona and obtains the certificate exempting him from military action. On hearing the news that the Austrians are about to be forced out of Verona, Livia fears for Mahler's safety. She leaves her home and travels through the battlefield of Custoza to be with him. She discovers him living in luxury with a prostitute. He denies that he ever loved her, and taunts her for her gullibility. She gains revenge by reporting him to the Austrian authorities. He is arrested and executed.

There is a web of interconnections between Verdi, Camillo Boito, and the plot of Boito's 1882 novella, *Senso*, on which the film is loosely based, that lends artistic and historical verisimilitude to Visconti's choice of *Il trovatore* to open the film. Several of Verdi's operas (though not *Il trovatore*) premiered at La Fenice, the theatre in which the film's opening scene takes place.[5] Boito (1836–1914), architect, scholar, and writer, shared Verdi's political views. It is likely that he was first introduced to Verdi by his brother, Arrigo (1842–1918), whose close collaboration with Verdi on the libretti of *Otello* (1887) and *Falstaff* (1893) is well known.[6]

Boito's account of the events of the 1860s is through the experiences of the egotistical, totally self-absorbed Livia, as told across several time frames in her secret diary. Boito's Livia has no political consciousness and indeed she seems amoral, her sole preoccupation being her own pleasure. This is not to suggest that Boito ignores the political: Livia is depicted in a number of politically loaded contexts, not least of which is the dramatic coach ride through the battlefield of Custoza, retained in Visconti's film. Her relentless self-absorption in the face of this event (and others like it) is in itself an ironic comment that is not likely to have been lost on Boito's contemporary Italian audience. Other ironies are present as well, many relying on the distinction between the private perception of self and the public reality that is readily deduced by the reader of Boito's novella, who is exasperated by Livia's extravagant posturings, and appalled by her glib appropriation of the profound to her own superficial analysis of her situation. The successful projection of this irony is no mean literary feat. Boito's considerable skills as a writer are evident also in the originality and complexity of the novella's structure, and the economy of his prose.

Boito the writer was linked with Verdi by the film director Luchino Visconti (1906–76). Visconti's early years as a film director coincided with the Second World War, during which he was active in the Resistance. In the years immediately following the war, Visconti, by now a committed socialist, was disillusioned with the lack of social change. The reissuing of Boito's writings, including *Senso* in 1952, provided Visconti with a means of exploring the parallels between Italy in the mid-1860s and postwar Italy.

Visconti's Livia is a very different character from Boito's. Although vain, she is by no means as self-absorbed as the character in the novella. At the opening of the film, she is seen to have strong partisan sympathies, and despite her gullibility and betrayal of her ideals she elicits a degree of sympathy, which is something Boito's Livia could never do. The events of the film are more immediate: Visconti has removed the flashbacks in Boito's text, and the action is traced chronologically. In making these substantial revisions, Visconti creates a more conventional, more realist narrative.

While Boito's political commentary is inferred, Visconti's is overt. In his comparative study of the novella and the film, Colin Partridge has suggested that Boito's primary subject matter is the personal, as social tensions are turned inward (as a consequence of the diary format of the novella). By contrast, Partridge continues, Visconti turns these social tensions outwards, making them public and therefore politicizing them.[7] Visconti exposes a central theme that is incidental to Boito's text, but inescapable in his own. The fierce idealism of the partisan movement is set against the divided loyalties, the compromise and opportunism typical of the ruling class, both Austrian and Italian. Central to Visconti's politicization of the film is his invention of the character Roberto Ussoni.

Partridge has drawn an analogy between the postwar years 1944–47 and the years following the Risorgimento, when "vast reforms were promised but no structural changes in fact occurred."[8] This parallel in timeframes was certainly recognized by the film's censors, who were particularly concerned with the scene depicting a meeting on the eve of the Battle of Custoza between Roberto Ussoni and Captain Meucci, an officer in the Italian army under General La Marmora. This scene was cut by the government censor after the film was premiered at the 1954 Cannes Film Festival. As Partridge describes it, Ussoni pleads for the irregular forces to be allowed to fight alongside the regular army in the coming battle; Meucci refuses permission, claiming that the decision has been made at a higher level. The ensuing battle is a disaster for the Italian forces, and Partridge suggests that Visconti's "flat and negative presentation" of the battle, and the "meek and submissive" appearance of the Italian forces was a factor in official disapproval. But the most significant factor Partridge claims was the implicit link between Roberto Ussoni and the Resistance leadership of 1943–45, when recognition of the irregular "Garibaldi divisions" of the Resistance was denied (in this case by the Anglo-American commanders). And, once again, as Partridge points out, the "privileged class" negotiated with an occupying force in order to protect their position and privilege.[9]

Partridge sees Ussoni as "the real hero" of the film, its "only source of positive values."[10] His discussion of Ussoni and the other characters (and indeed of the film in general) tends to focus on the visual dimension, with little reference to Verdi's music beyond acknowledging its presence. Many earlier writings on film, showing the ongoing influence of classical Hollywood aesthetics, share a tendency to regard music as an additional, supportive element rather than as a significant conveyor of information in its own right.[11] The argument here is that the soundtrack, and in particular Verdi's opera, plays a central role in shaping our interpretation of the film's narrative. The essence of the film is the extent to which individual behavior deviates from the ideal, and that ideal which is revealed so dramatically at the very beginning of the film is the altruistic heroism of Leonora and Manrico. Far from being additional or supportive, Verdi's opera is the mainspring of the film's narrative, setting into motion a chain of actions both political and personal: even Roberto Ussoni, who most represents the ideal in the course of the narrative, is seen to act in response to Verdi's music. And once the operatic performance is over, it remains as an ironic reference point: the ideal against which subsequent actions and events are measured.

The centrality of Verdi's opera to the film's plot is apparent from the very opening shot of the film, which shows the operatic stage set up for the second half of Part 3 of *Il trovatore*. Only after several minutes does it become fully clear that the opera is not, in fact, the substance of the film. Once the camera leaves the stage action to reveal the audience, we see the main characters of the subsequent action for the first time, but as members of the audience differentiated only by social standing, rather than as individuals. During the interval between Parts 3 and 4 of the opera, we become acquainted with the main characters of the film. Thus, when the opera performance resumes with Part 4, we understand the actions of the film's characters on a more personal level, and are by now predisposed to identify links between onstage and offstage action. By this means, Visconti sets up a mechanism for ironic comment that endures even after the operatic performance is at an end. By juxtaposing on and offstage action, and demonstrating links between them, our expectations are aroused, and we are inclined to measure the subsequent behavior of the film's characters against that of Leonora and Manrico.

The opening shot of the film shows Leonora and Manrico on stage beginning the duet "L'onda dei suoni mistici . . ." ("Let the wave of holy sounds descend, pure into our hearts"): the lovers are about to be married.[12] The duet proceeds as the opening credits are superimposed. This initial view of the stage seems to be shot from one of the lower boxes of the theatre. As the brief duet progresses, the distance between (film) viewer and stage action is reduced until the closing phrase "Gioie di casto amor" ("the joys of chaste love"), when flames are seen through the stage window behind the singers.

Ruiz enters in haste to tell Manrico that the Count has captured Azucena, Manrico's supposed mother, and that she is to die at the stake. After some frantic discussion, during which the explanatory text appears superimposed on the stage action ("Venezia—Primavera 1866 . . ." etc.),[13] Manrico calls his men, strides forward melodramatically to center stage, draws his sword, and launches into "Di quella pira . . ." ("The horrible blaze of that pyre burns, enflames all of my being!"). This cabaletta was one of many items from Verdi's operas that provoked audience uproar during the Risorgimento, the patriots associating "Italy" with "mother" in this instance.[14] As the cabaletta begins, the camera pans from the stage, across the orchestra pit to the parterre, where a number of Austrian officers are seated. These were the cheapest seats in the theatre, popular among the military for the close view they gave of females on stage.[15] At Manrico's text "Empi spegnetela o ch'io fra poco . . ." ("Monsters put it out; or very quickly I'll put it out with your blood") we see the most expensive and prestigious boxes along the side of the theatre, which normally accommodate the upper classes. In this case a number of high-ranking Austrian officers are seated amongst wealthy-looking men and women, suggesting that the occupying forces have the support of the upper classes, and both seem to be the target of Manrico's threat.

The camera now moves up past the tiers of cheaper boxes to show the crowd in the gallery, and pans along the row of ordinary men and women. These are the patriots, come to demonstrate against Austrian occupation. Once again Visconti matches Manrico's text to the portion of the audience we are seeing: the text switches from threats against the enemy to a declaration of duty towards his mother (metaphorically towards Italy), even if it were to cost him his life ("Era già figlio . . ."—"I was her son before I was your lover, your suffering cannot restrain me. . . . unhappy mother, I hasten to save you, or to die with you"). Manrico gives a clear statement of priorities: filial (national) duty must prevail over the personal. Disregard of this statement encapsulates the essence of the film, the pursuit of sensual pleasure (*senso*) at the cost of political loyalty.

Visconti brings all his characters together in the opening scene, and by the judicious matching of image with sound is able to suggest their political differences before a single word is spoken. Note that it is the soundtrack that is driving the pace of the images here: Verdi's score is faithfully adhered to, and it is the images that are cut to suit. As Manrico hits the high C at the end of this cabaletta, the camera reverts to the opening view of the stage, but now apparently from the gallery. The circle has been completed, but with a shift in viewing position from the boxes (the opening love duet) to the gallery (the end of Manrico's cabaletta). Only in retrospect can we recognize the significance of this shift: it is in the box where the offstage flirtation takes place, and in the gallery where, as the opera's action switches from the personal to the political ("Era già figlio . . ." etc.), the film's political action originates.

The following section of the opera is cut (as indeed it often is in real productions), and the cabaletta moves straight into the highly charged call to arms, "All'armi," from Ruiz and the soldiers who have gathered. Our view of the action is front-on to the parterre, where we see Livia's cousin, the activist Roberto Ussoni, arrive; he looks up to the gallery and assesses the situation. At the second call to arms we are at the back of the gallery, where we see pamphlets being surreptitiously distributed. Manrico sings "Madre infelice!" ("unhappy mother!") above the chorus; at the text ". . . corro a morir" ("hasten to die with you"), the women take out their tri-colored bouquets. The end of the operatic scene is shown in a long shot. Manrico runs off stage; we look around the theatre again as applause breaks out, and then up and down from the pit to the gallery as the demonstration begins. The patriots shout "Viva l'Italia!" and "Viva La Marmora!" (General of the Italian forces); pamphlets and bouquets rain down on the Austrian soldiers; Livia, framed in her box, catches the bouquet that Roberto throws over to her. Chaos breaks out in the theatre, the audience galvanized into action by the power of Verdi's music.

As a focus of social life in nineteenth-century Italy, the opera reflected the mood of the people in times of instability. The Austrian administration recognized the dangers of these gatherings, and ensured that there was a strong police and military presence, with one senior officer (in *Senso,* it appears to be the Colonel) authorized to clear the theatre if necessary.[16] Visconti's depiction of the scene, then, is largely in keeping with his concern in general for historical accuracy.[17]

After this dramatic opening, the action of the film is advanced considerably during the interval of the opera. We learn that Count Serpieri (Livia's husband) is indeed a supporter of the Austrian authorities; we see the confrontation between the patriot Roberto and the Austrian soldier, Franz Mahler; and Livia's subsequent meeting with Roberto confirms her support for the patriots. As the orchestra begins tuning for Part 4 of the opera, the conversation in the box between Livia, Count Serpieri, and the Austrian General turns to Franz Mahler, and Livia expresses a desire to meet him.

The final scene of Part 3 provided a highly dramatic rallying point that prompted a political response from the audience in the theatre. As Part 4 of the opera is played out on stage, Visconti's concern is to depict the more personal interaction between Livia and Mahler. Here the onstage and offstage actions seem to merge: the placement of the box in which Livia sits, at the lowest level of tiers and side-on to the stage, allows her to be framed against the stage. We have seen her in previous shots reflected in the wall mirrors of the box; in this scene it is almost as if Leonora is a reflection of Livia.

While the comparisons in this scene between on and offstage action are striking, Livia's status as a heroine is already beginning to falter. Livia is visually and aurally juxtaposed with Leonora, the romantic heroine, but although she inhabits the "real" world, Livia appears the more superficial figure. Leonora faces death while Livia faces, at worst, an attempted seduction by Mahler; Leonora sings of "the pangs that rack [her] heart," while Livia feels ill, and must go home. Even as he is setting up Verdi as a reference point, at our first meeting with these characters Visconti introduces a note of irony. As the film plot unfolds, the contrast between the heroic action on the operatic stage with Livia's weakness and Mahler's opportunism becomes increasingly stark.

That is the last we hear of Verdi in the film, and Bruckner's 7th Symphony becomes the dominating musical presence on the soundtrack.[18] Visconti's appropriation of the Austrian composer's work to underpin the playing out of the narrative after the night at the opera is calculated: to the very end, the film's action is motivated by the Austrian domination of the Veneto region, and the Italian characters act largely in response to the public and private moves of Austrian characters and institutions. Nevertheless, despite Verdi's subsequent absence from the film's soundtrack, his opera continues to loom as a narrative and visual reference. The connections established throughout the scene at La Fenice remain with the film's audience, so that this partial performance of *Il trovatore* becomes that offstage opera that Livia professes to disdain.

A number of oblique references to *Il trovatore* occur in the scenes at the Serpieris' country estate at Aldeno. The first of these is a narrative reference. Livia is in bed, and there is a disturbance outside the house. Franz Mahler is on her balcony, and she lets him into her room; she tells her maid that all is well, but the Count is convinced that there is an intruder in the garden and tells his men to keep searching. This is strongly reminiscent of the opening scene of *Il trovatore*. Count di Luna is jealous of Manrico's attentions to Leonora. The troubadour has been seen in the garden, and the Count urges his men to be on the lookout for him. Further operatic references—this time visual—emerge once Mahler is inside Livia's room attempting to seduce her. The setting itself, with its mirrors and curtains, is reminiscent of the scene at La Fenice. Behind Livia we see a painted mural of a male figure in archaic costume. At first glance, his arm appears outstretched in a gesture that is strikingly similar to that of Manrico as he sang "Di quella pira . . ." Is this Livia's romantic hero? The following day, Livia's betrayal of the patriots is watched by another painted troubadour figure. This one, however, looks distinctly shifty, his eyes glancing to the side, his posture shrinking, in contrast with the extravagantly outward gestures of Manrico.

Later in the film, we travel with Livia through the battlefield (with its cries of "All'armi!") to Verona. Mahler tells her, "I am not your romantic hero, I don't love you any more. . . . I'm also an informer. It was I who denounced your cousin to the police." Here the destruction of Mahler as Livia's romantic hero is complete and she sets out to obtain vengeance, surely one of the principal underlying themes of *Il trovatore*. The final scenes of the film take place in the dark streets of Verona, which visually recall the setting of Part 4 of the opera, with Leonora in a dark cloak, dwarfed by the imposing walls of the tower. Livia is similarly dressed, and is silhouetted against the blank walls. Mahler is executed, and the Austrian soldiers sing the military song "Viktoria" (in the opera, the monks sing the Miserere). The opera also ends with an execution (Manrico is beheaded) and the extraction of vengeance. In the film, Livia still calls out for her lover, and has, we assume, brought about her own downfall as well.

Thus Visconti's *Senso* opens and also, in a sense, closes with Verdi's opera. The operatic performance at La Fenice ended (prematurely) with Leonora's arrival at the tower in which Manrico was imprisoned; the film ends with Livia's playing out of an alternative, anti-heroic version of the end of the opera. Like Leonora, Livia takes direct, decisive action, but while the consequences are similar (both Manrico and Franz Mahler are executed), Livia's motives are as base as Leonora's are noble. Livia betrays her lover in order to destroy him; Leonora's supposed betrayal of Manrico was a ploy intended to save his life at the cost of hers.

Despite the relatively brief appearance of his music, Verdi is a strong presence in this film. The performance of his opera provides a convenient opportunity to demonstrate the political mood of the time and place, and Verdi's historical part in it. The opera sets in motion the political and personal action of the film. But so striking is this opening scene, and so cunning the analogies implied between on and offstage characters and action, that the opera remains as a measuring stick for the characters' actions long after it has disappeared from the screen and the soundtrack.

From this juxtaposition of operatic drama and "real life," the viewer might conclude that truly noble action can happen only on stage. Hence Visconti's invention of the character of Roberto Ussoni. Partridge's claim that Ussoni is the "real hero" of the film and its "only source of positive values" is true to the extent that he is the "real world" reflection of Manrico. Ussoni as a character is hardly developed, but the presence of this genuine hero in Livia's world renders her distortion of the reflected Leonora all the more powerful.

Visconti's focus is not on the heroic acts of Roberto and the other patriots: rather he is concerned with the individual's response to conflicting loyalties. Of all the characters in the film, it is Livia who most faces this dilemma. Manrico's solution to the dilemma is of no interest to the Austrians and their sympathizers, and in addressing the patriots Manrico is preaching to the converted. Livia, caught in the middle, might be inspired by the example on stage to true heroism: she might either use her position to further the patriot cause, or else forsake her position to join the patriots. She chooses neither of these options, nor does she explicitly make a stand against the patriots. Instead, Livia pursues a purely personal agenda of sensuality (*senso*). During their conversation at the opera, Livia told Mahler, "I like opera, but not when it happens offstage. You can't live your life as if in a melodrama, without regard for the serious consequences of your actions." Ironically, this is exactly what Livia does, and Visconti's subtle treatment of the opening scene at La Fenice ensures that, as the narrative unfolds, the viewer is constantly reminded of the increasing gap between the ideal and reality.

## LETO'S *LA VILLEGGIATURA* (A.K.A. *BLACK HOLIDAY*) (1973)

Leto's debut film attracted largely favorable reviews when it premiered. It is still mentioned with respect, but without detailed analysis, in standard works on Italian cinema. Yet it is far from dated, above all in its use of the music of

Verdi.[19] The dominating presence is that of *Don Carlos*, alongside excerpts from *Macbeth* and very briefly *Rigoletto*, plus crucial set pieces from *Nabucco* and *Il trovatore*. The manner of presentation of this music also covers a wide range: however, the examples are unified in the way that they are woven into the texture of the visuals, rather than being dazzling or "operatic" as in the opening scene of *Senso*. Most is non-diegetic orchestral music, doubling as conventional film music and as opera music emanating from a hidden pit. The only operatic excerpt that is sung (the Miserere from Part 4 of *Il trovatore*) seems to be functioning spatially the same way until the camera returns us to the source of the music, namely an onscreen radio speaker. Even the chorus "Va pensiero" from *Nabucco* is not rendered in a vocal version, but in the standard piano transcription, as performed onscreen by the main figure. The convergence of opera and cinema in this film then lacks the standard tension, whereby "cinema, at least mainstream cinema, tends to strive for realistic and naturalistic representation" whereas "opera, even verismo opera, is fundamentally anti-realistic because of the very presence of singing."[20]

A central dialogue revolves around Verdi as a symbol of freedom, while in the Commissioner's office a bust of the composer is prominent visually as a cultural icon. The film is thus permeated by Verdi, and seemingly not just as an eclectic soundtrack compilation. In a film of dramatically contrasted forces, the question arises: Whose Verdi is at stake? And what has dictated the choice of these particular operatic excerpts? The following plot summary of the filmscript will show some parallels with the dramatic situation of *Don Carlos*, but also indicate how far the film is from being a reworking of it or any other Verdi opera.

Rossini, a professor of history, has refused to take the oath of loyalty demanded of academics in 1931 by Mussolini's régime. He is incarcerated on an island, alongside communists and others deemed radical. In charge of prisoners on the island is Rizzuto, formerly a student of Rossini's father. Softened by his admiration for his earlier mentor, Rizzuto attempts to make life on the island tolerable for Rossini: he allows Rossini to move into a rented house, and offers to find him some work as a teacher. Rossini has already undertaken to coach some of his fellow prisoners—earnest communists—in Italian history, even though these activities are banned. The gulf between his academic understanding of the subject and their more practical, ideologically based approach soon becomes apparent. Rizzuto learns of Rossini's illicit teaching, and suggests that Rossini's wife join him on the island. Milena arrives with their young child, but Rossini becomes increasingly frustrated by the curtailment of his political freedom. At the same time, treatment of the other prisoners becomes ever more oppressive, leading ultimately to the death of Scagnetti, the communist. Rossini is offered the opportunity to retract his opposition to the Fascists, but refuses. Instead, he escapes by swimming out to a waiting boat. Superimposed text tells us that he goes on to fight in the Spanish Civil War and in the Italian Resistance in the Second World War.

The relationship between Rizzuto and Rossini is not unlike that between the Emperor and his son, Don Carlos, combining power with a growing mutual affinity (the Commissioner speaks at one stage of Rossini as his alter ego). The idealistic strand linking Don Carlos and Rodrigo has some similarity to what proves to be the two-way political education of Rossini and the communist Scagnetti. But the truly complex presence of Verdi within this film goes well beyond any direct match between opera plot and film script, as an analysis of key scenes will reveal.

The first snippet of Verdi, just a couple of minutes into the film, is synchronized with a shot of the face of Rossini, as if his inner thoughts were dwelling on a past performance. Reinforcing this impression is the operatic costuming of his guards. The news of the boat's imminent arrival is brought to the Commissioner, first seen with his caged birds on a terrace. This is the situation of the internees on the island, caged while still able to breathe fresh air. Apart from a catalogue of items banned and allowable, and the cursory announcement of the prisoners' arrival, there is no dialogue in the first seven-and-a-half minutes of this film, just some minimal sound effects (for example, waves lapping) and the orchestral Verdi excerpts.

The starting note of the first Verdi excerpt has been anticipated by the matching pitch of the ship's foghorn. The accompanying music is *Don Carlos*, orchestral introduction to Act 4 (bars 1–4, 1–2, 8–16), then a cut to the *Nabucco* Sinfonia (bars 14–24), a seamless transition in which key, register, and meter are matched. These musical excerpts from two different operas to feature in the film (and followed shortly after by a third, *Macbeth*) function as a kind of overture to the film's soundtrack. Far from clichéd Verdi, this mood-setting music is likely to defy ready identification beyond its composer. At the point where the prisoners file up the hill as a human chain, it is typical of Leto's emphases that we do not hear the referentially obvious Hebrew Slaves' Chorus. Instead he employs the orchestral introduction to Part 2 of Act 3 of *Don Carlos*: "The Death of Rodrigo." At the end of the film, there is neither this, nor any other music to accompany the procession of reverence for the dead Scagnetti, the reminder of Rodrigo. The film then largely avoids tugging the viewer's heartstrings through the convenient device of clichéd melodramatic music.

The musical choices are nonetheless dramatically persuasive, all the more so because they avoid a shallow parallelism between Leto's script and Verdi's plots. Verdi's *Don Carlos* (1867), for instance, refers to the problematic relationship between the Roman church and the Italian state during the Risorgimento. The inflexible dogma decreed by the church is administered by the much-feared Inquisitor, whose power and influence extend to the highest level of politics. In the uneasy relationship that is depicted between church and state, there is little doubt that it is the former that holds real power. The criticism was not lost on Verdi's audiences, and as recently as the 1950s there were objections to the opera's anti-church stance.[21] Any plot resonances behind Leto's use of orchestral music from *Don Carlos* invoke, first, a historical rather than a melodramatic parallel, but then, second, a parallel that is far from direct. The balance of power formalized by the Lateran Treaty implied a secular inquisitor.

This inspires the cinema audience to look beyond the comfortable assimilation of the events as a twentieth-century reworking of a (timeless, melodramatic) Verdi opera story and involves the defamiliarization of historical opera-going habits. In this way, the music is mobilized such that it signifies far beyond a more predictable match between image and sound. While not a Brechtian "Verfremdung," the music's associations are recast to reflect the gulf between its mid-nineteenth-century origins and the film's political context. This liberating of the historical Verdi, himself deemed an icon of liberation from political oppression, is transferred from Verdi's music to his visual image in the scene that follows.

When Rossini first enters Rizzuto's office (the music is cut at this point), Verdi appears as a striking visual icon. In fact, well before we see Rizzuto at all, we see a bust of Verdi on his desk. Positioned in the lower right-hand corner of the screen, the figure appears as the logical interlocutor for Rossini, it being almost lifesize in proportion to Rossini in the middle ground. Verdi, then, is the purely visual bridge between the two men, just as he clearly represents a cultural bridge in their educational backgrounds. He stands for a shared cultural tradition that has now bifurcated politically, as is borne out by the framing of shots from this point in the sequence. Initially present via his out-of-frame voice, Rizzuto is first seen in a front-on shot, sitting behind his desk. Directly behind him on the wall is a photo of Mussolini. Rossini is shot from the side and then from behind, and the gaze of the statue of Verdi frequently converges with his, meeting at Rizzuto. The lines of visual confrontation are then clearly drawn and sustained throughout the scene, with Rossini and Verdi allied on one side and Rizzuto and Mussolini on the other. Verdi the composer might seem to bridge the gap as a cultural link between both sides, but Verdi the political figure is allied with Rossini. This both anticipates the political education of the fictitious Rossini during the film and elides an imbalance in the national fervor attributed to the composers Verdi and Rossini, this Rossini having come to be regarded by some in the 1860s as an "unpatriotic reactionary."[22]

When the camera does take in Rossini front-on, what is positioned above him on the wall (the matching pendant to Mussolini above Rizzuto) is a map, seemingly of the island. When Rossini sits down and is asked about his father, whom Rizzuto revered, the camera frames him front-on alongside Verdi side-on. A sequence of shot/reverse shots from the respective points of view of interviewer and interviewee reinforces the visually opposed players, or in some frames, pairs of players. The soldier who removes Rossini's handcuffs on command even seems to look briefly at Verdi after he's "freed" Rossini. After a second wall photo becomes visible, namely the King, the power play via framing is completed with a shot finally combining Rossini and Rizzuto in the one frame, but with the

King on the wall behind Rizzuto who in turn is standing behind a seated Rossini. All three are viewed front-on, so that each seems controlled by the figure one step further away from the camera and higher up from eye level.

But that is just the outer power play. The camera's circling of the desk has animated the marmoreal figure of Verdi so that he's far from being an incidental detail of the room's furniture. And the combination of history professor, national icon as composer *and* as political inspiration, and map of the island seems irresistible, however much their outward submission to control is beyond question at this point in the story. Through the circling travelling shots, the camera renders Verdi three-dimensional, and this plus his free-standing quality stake out significant spatial claims over those of the two-dimensional rendering of Mussolini and the King, their space further constrained by frames. This is to remain the defining representation of Mussolini. Rossini's true inner freedom is thereby proclaimed by the configuration of the two groupings, while Rizzuto, as protégé of the frozen historical guardians, is projected as the true prisoner. In a scene devoid of musical accompaniment, all this has been mediated by the purely visual presence of Verdi establishing what is at stake.

Despite the battle lines being thus drawn, there is no clearcut alignment of the historical Verdi and the myth created in his name, both present visually in the bust on Rizzuto's desk and acoustically at different stages of the soundtrack. Near the end of a chess game with Rossini somewhat later in the film, Rizzuto, speaking of the State, proclaims that continuity is what matters. An abrupt cut then transposes the viewer to a musically raucous military procession, with the believers bearing aloft successive posters of Mussolini and the Pope, a celebration of the Lateran Treaty that resolved the Roman question in 1929. Where is Verdi to be situated between these twin pillars of power in Italian history, here shown as historically reconciled and hence all the more powerful in combination?

A quite different Verdi quotation in *La villeggiatura* is drawn from the earlier opera *Il trovatore* (1853). About a third of the way through the film, the Commissioner is shown in his office, censoring the prisoners' mail. He reads a letter from Rossini's wife from which it emerges that she is unable to afford the trip to visit her husband. A front-on shot shows Rizzuto standing alongside the radio, from which music is emitting, the Miserere from Part 4 of *Il trovatore*. This is the sole vocal excerpt employed. We hear a lengthy segment: the monks' chorus (Miserere), Leonora's "Quel suon, quelle preci," Manrico's "Ah! che la morte ognora," and the following duet between Manrico and Leonora above the return of the monks' chorus. In the opera, the scene is set outside the prison tower, with the imprisoned Manrico bidding farewell to the free Leonora (who is about to attempt to free Manrico by agreeing to marry the Count). In the film, the radio is turned down in favor of a voiceover reading the second violated letter, but the sound swells as Rizzuto walks to the radio speaker and says "Ècco!" at the end of the scene.

Rizzuto mirrors this Verdi, the Verdi of melodramatic plots, to become the ultimate stage manager of the drama enacted on the island. Verdi provides the dramatic solution, while Rizzuto turns art into life by reuniting Rossini with his wife (even if the analogy with the opera extends only as far as the physical presence of Rossini's wife at the prison). The summoning to the island of Rossini's wife is an outward concession, while the real reins of power remain unchallenged. But the reestablishment of a domestic idyll is confounded by the final images of the film, when Rossini swims out to a boat. He thereby escapes his comfortable captivity and abandons his wife.

The crucial Verdi scene of the film comes approximately halfway through, with the Rossini family now firmly ensconced in their new lifestyle. Starting with "Va pensiero" from *Nabucco,* the most famous operatic rendition of longing for a distant homeland, the scene is immediately preceded by Scagnetti and two of his comrades, plotting their escape. While Leto seems to be using the chorus with its hallowed associations of being a thinly veiled patriotic rallying cry, it is worth noting that the music in turn has undergone a process of mythologizing after the event.[23] For Rossini, playing a piano transcription of the melody, its phantom text recalls the turbulent past as much as being a poignant comment on his present. His instrument is the only piano on the island; this, too, he owes to Rizzuto. Its tones fill the house as the camera roves across the bourgeois décor of their dwelling, every piece of furniture being recorded in lingering detail. The exultant upbeat of the chorus coincides with a flashback to a political leaflet being passed between husband and wife, a sign of Rossini's earlier involvement in an opposition movement. As the music flows without interruption, the drawing room setting is punctuated by further flashbacks to Rossini and Milena escaping over a balcony, whereupon in the present the pianist loses the thread of the music and rubs his hands, an image prefiguring a flashback to a close-up of his hands manacled. In other words, for Rossini this is music whose subject matter he himself has lived through and been intensely bonded to. And that amalgam locates Verdi for him in the dual camps of art and politics. The constant oscillation of time levels between the *then* of Rossini's insurrectionary activities and the *now* of his political punishment is paralleled by Verdi's presence. The continuity of his music combines the highly charged Risorgimento call to rise up (at least according to the annals of Verdi reception), side by side with his ongoing effect as an icon of opposition to Mussolini (as analyzed above in an early scene).

As Milena goes out onto the terrace, a high-angle shot picks out the figure of Rizzuto behind the grating of their garden gate. He is drawn by the sound of the music, a rare live performance on the island, and is at the same time deferential to the privacy of his "prisoner" well beyond the latter's rights. The complex combination of longing and exclusion he undergoes is captured by the framing of him as the true prisoner, the bars of the gate and the shadows behind him being prominent, while counter-shots from below show a backlit, radiant Milena freely striding the open balcony, for all the world like an opera stage. Beyond this physical gulf, there is the strong sense, via the earlier scene with *Il trovatore* on the radio, of Rizzuto as rapt but passive recipient of Verdi's music, and Rossini as its faithful and natural performer, enriched with an inside perspective on its material.

Awkwardly, the Commissioner is finally tempted indoors, whereupon the music ceases, a suggestive but ambiguous silence. Would playing Verdi in his immediate presence be a blasphemy against the political import of this music? Is it to be seen as the preserve of Rossini? Whatever the implications, this is clearly the one area where Rizzuto does not or cannot impose his will, even indirectly, and hence the area best exemplifying an untouchable inner liberty enjoyed by Rossini. Leto's rendering of "Va pensiero" in this scene is complex in the extreme. There is considerable ambiguity both in script and cinematography as to who is the true prisoner, the gaoler or the captive. Then the necessarily reduced scoring and the domestic setting of the performance divest the music of operatic brilliance. The series of flashbacks creates tension between persecution when in the homeland, and Rossini's "holiday" from punishment in his preferential treatment on the island. Leto avoids a directly referential use of one of Verdi's most familiar melodies of all, not seeking to swim impossibly against the tide of its traditional connotations, but lending these considerable psychological and political nuances.

Despite the music going underground once the Commissioner enters the Rossini residence, Verdi does not disappear, nor do the germs of the Italian Resistance movement. Instead, he remains as a centerpiece of the following dialogue over coffee.

> Rizzuto: For me Bach is like a Gothic cathedral. Space and volume. Architecture.. . . . I recall the première of *Parsifal* in Palermo. Those were the years of controversy over Verdi.[24]
> Rossini: But Wagner . . .
> Rizzuto: Wagner . . .
> Rossini: Too many irrational myths.[25] Verdi was ours. His music was a weapon for our freedom.
> Rizzuto: Freedom for the nation.
> Rossini: Freedom for everyone.

Whereupon Rizzuto looks considerably discomfited. The final thesis/antithesis finds no synthesis: it is strongly reminiscent of the Nazi containment of Beethoven's 9th Symphony because of its message of universal brotherhood. The Wagner première cited may imply either an aesthete image of Rizzuto, one who will welcome the Axis alliance, or else one who simply follows the current trend (a tendency that, extended beyond musical tastes, will make of him a Fascist). For all Leto's striving to approach Verdi freshly, the attempt is confounded by the historical continuity of the Verdi myth, which has not changed significantly. When it comes to Wagner, on the other hand, Leto's '70s viewing public cannot but endorse and amplify Rossini's view expressed in this interchange.

The way the space and volume of this scene are shot deserves comment. For alongside its lingering on the piano, the camera in its inventory of the interior has twice picked out the trumpet of a gramophone. And so again, as with the meeting in Rizzuto's office, the spatial accompaniments of Rossini's musical life indicate at the very least his own choice of music played. Beyond that, the piano enables him to enter into a creative relationship with the composer as a performer of the score. All this is a far remove from the wholly passive reception on the part of Rizzuto. His office radio may be playing Verdi the one time that we hear it, but it will also, between the lines of the film's political message, emit propaganda broadcasts on behalf of the ruling Fascists, state-controlled messages no longer respecting individual choice. Moreover, the scene seamlessly combines both aspects of Verdi, first the composer, with the potentially incendiary messages of his operas' libretti, and second the Risorgimento icon, the person whose name sufficed as an oath of allegiance to national unity. Rizzuto remains excluded from the first sphere, except as a pathetic listener in the wings, and in the second fails, even rhetorically, to clinch the argument. The kind of political dispute that in public life is banned takes place under the mantle of a conversation about Verdi, with the master the loser. The battlelines for internal Italian politics in the early '30s are clearly drawn with competing claims to Verdi the icon.

Elsewhere in the film, quotations from Verdi have a significant structural function, going beyond any reference to the dramatic situation of the opera they are drawn from. When the same excerpt is used in different parts of the film (e.g., the "Death of Rodrigo" music from *Don Carlos*), it not only creates a link between all these instances and the plot of the opera, but also has the effect of an acoustic flashback, linking scenes in the film where no linkage is provided by the visuals. An example combining the various possible uses is the scene in which Rossini learns of the death of Scagnetti. Before the news emerges, the brass chorale from the opening of the *Nabucco* Sinfonia is heard on the soundtrack. After that, the "Death of Rodrigo" functions as funeral music for Scagnetti as Rossini assimilates the news. Both these works, and on a number of occasions this particular *Don Carlos* excerpt, have figured prominently in the film. Both were seamlessly linked in the very first Verdi quotation. By this stage, they have generated a musical cohesion in relation to the film that goes beyond the purely musical and/or dramatic energy they provide. A similar parallel is created by the repetition of the opening of Act 4 of *Don Carlos*, which is played when the Commissioner suggests to Rossini that his wife should come and join him, an echo of the very first musical extract heard as Rossini himself arrives at the island. Originally composed film scores can, of course, provide this linking function internal to the film's plot. But the use of preexisting music, especially by a composer whose reception is as ideologically loaded as that of Verdi, adds further dramatic, narrative, and frequently historical dimensions. The effect of the soundtrack is then akin to the power of visuals—the portrait of Mussolini or the bust of Verdi—that form a background to the main plot but significantly frame this plot, and are captured accordingly by the camera.

At the conclusion of the film, Rossini forsakes his family for the cause. "La villeggiatura è finita," he says, and indeed the phony holiday and the phony war are over. Scheduled to stay on the island for five years, Rossini leaves much earlier, and survives the Spanish Civil War as curtainraiser to World War II, and the War itself. He has two dates with death, the concluding text on the screen tells us, first in 1936 in Spain, and then on April 18, 1948, after the days of Resistance. The first would have put Rossini in direct conflict with the Italian régime, engaged on Franco's side in the Spanish Civil War. The second and more precise date is that of the election that cemented the postwar prominence of the Christian Democrats and dashed the politically realistic hopes of the Italian socialist and communist wings, with their claim to being the true heirs to the Resistance myth. This pessimistic gloss from Leto's early '70s vantage point does not compromise the significant development in the figure of Rossini during the closing minutes of the film. His earlier refusal to take an oath is ultimately untenable as an effective political stance, with the negation of power through words that never seriously threaten that power. But he finally progresses to an active profession of his political belief. He, the would-be history teacher of Scagnetti and his comrades, has become their pupil.

Again Verdi's music is an apt choice to accompany the final frames of the film, whose political narrative extends well beyond these frames. As Rossini swims out to the boat, the viewer hears the last of a number of excerpts from *Macbeth*, a section of the overture that is also heard in the sleepwalking scene of Act 4. The broad dramatic context of *Macbeth* is clearly relevant to Leto's design, the centrality of political ambition and the uncompromising realization of that ambition.[26] The first Macbeth extract to be heard in the film accompanied the disembarkation of the prisoners in the opening minutes. It is played at a low volume, further concealing the source of a few bars only from Act 1, the point in the opera when Lady Macbeth waits in her chamber while Macbeth murders Duncan. Short silences separate this from the surrounding *Don Carlos* and *Nabucco* references, disguising a change of key. There is no direct parallel to Leto's plot at this point, although possibly a foretelling (akin to the witches' prophecies) of the death of Scagnetti much later in the film. But the main purpose is to hint from the outset at treachery in high places. The lengthiest *Macbeth* excerpt, well into the film, accompanies a scene in which Scagnetti and other prisoners are swimming in the sea in the wake of plotting an escape from the island, resentful of surveillance by the authorities. The music here is the opening of Act 3, the scene in the witches' cave before they conjure up the spirits for Macbeth. Here plot parallels are tenuous. Nonetheless, it is worth pointing out that, like the witches, Scagnetti and his group are more "knowing" and have more experience of the real world than the naïve Rossini, and that they, too, are deemed to be outlaws.

Finally, we hear the sleepwalking excerpt leading up to the closing text on the screen, finishing on an impassioned upbeat but without musical resolution, in harmony with the defiant, open-ended "resolution" of the film. The music, particularly prominent as the "final chord" in the film score, would also seem to be a commentary on the rude interruption of the sleepwalking of the class of people represented by Rossini. Understood this way, Verdi the composer survives, but Verdi the political icon is superseded by reference to direct, not legendary, politics. This deployment of Verdi signals the presence of the film director, more strongly than other musical excerpts used on the soundtrack.

The sober tone of this film is matched by the bypassing of vocal excerpts in all but one case. Remote from the sumptuous, highly charged production of Verdi (and of a Verdi legend) in *Senso*, Leto's film avoids vocal color, film color, and indeed melodrama itself. Verdi's music, and his alone, in a film without melodrama would seem to be an impossible challenge for an Italian director. But the highly intelligent choices of opera excerpts underpin the protest voiced by this film, and the musical and political personae of Verdi are interwoven convincingly. Leto both reassesses the composer as myth, and reasserts his role in orchestrating Italian politics far beyond the Risorgimento.

For Italian audiences during the Risorgimento, the chronological setting of many Verdi operas functioned as a musical *roman à clef*, with past events as a gloss on the present. Citing Verdi on the soundtrack of postwar Italian films operates in similar fashion, invoking both ostensible and intended setting (above all, political setting) of the works chosen, as well as the state of cinematic Verdi reception contemporary with the making of the film. This ever-present, multi-level structure—first and "second" Risorgimento, to oversimplify, plus a retrospective view of the "second Risorgimento"—is a powerful device of cultural and historical commentary. Inasmuch as World War II and its aftermath are reassessed from an ever more distant perspective, the same process of image and afterimage is at work. And part of what Verdi's music evokes in these films—whether tenable historically or not—is the mythology of the Resistance as a convenient postwar view of Italian history.

The current state of the debate on postwar Italy's lack of national unity, with "neither the Resistance nor the anti-Fascist legacy" filling the gap, is summarized by David Ward: "Italy was not France where a figure like de Gaulle could rise above the in-fighting of partisan, domestic politics and become a truly national figure. France had de Gaulle, Italy has no such figure."[27] But it did have Verdi as perhaps its strongest national signification, before the three tenors furthered his transition into world music. And within and beyond the films treated here, this is how Verdi, the figure, the myth, and the icon, functions, quite independently of the way the music is used as part of the films' drama. The historical Verdi of pre-Fascist days is elided in potency with a post-Fascist construct of Verdi. This is not without considerable irony. For, as Jonathan White comments on a pronouncement made by Verdi in the heady year of 1848, "events on the national stage are the only 'stage' worth attending to, and far more heroical in form than any which has been musically 'composed.'"[28] If indeed Rossini and "his" domesticated Verdi are found wanting at the end of Leto's film, then this director also seems to be endorsing Verdi's sentiments in the year of European revolutions. Visconti, on the other hand, is acutely conscious of the limited applicability of parallels between a first and a "second" Risorgimento. But his film's timeframe keeps evoking them, even while his use of Verdi is unashamedly dramatic.

The films analyzed here both exploit the dramatic potential of Verdi's operas and reinforce a historical myth; citing Verdi combines cultural memory with an often-transfigured version of recent history. In *Senso,* Visconti draws on parallels between the Risorgimento reception of operas with potentially incendiary plots and Italian "occupation" by the alien force of Fascism, leading to direct occupation of Italy by Nazi Germany. On the other hand, Leto traces the continuation of bourgeois humanism into the prewar years of Fascist ascendancy, with Verdi an icon once shared and now contested.[29]

The deployment of nineteenth-century opera in Italian postwar cinema conjures an era when opera represented the cultural language of Italian society as a whole, a society yet to be united at both political and linguistic levels. Opera reception played a key role in Italian self-perception. Of no other country is it equally true that "opera elides with spectacle and national self-representation."[30] Antonio Gramsci accused the Verdi-style opera of being nothing less than a melodramatic trivialization of Italian life, functioning as a kind of musical pulp novel.[31] This melodramatic tendency is avoided by these film directors. Even at the beginning of *Senso,* Verdi as spectacle is positioned by the characters' discussion of on and offstage melodrama. Leto in turn avoids the danger spelt out by Gramsci in his integration of Verdi into the film's narrative. The combination of the operatic and the cinematic via Verdi nonetheless provided a theatricalized version of Italian history, the ultimate validation of self-representation through spectacle.

## NOTES

As a sounding board for all things Italian, but especially film matters, our thanks to Gino Moliterno.

1. Roger Parker, "'Va pensiero' and the Insidious Mastery of Song" in *Leonora's Last Act: Essays in Verdian Discourse* (Princeton: Princeton University Press, 1997), 20–41.

2. Quoted in Andrew Porter, "Verdi, Giuseppe," in *The New Grove Dictionary of Music and Musicians,* ed. Stanley Sadie (London: Macmillan, 1981), 19: 638.

3. The phenomenon of the decline of Verdi's popularity in Italy during the period 1900–1924 and his subsequent "renaissance" is discussed at length in "Franz

Werfel and the 'Verdi Renaissance'," George Martin, *Aspects of Verdi*, (London: Robson Books, 1988), 61–77.

4. Introduction to *Italian Fascism: History, Memory and Representation*, ed. R.J.B. Bosworth and Patrizia Dogliani (London: Macmillan, 1999), 7. In the same volume, see too David Ward, "From Croce to Vico: Carlo Levi's *L'orologio* and Italian Anti-fascism, 1943–46," esp. 64–66.

5. Five of Verdi's operas were premiered at La Fenice (a number exceeded only by La Scala of Milan): *Ernani* (1844), *Attila* (1846), *Rigoletto* (1851), *La traviata* (1853) and *Simon Boccanegra* (1857). *I due foscari* (1844) was to premiere at La Fenice, but was banned by the censors because of unflattering reference to old Venetian families. Verdi's operas in general were of course prominent among productions, from the time of their composition until the destruction of the theatre by fire in 1996.

6. The collaboration between Verdi and Arrigo Boito in fact goes back as far as 1862, when the young Boito provided the text for Verdi's cantata *Inno delle nazioni*: a hymn of nations written for the London Great Exhibition of that year. Arrigo Boito was an active participant in the fighting of 1866 as a volunteer in Garibaldi's campaign.

7. Colin Partridge, *Senso—Visconti's Film and Boito's Novella: A Case Study in the Relation Between Film and Literature*. (Lewiston N.Y.: The Edwin Mellen Press, 1991), 78.

8. Ibid., 73.

9. Ibid., 94–96

10. Ibid., 96, 94

11. A film's credits, too, often reflect this bias. An oddity of the credits of this film is that Bruckner's Symphony is acknowledged along with its performers, but Verdi's opera is nowhere mentioned, its cast, conductor and orchestra destined to remain anonymous. In fact, it seems that the opera scenes are staged, and not merely recorded voiceovers.

12. Throughout the discussion of *Senso* we used William Weaver's translation of the libretto, which accompanies the EMI recording of the opera (*Il trovatore*, EMI disc SLS 869, 1958).

13. "Venice—Spring 1866. The last months of the Austrian occupation of the Veneto region. The Italian government has made an alliance with Prussia, and the War of Liberation is imminent." This and subsequent translations of the film's dialogue are taken from the subtitles of Visconti's *Senso* screened on SBS Television (Australia). The same applies for *La villeggiatura*.

14. Martin, *Aspects of Verdi,* 283, n.13.

15. John Rosselli, *Music and Musicians in Nineteenth-Century Italy* (Portland: Amadeus Press, 1991), 59. Elsewhere Rosselli observes that the military were often on the free list for parterre seats at this time. See *The Opera Industry in Italy from Cimarosa to Verdi: The Role of the Impresario*, (Cambridge: Cambridge University Press, 1984), 44.

16. Rosselli, *Music and Musicians in Nineteenth-Century Italy*, 63–4.

17. He does take poetic licence, however, in setting his opera at La Fenice: this theatre was in fact closed from 1859 (after the signing of the treaty of Villafranca which ceded the Veneto to Austria) until October 1866, when the Veneto was reunited with Italy. See Luca Zoppelli, "Venice," *The New Grove Dictionary of Opera*, ed. Stanley Sadie (London: Macmillan, 1992), 4: 918.

18. The role of Bruckner's music in this film is discussed in detail in Roger Hillman's article "Sites of sound: Austrian/German music and Visconti's *Senso*," *Cinefocus* 4 (1996): 46–52.

19. The composer's name is signaled in credits at the beginning and end of the film, but without acknowledgement of which works are quoted.

20. Jeongwon Joe, "Hans Syberberg's *Parsifal*: The Staging of Dissonance in the Fusion of Opera and Film," *Music Research Forum* 13 (1998): 2.

21. Anthony Arblaster, *Viva la libertà! Politics in Opera* (London: Verso, 1992), 138. The particular interest shown in *Don Carlos* by film directors exemplifies the problematic relationship between church and state in postwar Italy. Visconti and Zeffirelli have both directed films of the opera. See Alan Blyth, *Opera on Video*, (London: Kyle Cathie Ltd, 1995), 95–98.

22. Arblaster, 66–67. Balancing *William Tell*, a "Hymn to Independence" and a few other works, Rossini also composed a cantata at the request of Metternich for a congress of European powers, and a hymn to Napoleon III. Later in Leto's film we learn that (Professor) Rossini's mother's maiden name was Tancredi.

23. Summarizing its reception, Parker (see n.1) writes that "'Va pensiero' moved fairly uneventfully through a historical period of great political tension, but later emerged as the representative music of that period." (38)

24. *Parsifal* was first seen in Italy on January 1, 1914: the copyright limiting performances to Bayreuth expired the day before and a number of theatres around the world seized the earliest opportunity to stage the work. It was staged in Bologna and Rome on January 1; other Italian cities, including Palermo, are likely to have followed shortly after. The controversy Rizzuto refers to is most probably the Wagner–Verdi debate (see n.3) which followed Italy's gradual coming to terms with the music dramas of Wagner.

25. See Marion S. Miller, "Wagnerism, Wagnerians, and Italian Identity," in *Wagnerism in European Culture and Politics*, ed. David C. Large and William Weber (Ithaca: Cornell University Press, 1984), 167–97.

26. Frits Noske sees *Macbeth* as a turning point in Verdi's depiction of the death topos. His following description harmonizes with Leto's unmasking of Fascism (notably in Scagnetti's death) and hence reinforces the aptness of his use of *Macbeth*: "Death is no longer the (mostly unwanted) consequence of mere violence stirred by feelings of vengeance, jealousy, or rivalry; it is the compelling result of thirst after power." Frits Noske, *The Signifier and the Signified: Studies in the Operas of Mozart and Verdi* (The Hague: Nijhoff, 1977), 186.

27. David Ward, "Fifty Years On: Resistance then, Resistance Now," in Borden W. Painter et al., "Behind Enemy Lines in World War II, the Resistance and the OSS in Italy," in *Journal of Modern Italian Studies* 4, no. 1 (spring 1999): 63.

28. Jonathan White, "Opera, Politics and Television: Bel Canto by Satellite," in Jeremy Tambling (ed.), *A Night in at the Opera: Media Representations of Opera* (Guildford, UK: John Libbey, 1994), 292.

29. Bertolucci offers a different slant again. At the beginning of his film *1900*, the death of Verdi (proclaimed by a character called Rigoletto!) seems to signify the passing of the bourgeois age. For Bertolucci's "take" on *Rigoletto* itself among other Verdi operas, see Deborah Crisp and Roger Hillman, "Verdi and Schoenberg in Bertolucci's *The Spider's Stratagem*," *Music and Letters* 82, no. 2 (2001): 251–67.

30. Jeremy Tambling, *Opera and the Culture of Fascism* (Oxford: Clarendon Press, 1996), 7.

31. See Simonetta Falasca-Zamponi, *Fascist Spectacle: The Aesthetics of Power in Mussolini's Italy* (Berkeley: University of California Press, 1997), 262, n. 147.

# 10

# Chinese Opera, Global Cinema, and the Ontology of the Person

## Chen Kaige's *Farewell My Concubine*

### Teri Silvio

ITHIN THE HISTORY OF CHINESE-LANGUAGE CINEMA, THE CHINESE opera has served as an ambivalent parent-figure.[1] The opera-film has inaugurated several phases in Chinese cinema history; it has also been a reviled object against which the Chinese cinema defines itself as modern. The first dramatic feature films made by Chinese artists in the first decade of the twentieth century were films of Peking Opera performances. The dialect cinemas of Taiwan and Hong Kong were also inaugurated by the opera-film genre in the 1940s. And in the People's Republic of China (PRC), during the Great Proletarian Cultural Revolution (1966–1976), films of the twelve "model operas"—a genre that combined Peking Opera with Russian ballet and socialist heroic narratives—were among the few approved for public consumption, defining a generation's experience of the cinema.

Yet, in each case, the prominence of the opera-film was transitory. By the 1920s, the Peking Opera feature was largely abandoned for the social(ist) realist dramas and slapstick comedies of the Shanghai studios. The opera-film virtually disappeared from the cinemas of Taiwan and Hong Kong by the 1970s, although popular genres that draw on operatic traditions, such as the martial arts film, have flourished. In the PRC, both the style and ideology of the model opera-film were immediately abandoned after the death of Mao in 1976. In the project of constructing a new Chinese cinema that breaks completely from the didacticism of the Maoist era and can "go out to the world," the opera-film has had no place.

The 1980s saw the development of a dual structure in the PRC cinema. As China's economy opened up to foreign trade, imports from Hong Kong and Hollywood came to dominate the popular cinema. A local commercial cinema also grew up—the first since 1949—producing mostly films in the Hong Kong genres. Cooperation between mainland filmmakers and producers and distributors from Hong Kong and Taiwan increased.[2] At the same time, the state-sponsored cinema was revived. The Beijing Film Academy, which had been closed during the Cultural Revolution, was reopened in 1978. The directors, cinematographers, and screenwriters who graduated were assigned to work at state studios in various provinces. These "Fifth Generation" filmmakers—including Chen Kaige, Zhang Yimou, and Tian Zhuangzhuang—were committed to developing a new art cinema that would break free of the generic conventions of both propaganda and commercial films.

As the film industry expanded, so did critical film theory. During the 1980s, writers such as Andre Bazin, Siegfried Kracauer, and Christian Metz were translated into Chinese, a much wider range of foreign films were finally available to film workers and academics, and film theorists from the U.S. and Europe were invited to give papers at Chinese film conferences. Inspired by this new range of material and theory, Chinese filmmakers and academic theorists debated such issues as the applicability of Western film theory to the Chinese cinema, the social value of entertainment films versus art films, and the ontology of cinema.[3]

One of the earliest and most influential of these arguments centered on the relationship between film and theater. In 1979, Bai Jingsheng argued that the Chinese cinema needed to "throw away the walking stick of drama" if it was to "catch up" with the cinemas of the U.S. and Europe.[4] The elements of Maoist film aesthetics that Bai repudiated are those generally seen as carryovers from the traditional opera into the socialist theater: reliance on coherent narrative driven by heroes and villains. Thus, within three years of Mao's death, the trauma of the Cultural Revolution was retrospectively linked to theatricality, and the project of cinematically constructing a new Chinese identity was predicated on a disavowal of the theater (and, implicitly, its operatic heritage).

Yuejin Wang identifies two stylistic trends in post-Cultural-Revolution Chinese state-sponsored cinema of the 1980s. In the early 1980s, the films of directors such as Xie Jin were characterized by emotional restraint, narrative ellipsis, and melancholy. Then, the mid-1980s saw the development of the violent, exoticist, allegorical cinema of the Fifth Generation directors. Wang sees both of these styles as reactions against the Chinese cinematic tradition of "the theatrical impulse, mounted onto Hollywood montage regulated by Soviet ideological dogmatism."[5] Chen Kaige's *Yellow Earth* (*Huang Tudi*, 1985), which blended elements of both styles, was one of the most influential films of the decade.

## FAREWELL MY CONCUBINE

*Farewell My Concubine* (*Ba Wang Bie Ji*, 1993), Chen's second film after his return to China from three years in New York, proved to be as much of a watershed in

Chinese cinema history as *Yellow Earth* had been. *Farewell* was Chen's attempt to combine popular and art cinemas, both in terms of production and in terms of style. It was filmed in Chinese studios with international funding and big-name stars from both the PRC and Hong Kong. The producer, Hsu Feng, was a former Taiwanese film star who had moved to Hong Kong. The script was based on the novel of the same name by Hong Kong writer Lillian Lee (Li Bihua).[6] *Farewell* was seen by both Chen Kaige and his critics as joining the international festival appeal of the Fifth Generation directors with the commercial appeal of Hong Kong cinema, a definitive step towards the creation of a truly global Chinese cinema. It was the first Chinese film to win the Palme d'Or from the Cannes Film Festival, and was nominated for an Oscar. It received wider distribution, both in cinemas and on video, than any previous film made in the PRC.

I believe it is no coincidence that this border-crossing film is a sort of meta-opera film, a backstage drama about the lives of two Peking Opera actors. The first half of the film covers the training of two boys, Douzi and Shitou, in Master Guan's Peking Opera academy. In the harsh environment of the school, Shitou protects the stubborn, but younger and weaker Douzi. Douzi is assigned to play the *dan*, or female roles, Shitou the *jing*, or "painted face" male roles. They graduate and become stars. Douzi takes the stage name Cheng Dieyi (played by Leslie Cheung Kwok-hing), and Shitou takes the name Duan Xiaolou (played by Zhang Fengyi). Their signature piece is the *kunqu* opera *Farewell My Concubine*. Xiaolou plays the brave King of Chu, who is surrounded by enemy troupes and knows he is doomed; Dieyi plays his loyal concubine, Yu Ji, who kills herself after performing a final sword dance for him. Xiaolou marries the prostitute Juxian (played by Gong Li), and Dieyi, clearly as a sort of reply to Xiaolou's abandonment, has an affair with a wealthy patron, Yuan Shiqing (played by Ge You). Dieyi and Juxian's battle for Xiaolou's affections is intertwined with the rapid overturn of political regimes as the Japanese occupy Beijing, then are replaced by the KMT (Chiang Kai-shek's Nationalist Party), and the KMT is in turn replaced by the CCP (Mao Zedong's Communist Party). Both Dieyi's artistic passion and Xiaolou's pragmatic patriotism land them in jail at different times. During the Cultural Revolution, the two actors are harassed by Red Guards. Xiaolou and Dieyi are pressed into mutual public betrayals, and Xiaolou publicly renounces Juxian, after which she hangs herself. In 1977, after the death of Mao and the trial of the Gang of Four, Xiaolou and Dieyi, now old men, return to the theater. As they rehearse *Farewell My Concubine* in their old costumes on an empty stage, Dieyi substitutes a real sword for the usual wooden prop, and slashes his own throat.

Many Chinese critics saw *Farewell* as a "sell-out," a leap from Chen's previous intellectual, anti-theatrical style to crass commercialism. I propose instead to read it as a dialectical return, a reevaluation of the disavowed theatricality of the Cultural Revolution. I see this film as a complex meditation on the distance between the Chinese opera and the global cinema. The specific combination of pain and pleasure produced by this distance can be read as a synecdoche for the Chinese experience of "modernization" and "globalization" in the post-Mao era.[7] *Farewell* condenses a specific sense of nostalgia produced by China's rapid transformation from a performance-based culture to an increasingly screen-based one.

## OPERA AND NOSTALGIA

Nostalgia for cultural heritage is rarely a yearning simply for lost objects or even for the ways of life and social structures that those objects conjure. In longing for "tradition," we do not simply long for an objective world that we perceive to be waning or lost. We also yearn for specific *relationships* between the world and the self, for alternative ways of being a person. In other words, nostalgia provokes the desire for ontologies of self that seem impossible in our present world, for a different set of relationships between exteriority and interiority, body and mind, practice and mentality.

In this sense, nostalgia and theater function in a similar way. Both theater and nostalgia set up a contrast between two worlds, one present and one imagined. Both grab us through physical sensation in the present world and pull us into the imagined one. Both work through a tension between intimacy and distance, between identification with the world of the past or the world on stage, and the awareness that we cannot enter that world. And like the inhabitants of memory, characters on stage present us with alternative ontologies of the person. As Bert States puts it, "The intimacy of the theater is not the intimacy of being within its world but of being present at its world's origination under all the constraints, visible and invisible, of immediate actuality." The "weakly disguised reality of the actor" enables us to witness not only how other people might live their lives, but also how those people might be brought into being.[8]

The connection between the theater and nostalgia is heightened in the Chinese opera. For one thing, the operas are always set in the past. The world created on stage is inhabited by emperors and their concubines, scholar-poets and warrior women, mythical heroes and supernatural beings. Periodic attempts to create operas with contemporary settings have always failed to capture the audience.

But even more than the setting, it is the stylization of the performance that creates a balance of distance and intimacy in the relationship between the onstage and offstage worlds. The active construction of the world and the characters is particularly weakly disguised in Chinese opera. Sets are minimal, usually just a chair and a table. Sense of place and time are created solely by the actors. The distance between the characters and the actors creating them is visible in two ways. First, there is no necessary correspondence between the sex and age of the actor and that of the character he or she plays. In many southern Chinese operas, it is standard for women to play both male and female roles; in Peking Opera and other northern operas, it was standard for male actors to play all the roles. Child actors often play elderly characters, and adult actors also frequently play children. Second, every movement is choreographed. Chinese opera actors learn a repertoire of gestures in much the same way that ballet dancers learn their steps.

For Chinese audiences, the difference between the onstage and offstage worlds measures the distance between past and present. Chinese opera fans know that the people of imperial times moved and spoke differently from contemporary men and women. For an actor to carry his physical comportment from offstage into the role of an ancient hero would be a jarring and ridiculous anachronism. Even the practice of cross-gender performance is seen in terms of historical, rather than critical, distance. For instance, fans of southern operas claim that women are better at playing the male roles because the men of the past were more delicate and refined than modern men. The introduction of realistic theater in the early twentieth century, and of cinema shortly thereafter, only intensified and overdetermined the association between Chinese opera and nostalgia.

It is not surprising that Chinese efforts to mourn and recapture a lost sense of identity should center around the vicissitudes of the traditional theater. The figure of the actor trained for a genre that has lost its place, who must face changing audience expectations in order to survive, provides a perfect trope for the experience many people have of identity crisis in times of rapid social reorganization. In China, Taiwan, and Hong Kong in the 1990s, narratives about local opera actors have become popular in literature and reportage, as well as in cinema, but they are most poignant in film form.[9] These films about Chinese opera actors manifest a sort of double, or reflexive, nostalgia. They are 1990s representations of early- to mid-twentieth century representations of imperial China; they use the "modern" technology of film to show us how the "traditional" technology of the theater shows us "ancient" China and its heroes coming into being.

## PAIN AND PRESENCE

I first saw *Farewell My Concubine* on scratchy pirated video in Taipei, Taiwan, in 1994.[10] I watched it and discussed it with several friends who were either professional or amateur actors in various Chinese regional opera genres: Peking Opera, Taiwanese Opera, and Fuzhou Opera. Most of these friends also had experience working in cinema or television. There was one scene with which they all identified strongly. It is the early 1930s. A group of Master Guan's students are relaxing in the academy's courtyard, talking about their favorite foods, what they would most like to eat if they were free. One boy, Laizi, sings the praises of candied crab apples, and just then they hear the cry of a candied crab-apple vendor over the wall. Laizi and the other children run to the front gate and pull it open to see a wall of beautiful paper kites. Laizi decides to run away. Douzi goes with him, despite the pleas and curses of Shitou. The boys have been confined to the academy since they were indentured as young children, and the bustling street market thrills them. They come to a theater, where they see adult Peking Opera stars being greeted by hundreds of fans. They sneak inside and watch a performance of *Farewell My Concubine*. Douzi watches the actor performing the role of the heroic but doomed King of Chu with tears streaming down his face. Laizi, also in tears, wails, "What does it take to become a star? How many beatings? Will I ever enjoy such fame?" In the next scene, the boys go back to the academy where Douzi is beaten and Laizi hangs himself.

Although he is a relatively minor character, it was only Laizi's despair that moved my friends to tears. "Yes!" A woman who had recently given up acting in Peking and Fuzhou Opera to sell insurance nodded her head, "That's just what it's like!" A rising star in televised Taiwanese Opera sighed in agreement, "So pathetic!"

The entire first half of the film focuses on the cruelty of the training process at the school, including severe beatings and painful, extended stretching exercises. But the scenes of beatings are interspersed with lush, painterly shots of snow falling in the courtyard, the students standing in a row along the riverbank singing, boys bathing by candlelight. Critics of the film have been suspicious of this aestheticization of child abuse, but they have also noted that the first half of the film is more compelling than the second. I think that my actress friends' reactions are telling; it is precisely the combination of physical pain and beauty that grabs Chinese viewers. Laizi's tears in the theater condense the nostalgic ambivalence with which many Chinese people view the opera world of the past.

While none of them would ever again want to put a child through the kind of torture depicted in the film, Chinese opera fans often lament that the world will never again see the likes of the stars of the past. The younger generation, they say, does not "eat bitterness" as the students of the past did; because they have not had their roles literally beaten into them, their performances will always lack the intensity that the older generation was able to achieve.[11] This ambivalent nostalgia is summed up by none other than Jackie Chan, the living embodiment of the transition from Chinese opera actor to international screen star:

> As harsh as it may have seemed, it was a system that had worked for decades, even centuries, producing the very finest acrobats, singers, and fighters that the world has ever seen. The kind of training we received just doesn't exist anymore. There are still opera schools, but they don't allow you to punish students physically; that kind of discipline is now against the law. And to tell the truth, younger generations of performers aren't as good as we were, and the ones who went before us.[12]

The erotic presence of the body disciplined through years of pain was a necessary sacrifice exchanged for the benefits of modernity (self-determination, prosperity); the figure of the traditional opera actor, therefore, always carries the weight of emotional ambivalence that is the essence of sacrifice.

It is significant that the objects that lure Laizi and Douzi out into the world, the candied crab-apples and the kites, are symbols associated with Old Beijing, specifically, with the street market and holiday fairs. In returning to Master Guan, the children reverse the direction of both Marxist and classical economic concepts of progress; they sacrifice the pleasures of the market for a chance at the charismatic presence offered by the "feudal" system of bondage.

NOSTALGIA FOR MAOIST SELVES

*Farewell* draws clear parallels between the violence of Master Guan's academy and that of the Cultural Revolution. This analogy is usually read as a critique: the film implies that, for ordinary people, life was just as precarious and enclosed under Mao as it was in the "old society," punishment equally arbitrary and cruel. Thus, the film's portrayal of the Maoist era is often read through what Lisa Rofel calls "the allegory of post-socialism," a historical narrative that runs, both explicitly and implicitly, through post-Mao policy statements and cultural productions (including Fifth Generation films). In the post-socialist narrative, Maoism violently suppressed the "natural humanity" of ordinary Chinese people: the desire to excel, the desire for aesthetic pleasure, (hetero)sexuality, maternal instinct. Post-Mao reforms have emancipated the Chinese people by providing an environment (the market, the nuclear family home) in which these "natural" desires can be fulfilled.[13] But if we read *Farewell* through the nostalgia for the opera actor's presence, the film's representation of the Cultural Revolution becomes much more complex. Rather than being just a straightforward condemnation of Maoist violence, *Farewell* is also a work of mourning for the ("unnatural") ways of being a person that that violence once promised to create.

The analogy between the opera and Maoism is established through a series of parallels between the practices of opera training and the Maoist "struggle session." In both the opera academy and Cultural Revolution struggle sessions, identities are violently unmade and remade. Both processes involve a dialectic between interiorization and exteriorization, between the division of the self into an observer and an observed (performer and audience) and the unification of the self into an undivided consciousness (a self that knows no boundary between onstage and offstage, public and private). And these dialectical processes are both initiated and maintained through violent work on the body.

The tranformation of the boy Douzi into the opera star Cheng Dieyi involves a series of traumatic events. The initial trauma occurs when Douzi's mother, a prostitute, chops off an extra finger on one of his hands in order to get him into the academy. Later, after Master Guan has assigned him to train in the *dan* role, he is continually beaten for one particular mistake. Douzi cannot memorize a line from the opera *A Nun Dreams of the Outside World (Si Fan)*: "At sixteen, I am a nun, my hair shorn at youth's prime. I am by nature a girl, not a boy. Why must I wear these sexless robes?" Instead, he says, "I am by nature a boy, not a girl." Each time he makes this mistake, he is beaten more severely. In what is probably the most controversial scene in the film, a theater agent comes to observe the children's progress. The agent asks Douzi to recite from *A Nun Dreams of the Outside World*, and Douzi again says, "I am by nature a boy, not a girl." Shitou, who is practicing nearby in the costume of a general, seizes a hot pipe and forces it into Douzi's mouth, shouting, "I'll teach you how!" With blood running from his mouth and tears from his eyes, Douzi stands up and, for the first time, recites the passage correctly, with an intensity he has never displayed before. The camera closes in on him as he walks toward it, letting us know that he has now transformed, he is now a future star. Few reviewers have failed to note the obvious sexual symbolism of the pipe, and this moment clearly "fixes" the intertwined passions of the man that Douzi will become: a passion for the opera and a passion for his costar.

The scenes of Cultural Revolution struggle sessions parallel this scene in several ways. First, the general theatricality of Maoist political practice is emphasized. When Xiaolou is grilled by the Red Guards, he is seated alone on a stage, under a glaring spotlight. Later, Xiaolou and Dieyi are paraded through the streets. Their confessions and mutual betrayals are elicited for an audience, and reverse shots of this audience maintain the sense of spectacle. Second, the person who is being "struggled," like the opera student, is forced to admit to an essentialized role. Douzi is made to declare that he is "by nature a girl"; Xiaolou is forced to answer yes to the question, "Aren't you the King of Chu?" Both Douzi and Xiaolou are resistant to taking on these identities, and in both cases, physical violence is used to break their resistance. Third, once this breaking down of resistance has occurred, the person being remade must exteriorize, or spectacularly embody, their newly assigned identity. At the end of his interrogation, Xiaolou is forced to break a brick over his forehead, something he once did as a boy to placate an angry audience. During the final struggle session, Xiaolou and Dieyi are made to wear their costumes and stage makeup, as well as placards that identify them both by their stage names and as "the King of Chu" and "Yu Ji" (as opposed to the more usual "class enemy" or "rightist"). Covered in the trappings of the theater, their ideological status is literally on display.

The film focuses more on the breaking down of identity rather than its rebuilding, but it is important to note that the process by which people were remade into New Socialist Persons was also parallel to opera training. As Ann Anagnost has noted, the Maoist practice of "speaking bitterness" was a performative and embodied one in which "new conceptions of the social and historical became 'real-ized' through the visceral experience of the speaking subject."[14] Manual labor was an important part of the remaking of urban intellectuals into model citizens. Through pulling ploughs, hauling rocks, or working twelve-hour days over a weaving machine, they were supposed to internalize the spiritual qualities of the ideal worker/peasant. Muscles and calluses became the sign of a pure socialist consciousness. The ideal socialist subject, like the star actor, was made through a dialectic between mind and body.

Chen Kaige's personal attitude towards the Cultural Revolution is extremely ambivalent, as is evident in his earlier films, particularly *Yellow Earth* and *King of the Children* (*Haizi Wang*, 1987). When he recalls his own days as a Red Guard in autobiographical writings and in interviews, Chen expresses both horror and longing. He speaks with deep regret of the part he played in leading struggle meetings, particularly against his father, also a film director. Yet he also remembers the time as one of idealism and promise. As Godfrey Cheshire noted after an interview, "Given the anguish he suffered, it's a bit surprising to hear him call the Cultural Revolution 'a great time . . . the beginning of the new China and the end of the old.'"[15] No such Maoist idealism is immediately visible in *Farewell*. After the brutal crackdown on the Tiananmen Square demonstrators in 1989, there are compelling moral and political reasons for this. However, I believe that Chen's ambivalence is not absent from *Farewell*, but displaced onto a juxtaposition between the two main characters and their relationship to Peking Opera. While Xiaolou's insistent separation of his onstage role and his offstage life make him a post-socialist "natural" man, Dieyi's refusal to separate onstage from offstage make him a trope for lost socialist ideals.

The overt allegorical figure for the unnatural Maoist person is Xiao Si, an abandoned baby rescued by Dieyi who later becomes his combination personal servant/adoptive son. When the Cultural Revolution begins, Xiao Si joins the Red Guards, steals the role of the concubine Yu Ji from Dieyi, and gleefully leads the struggle sessions against Dieyi, Xiaolou, and Juxian. Like the treacherous child in Zhang Yimou's *Ju Dou* (1989), he embodies the post-socialist vision of the Cultural Revolution as the unleashing of a monstrous Oedipal complex.

If Xiao Si represents the monstrosity of the Maoist era, Xiaolou and Juxian represent the humanity of the "ordinary folk" who survived it by maintaining a boundary between their public actions (the playing out of enforced roles) and their private sentiments. Xiaolou's response to Maoist didacticism is prefigured by his insistence to Dieyi that their onstage roles are "fake." But it is only the trauma of the Cultural Revolution that initiates a separation between his onstage and offstage personae. As a boy, he seems to have a natural affinity for the heroic male role. He embodies the virtues of the King of Chu in his protection of the weaker Douzi, in his willingness to play the rescuer for Juxian, and in his patriotic refusal to perform for Japanese and KMT officers. It is only the increasing pressure of Maoist politics, beginning with the execution of Yuan Shiqing, that forces him to see the gap between his onstage heroism and his offstage limitations.

## DIEYI'S HOMOSEXUALITY AS MAOIST PURITY

In contrast to Xiao Si and Xiaolou, Cheng Dieyi provides an ironic commentary on the post-socialist allegory, a more nuanced vision of how the ideologies and practices of the Cultural Revolution worked at the level of identity. Dieyi's refusal to separate his onstage and offstage identities—that is, his "homosexuality"—represents a nostalgic vision of the New Socialist Person.

Many reviewers have criticized *Farewell* for its portrayal of same-sex relationships. The only actual sexual encounters Cheng Dieyi has are with the perverse Eunuch Zhang and with his patron, Yuan Shiqing, who is portrayed as narcissistic, decadent, and manipulative. While the relationship between Dieyi and Xiaolou is tender when they are children in the academy, once they are adults, Xiaolou is "crassly insensitive to Dieyi's feelings in a way that makes nonsense of the boyhood scenes."[16] Any direct expression of Dieyi's desire is elided in the film, in contrast to the heterosexual relationship between Xiaolou and Juxian, which is warm and fleshly. Perhaps most offensive to gay reviewers is Chen's "determination to emphasize that the homosexuality of [Cheng Dieyi] is the result of being forced to change his gender identity."[17] Not only is Dieyi's sexuality narratively linked to "emasculating" childhood traumas, but the adult Dieyi is hyper-feminine: "he pouts, slams doors, and flounces about, incarnating a homophobic fantasy of the hysterical faggot."[18]

I think it is a mistake, however, to read Dieyi as a failed realist portrayal of a gay man, or to compare *Farewell* to representations of modern Chinese gay life such as Ang Lee's *Wedding Banquet* (*Xi Yan*, 1992) or Wong Kar-wai's *Happy Together* (*Chun Guang Zha Xie*, 1997). Under Mao, homosexual acts or desires were seen as political, symptoms of a bourgeois class consciousness. The emergence of gay identity in the PRC is very recent, and is intimately linked to globalization and to the psychologism of the post-socialist allegory.[19] Dieyi is not gay. Rather, his sexuality is a synecdoche for a whole way of being a Chinese person that had to be sacrificed in order for "gay" to come into existence as a possible identity category.

Dieyi's overdetermined gender identification and the stereotypical affects of all the "homosexual" characters mark the same unbridgeable distance from an imagined national past as the empty landscapes and haunting folk music that gave *Yellow Earth* its melancholy tone. The relationship between Dieyi and his patrons resembles that between the boy actors and their literati patrons in the late-eighteenth century more than the relations between actors and fans in the mid-twentieth century. It is no accident that the scenes with Eunuch Zhang and Yuan Shiqing take place in rooms that are virtual museums, filled with more antiques than even the richest Chinese collector could afford. As Eunuch Zhang lowers himself onto the struggling Douzi, the camera pans up to a portrait of a beauty in her bath: perhaps the famous Tang Dynasty courtesan Yang Gui Fei, a character that Dieyi enacts on stage later in the film. Yuan Shiqing seduces Dieyi with sophisticated talk about the history of the opera and quotations of classical poetry. Thus, homosexuality is associated with the same ancient world that is created in the opera itself.

Chris Berry has noted that the opera "is emerging as a privileged Chinese site or trope in the discursive construction of homosexuality."[20] I would like to make the opposite point: that homosexuality is becoming a privileged trope for a Chinese allegorization of the opera. Dieyi's forced "gender conversion" stands for the process of transformation of subjectivity that was crucial to the creation of ideal Maoist subjects. Douzi's resistance to learning the female role is significant precisely in the context of the parallels between opera training and the violence of the Cultural Revolution. When women first began to perform in Peking Opera in the 1930s, many fans objected on the grounds that a female actress could not enact the idealized quintessence of Womanhood as well as the male actor did, precisely because they would inevitably fall back on their "natural" femininity. Xiaolou fails as a hero because he takes his masculinity for granted. It is only in overcoming resistance–that is, by denaturalizing one's own subjectivity—that the opera star and the New Socialist Person can come into being.[21]

Thus, although Dieyi is overtly the least patriotic character in the film, he is, allegorically, the most revolutionary, in a specifically Maoist sense. If Xiaolou represents the remembered real of the Cultural Revolution, Dieyi represents its lost ideal. This is why Xiaolou is the Everyman figure of the film, but also the most weak and morally culpable. Dieyi, on the other hand, is both an exoticized and pure figure. His status as an object of idealizing nostalgia and his homosexuality are intimately linked. Dieyi's homosexuality exists only insofar as it is the index of the unity between his on and offstage selves, of his perfection of the dialectic between the mental internalization of a role and the exteriorization of that role onto the surface of the body (in his gestures and voice). Dieyi's homosexuality simultaneously represents the Confucian purity of the concubine Yu Ji, who sacrifices her life for her lover/king, the Modernist purity of the artist who sacrifices all for his artistic vision, and the Maoist purity of the socialist New Person who sacrifices physical and psychological comfort—his historically naturalized inclinations—to remake his consciousness.

## MEI LANFANG AND CHEN KAIGE

Cheng Dieyi is modeled, at least in part, on the great Peking Opera star Mei Lanfang (1894–1961). The operas that are performed in *Farewell* are all ones for which Mei was famous, including *Farewell My Concubine*, which was written by Qi Rushan for Mei and Yang Xiaolou in 1921. The performances in the film are all identifiably in the "Mei school" style, and Leslie Cheung studied surviving film clips of Mei while preparing the role of Dieyi.

Yet there are also significant differences between Dieyi and Mei, differences necessitated by Dieyi's function as an object of Maoist nostalgia. Dieyi's purity is, as I have argued, predicated on the film's construction of a parallel between the world of Republican-era Peking Opera and the political environment of the Cultural Revolution. While those aspects of the Republican-era theater that mirror Maoist practice are highlighted in *Farewell*, similarities between the early twentieth-century theater and the culture of the post-Mao era are occluded.

The Republican era (1911–1949) was one of intense commercialization and globalization in China, a period of agonizing intellectual debates over how to maintain Chinese identity while "catching up" to the West. It was also the first period when the opera-film opened up new possibilities for a Chinese national cinema. Yet any hints of the cosmopolitanism of Beijing in the '20s and '30s, or that Peking Opera ever had any truck with the moving pictures, are missing from *Farewell*. It is these "failures" of historical representation that make the film interesting; *Farewell*'s cinematic self-consciousness lies precisely in the distance between the way the film represents the Republican-era Peking Opera and the way that Republican opera reflected the Chinese experience of modernity.

Mei Lanfang was not only an actor, but a producer, choreographer, archivist, publicist, and teacher; he largely defined the form of Peking Opera that we know today. He was a major figure in Republican-era negotiations between China and the West, tradition and modernity, stage and screen. Mei was internationally know as China's "cultural ambassador" in the '30s and '40s; he performed and gave speeches to foreign dignitaries in Beijing and abroad, and was the first Peking Opera star to tour Japan, Europe, and the United States. He met Bertolt Brecht, Konstantin Stanislavski, George Bernard Shaw, Charlie Chaplin, Mary Pickford, Douglas Fairbanks, and Sergei Eisenstein. Mei was also one of the first Chinese cinema idols; he scripted and starred in a number of opera-films, going from silents to sound films to color, cooperating with directors in China, Japan, the U.S., and the USSR.

These aspects of Mei's career, which are erased from the character of Dieyi, are precisely those that parallel the career of Chen Kaige. Like Chen, Mei mediated between the aesthetics of Chinese opera and those of Western cinema. Mei's artistic innovations, like Chen's, constructed a new image of Chinese culture and history for both local and global consumption.

GLOBALIZATION, REALISM, AND ANACHRONISM

Mei Lanfang made his professional debut at the age of fourteen in 1908, three years before Sun Yat-sen's Nationalist Revolution, at the height of Western imperialist incursion into China. At this time, the fate of Peking Opera was as uncertain as that of the nation. The literati who had been the opera's primary patrons had lost their place with the elimination of the imperial examination system in 1905. The new brand of modern intellectuals, often educated in Japan or Europe, were experimenting with a new theatrical genre, the "spoken drama" (*hua ju*). Inspired first by Japanese adaptations of Western realist dramas (Ibsen was particularly popular), the spoken-drama movement sought to reflect the "real life" of "the people." For the artists and intellectuals involved in the modernization projects of the time, Chinese opera's content was politically regressive and its style embarrassingly fantastic. Cinema, mostly imported from the U.S. and Europe, was also beginning to challenge the opera's hold on its urban audience, which furthered the perception that realism and modernity were linked and Peking Opera was antithetical to both.

Thus, Mei was faced with similar problems to those that faced the Fifth Generation filmmakers in the 1990s: How to appeal to a new, commercial audience whose values are different from those of the outgoing elite? How to reconcile local aesthetics with new concepts of realism coming from the West? How to construct a national aesthetic with global appeal?[22]

One of the most common critiques of *Farewell* made by Chinese scholars is that the film presents Peking Opera, and Chinese culture generally, as an Orientalist spectacle: a beautiful but inarticulate image frozen in an unspecified past. Ironically, in spectacularizing the opera, Chen was following a precedent set by Mei Lanfang. The actual strategies Mei used to reconstruct Peking Opera as a "national drama" for global consumption are evacuated from the film's representation of the opera itself, but they are repeated in the film's style. These strategies include visual reference to classical Chinese painting, the representation of Peking Opera as an anachronism, and the allegorical construction of China as Woman.

Mei Lanfang's efforts to adapt his training to the context of post-imperial China included several forms of experimentation. He tried performances in modern (female) dress based on current newspaper stories, but quickly abandoned this strategy. His more lasting legacy comes from his revival of the literary *kunqu* form (*A Nun Dreams of the Outside World* is a *kunqu* opera revived by Mei), and his development of the "new ancient costume drama," in which he brought characters from classical painting, history, and literature to life (*Farewell My Concubine* was one of these). The *tableaux vivants* of Mei's new ancient costume dramas thus prefigure the "painterly" cinematography of the Fifth Generation films. Like Mei's poses, framed by the proscenium, the nearly still shots that are placed throughout the first half of *Farewell* (snow falling in a courtyard, the backs of boys lined up in the mist on the riverbank), with their Daoist emphasis on negative space, are visual references to late imperial Chinese painting that lend the film an aura of classicism.

When he brought Peking Opera into an international cultural arena, Mei presented it as an anachronism. The introduction to the program for Mei's 1930 tour of the U.S., written by Hu Shih (billed as "the Father of the Chinese Renaissance"), begins with the sentence, "The Chinese drama is historically an arrested growth." It continues:

> [N]owhere in this modern world are to be seen such vivid presentations of the irrevocably lost steps in the slow evolution of the dramatic art as are seen on the Chinese stage today. There one sees every historical survival preserved and carried out with artistic perfection.[23]

This concept of the opera as a timeless bearer of Chinese history is evident in several aspects of *Farewell*: the anachronistic *mise-en-scène*; the way that the opera performances within the film never alter in content or style no matter how much the historical background changes; and the exoticism of European and U.S. publicity material for the film.

As a *dan* actor, Mei's success depended on the creation of a canon of operas in which the female characters dominated. This was one reason behind his revival of the *kunqu* form, because *kunqu* operas provided some of the best female roles. At the same time, Mei was one of the key figures in the transformation of "the opera of the capital" (*jing xi*) into the "national drama" (*guo ju*). In many of Mei's operas, therefore, the heroines were allegorical figures for China in both their patriotic sacrifices and their embodiment of Chinese ideals of grace and beauty. *Farewell* repeats this strategy in the character of the feminized Dieyi. Not only does Dieyi embody the patriotic, self-sacrificing Chinese woman (as created by Mei) on stage, but, as I have argued, his offstage femininity stands allegorically for a lost national ideal of the person.[24]

OPERA TIME AND CINEMA TIME

One area in which Mei and Chen differ significantly is in their engagement with Western ideas about the kind of reality that cinema is best suited to capture. We can see this difference in their solutions to the question of how to represent the passage of time. In Chinese operas, the passage of time is represented through symbolic action (for example, a character circling the stage represents a long journey). Sudden jumps in narrative time do not require explanation because the audience is usually already familiar with the story. Although a change in age may be represented by the donning of a beard or a change in clothes, it is never represented through a change in actors.

Mei believed that this mode of representing the passage of time was unsuitable for the medium of cinema. This is interesting, given the range of international film styles to which he was exposed. Implicitly, he favored the conventions of Hollywood narrative over Soviet montage. In his opera-films, Mei solved the problem of the disjuncture between operatic and cinematic narrative technique quite simply; he only filmed scenes in which narrative time and performance time were equivalent.

In *Farewell*, jumps in time are represented through a change in setting, changes in cast, and the insertion of still photography. The first time-jump moves the story from 1924 to roughly 1930. We see the boys from the academy lined up along the riverbank, singing an aria from *Farewell My Concubine* as the snow falls. In the next shot, we see a group of older boys similarly lined up along the riverbank, singing the same aria, standing in fresh green reeds. The second jump in time moves the story from roughly 1930 to 1937. We see Master Guan and his students arranging themselves for a photograph. The photographer's bulb flashes, and we are presented with a black-and-white photo of the group, replicating school photographs of the era. There is another flash, and the camera is suddenly pulling back from Leslie Cheung and Zhang Fengyi, posing in a photographer's studio. The next shot gives us an overhead view of the street, with a superimposed text explaining that it is now 1937, and Douzi and Shitou have become stars with the stage names Cheng Dieyi and Duan Xiaolou. The transition from the framing scene (in 1977) to the first scene of the narrative (in 1925), like the photo-flash transition, is marked by a temporary transition to an older medium. The scene in which Douzi's mother carries him through the market to Master Guan's academy begins in a sepia tone; the film gains color as the scene progresses.

Thus, *Farewell*'s sense of historicity lies in its replication of the history of visual technologies, from painting to photography to black-and-white film to color film. The history indexed here is not that of China, but of the media through which Chinese life has been represented.

## CONSTRUCTING THE CHARACTER: INTERIORITY AND EXTERIORITY

Mei Lanfang mediated between the aesthetics of Chinese opera and those of Western realism by developing a style that emphasized emotional realism while maintaining the opera's stylization. One of Mei's major innovations was that he was able to master all of the stock role types within the *dan* category (the virtuous elite woman, the flirtatious servant girl, the woman warrior)—no mean feat in itself—and blend them to create entirely new characters, including the concubine Yu Ji. The idea of gestural syntax was crucial to Mei's creation of these characters:

> Each stylized gesture/movement (*shen duan*) in Peking Opera is extracted from life and naturally has a definite meaning. But you cannot explain each gesture alone or mechanically. Some *shen duan* express a single idea, for instance climbing up or down steps or opening a door. . . . But some *shen duan* only have meaning when they are strung together. Sometimes, a *shen duan* can have a simple explanation in one situation, but when that same *shen duan* is placed in another situation, if you want to understand the ideas and feelings being expressed, you need to see it within the context of a whole choreography.[25]

In choreographing specific characters, Mei focused on creating sequences of stylized gestures that would express the character's emotional state as a flowing text. In Mei's choreography for Yu Ji's sword dance, a complex sequence of movements reveals her alternating and conflicting emotions: the smiling face she puts on to cheer up the king, the tears she wipes away when she turns to face the audience, and her increasing despair and her determination not to increase Xiang Yu's misery by letting him see.[26]

This kind of emotional tension is, significantly, also critical to Hollywood style. James Naremore writes in *Acting in the Cinema* that, "realist acting amounts to an effort at sustaining opposing attitudes toward the self, on the one hand trying to create the illusion of unified, individualized personality, but on the other suggesting that the character is subject to division or dissolution into a variety of social roles."[27]

Mei believed that film's distinctive ability to index physical reality was most valuable when it was focused on the human body. He wrote:

> An opera actor always regrets that he cannot see what he does on the stage. It is only on the screen that you can see your own performance, and only then can you really see both your good and bad qualities, and are thus able to criticize yourself and enjoy your own art. An actor can use film as a special sort of mirror, to show him to himself. . . . It is the film's use of facial expression that particularly inspires me. . . .[28]

In making his opera-films, Mei was always eager to use close-ups to emphasize the characters' emotions. What he found most frustrating in his cinema work was editing that interrupted the flow of the actor's movement, isolating *shen duan* from the sequences in which they had meaning. For Mei, montage was antithetical to emotional realism.

In *Farewell*, the emotional logic and reality effects of Mei Lanfang's style (that is, the expression of conflicting attitudes toward the self) are, in fact, evacuated from the diegetic opera performances and transposed to the style of the film itself. The physical presence and gestural syntax of the opera actor has been replaced with specifically cinematic modes of constructing the person. Where the actor's body and a gestural code held the Peking Opera role together, the characters in *Farewell* are given coherence through the star image of the cinema actor and an externalized symbolic code.

To explain what I mean by this process of evacuation and transposition, let me turn to the problem of casting. One of the reasons that the first half of the film has a different feel from the second half is that the young actors who play Douzi and Shitou (Yi Zhi and Ma Mingwei; Zhao Hailong and Fei Yang) were, in fact, students from Peking Opera schools, while Leslie Cheung and Zhang Fengyi, who play the adult Dieyi and Xiaolou, are cinema actors. I will focus here on Leslie Cheung. Leslie Cheung is one of a number of multitalented international stars of a type produced only in Hong Kong. He began his career singing Canto-pop and remains one of the most popular male vocalists in Hong Kong. As with many Canto-pop stars, his success as a singer made him prime material for film directors, and he was frequently cast in the romantic leads in genre films (he often sang the theme song, as well). By the time he was cast in *Farewell*, he had moved into more serious roles, such as the self-destructive playboy in Wong Kar-wai's *Days of Being Wild (Ah Fei Zheng Zhuan*, 1991).

The casting of Cheung as Cheng Dieyi presents a rather obvious question: If Chen simply wanted to capitalize on Cheung's international appeal by making a star vehicle, why choose to make that film about Peking Opera actors? And conversely, if Chen wanted to make a film about Peking Opera, why cast Cheung, who had no previous opera training and is not a native speaker of Mandarin? I would argue that this contradiction is one of the primary sites where the film's awareness of its conditions of possibility, and of the loss of other possibilities those conditions entail, is manifest.

Although Cheung did study Peking Opera with a private teacher in preparation for the role, he simply does not have a Peking Opera actor's physical presence, that particular bodily habitus acquired through years of painful training. My Taiwanese opera actor friends were genuinely impressed and moved by Cheung's performance, but they also laughed at the scenes in which he is shown performing Peking Opera.

The editing in these scenes strives to compensate for, or hide, Cheung's lack of opera training. When Dieyi is on stage, he is almost never shown in long-shot while moving. Most shots of him onstage are close-ups. (To anyone familiar with Peking Opera, this actually emphasizes Cheung's amateur status, because in the opera facial expressions, especially eye movements, are stylized and take years to learn). The shots also tend to alternate rapidly. When Dieyi's entire body is shown while he is onstage, it is usually during some moment of distraction or crisis, when Cheung's hesitancy can be given a diegetic justification: for instance, when he performs for Yuan Shiqing while drunk, or when the KMT soldiers are disrupting his show.

But if, for my Taiwanese friends, Dieyi's stage performances were not convincing, Cheung's performance of Dieyi was. Part of what gives the character of Dieyi a sense of coherence is Cheung's star persona. By 1993, rumors that Leslie Cheung is gay were an established part of his image. Many fans in the Chinese-speaking world saw *Farewell* as Cheung's "coming out" film, and Cheung's work since the film—particularly in Peter Chan's gender-bending comedy *He's a Woman, She's a Man (Jin Zhi Yu Ye,* 1994) and in *Happy Together*—has strengthened this perception. That Chen Kaige was consciously working with this aspect of Cheung's star image seems clear. Chen's first choice for the role of Dieyi was John Lone, the star of Bertolucci's *The Last Emperor* (1987). Lone is, like Cheung, a Hong Kong based star of international reputation. And, like Cheung, Lone's star persona also includes rumors of gay identity. The substitutability of the two stars is striking; Lone declined *Farewell* to star as the gay (in this case, self-identified) Peking Opera *dan* in David Cronenberg's *M. Butterfly* (1993).

As I've noted, some gay critics found Cheung's performance stereotypical, over the top, and hysterical. But Cheung was already associated with a flamboyant and melodramatic style in his concert performances, and for many Chinese fans, the mesh between Dieyi's and Cheung's flamboyance lent the performance a certain reality effect. Dieyi's offstage "flouncing" can thus be read simultaneously as the internalization of an imposed code and as the "free" expression of diva "personality."

Mei Lanfang consciously disassociated himself from the stigma of the *xiang gong* (boy actors of the late imperial era who were assumed to be the sexual playthings of their literati patrons) by clearly separating his onstage and offstage personae. In his stage work and in his writing about it, he made the body, rather than the psyche, the source of the self's coherence. Ironically perhaps, it is the emergence of sexual-identity categories that are seen to inhere in the psyche rather than the body, and of a cinematic star culture premised on a psychological affinity between actors and their roles, which allow Cheung's anachronistic portrayal of Mei-as-*xiang gong* to be read as realism.

Aside from Cheung's star image, what gives the character of Dieyi coherence is a set of symbolic motifs, such as the finger, the pipe, and the sword. What I mean when I say that Mei Lanfang's approach to the character is transposed in *Farewell* onto an exteriorized symbolic code is that Chen's deployment of Freudian symbolism most closely resembles the opera actor's process of dialectical internalization and externalization. The Peking Opera actor internalizes a gestural semantics into bodily, not psychic, memory, and then externalizes that memory into a performance text. In *Farewell*, an interior psyche is constructed for Dieyi through a symbolic language that belongs to the *mise-en-scène*, rather than the actor. I believe that the excessiveness of this psychological symbolism, the way it begs for a simplistic element-by-element translation (such as the finger-chopping as "castration" and the pipe scene as a "rape"), is a register of how far the distance between stage and screen has grown in post-Mao China. Compared with Mei's gestural syntax, the film's Freudian semantics must make up for the loss of quality ("presence") with quantity.

## OPERA, CINEMA, AND THE CHINESE PERSON

Chen Kaige has stated that as a film worker he has "always advocated the idea that in comparison with Western culture, the weak point in our Chinese culture is 'the problem of the attitude towards the individual.' Now, following economic development and the increasingly meticulous division of labor, the whole culture is changing. This change in the whole will make the individual grow stronger and stronger."[29]

This essay has attempted to examine how this particular concept of modernity works itself out in Chen's cinematic practice.

For the past half-century, representation of the individual has been one of the primary axes along which Chinese intellectuals measure their status as "modern." In the Republican era, Mei Lanfang made emotional realism one of his primary goals. In post-Mao Chinese cinema, emotional realism has taken priority over many other possible cinematic aesthetics. As Esther Yau notes:

> Whereas the notion of "documentary aesthetics" came to be neither widely nor uniformly adopted in practice, the creation of "realistic screen characters," freed from political predestinations, predictable virtues or vices, and even from

moral judgments, became a premise widely accepted in commercial filmmaking. . . . Contradiction and ambivalence as qualities applied to characters became an index for artistic sophistication in Chinese filmmaking in the early and mid-1980s.[30]

But although this focus on the construction of the "real" individual is a point of continuity between the Republican and post-Mao eras, the definition of "real" is not. *Farewell* does not simply show us timeless, universal human nature in a historically and culturally specific setting. Rather, it historicizes the ontology of the Chinese person. What I have tried to show is that neither *Farewell's* epic history nor Chen's statements about the development of the Chinese individual need to be read as narratives of progress. *Farewell*, through it's cinematic representation of the opera, makes visible a historical transformation in the nature of the Chinese person, a transformation that has meant the sacrifice of one set of ideals and human possibilities for another.

NOTES

1. The term "opera" is in some ways an inaccurate translation of the Chinese term *xiqu*, an umbrella term that covers many regional performance genres. Nevertheless, I use the term "opera" or "Chinese Opera" throughout this chapter to highlight the links between my work and that of the other writers in this volume.

I use the pin-yin romanization system for all Chinese terms, with the exception of names that are more recognizable in other spellings (e.g., Chiang Kai-shek). The names of Hong Kong performers and directors are given in their standard Cantonese romanizations.

2. For a detailed description of the development of the "Hong Kong/ Mainland alliance" see Jenny Kwok Wah Lau, "Farewell My Concubine: History, Melodrama, and Ideology in Contemporary Pan-Chinese Cinema." *Film Quarterly* 49, no. 1 (1995): 16–27.

3. See George Semsel, Xia Hong, and Hou Jianping, eds., *Chinese Film Theory: A Guide to the New Era*, (New York: Praeger, 1990).

4. Part of Bai's article is translated in Semsel, Xia, and Hou, eds. *Chinese Film Theory*.

5. Wang Yuejin, "The Cinematic Other and the Cultural Self? De-centering the Cultural Identity on Cinema." *Wide Angle* 11, no. 2 (1989): 37.

6. Many of Lillian Lee's novels have been adapted to the screen by Hong Kong directors, including *Rouge* (*Yanzhi Kou*, 1987, dir. Stanley Kwan).

7. Some of the most prominent post-Mao transformations include the the privatization of agriculture and industry and the decline of the state economic sector, the opening up of markets for both domestic and international trade and the encouragement of international investment through the establishment of Special Economic Zones, relaxation of political surveillance (punctuated by crackdowns), the emergence of new social classes (rich entrepreneurs and poor migrant laborers), the

growth of consumer culture, the movement of women out of paid labor and into the home in large numbers, and the rapid expansion of electronic communications technologies.

8. Bert O. States, *Great Reckonings in Little Rooms: On the Phenomenology of Theater*, (Berkeley: University of California Press, 1985), 154.

9. I believe that such narratives can be considered to be an emerging genre, one defined by its use of Chinese local opera as a synecdoche for lost ways of being. This chapter is part of a larger project in which I am exploring this genre and comparing how representations of the opera actor in Taiwan, Hong Kong, and the PRC reflect the experiences of those places' different traumatic modern histories. Examples from Taiwan include Ling Yan's 1990 novel *The Silent Thrush* (*Shi Sheng Huamei*), a 1991 film adaptation of the same, and Hou Hsiao-hsien's *The Puppetmaster* (*Xi Meng Ren Sheng*, 1993). Examples from Hong Kong include the novel *Farewell My Concubine* and Shu Kei's 1996 film, *Hu-Du-Men*. Homosexuality is a prominent theme in most of these works.

10. The film was banned in both the PRC and Taiwan at the time, but news about it was in the papers and videos were available. It eventually did play in Taipei later in 1994.

11. This nostalgic discourse may be more common in Taiwan and Hong Kong than it has been in China until recently. But with economic reforms since the 1980s, traditional opera schools are losing their long-standing state support (and control), and the opera is beginning to face the same market pressures in the PRC that it has long faced in capitalist Chinese societies. As young actors turn to the more lucrative arenas of film and television, we can predict that older fans and actors will lament their lack of dedication and the easiness of their lives.

12. Jackie Chan (with Jeff Yang), *I Am Jackie Chan: My Life in Action* (New York: Ballantine, 1999), 56.

13. Lisa Rofel, *Other Modernities: Gendered Yearnings in China After Socialism* (Berkeley: University of California Press, 1999), 217–18.

14. Ann Anagnost, *National Past-Times: Narrative, Representation, and Power in Modern China* (Durham, N.C.: Duke University Press, 1997), 19.

15. Godfrey Cheshire. "The Long Way Home." *Film Comment* 28, no. 4 (July 1992): 38.

16. Tony Rayns, "Ba Wang Bie Ji (Farewell My Concubine) [review]." *Sight and Sound* 4, no. 1 (January 1994): 42.

17. Shu Kei. "Letter to Chen Kaige." *Cinemaya* 20 (summer 1993): 19.

18. Chris Berry, "At What Price Success?" *Cinemaya* 20 (summer 1993): 21.

19. For more on the emergence and negotiation of gay identity in the PRC, see Lisa Rofel, "Qualities of Desire: Imagining Gay Identities in China." *GLQ* 5, no. 4 (1999). There is no doubt that the emergence of gay and lesbian subcultures has a lot to do with the increasing Western presence in China since Deng Xiaoping's economic reforms: a presence which includes not only gay men and lesbians who travel to China from San Francisco, Hong Kong, and New York, but also the publication

of translations of Western texts on sexology, AIDS, and international activist groups like ACT-UP. Yet we should not assume that this is a straightforward example of "Westernization." Rather, the recent explosion of interest in homosexuality in China is related to an obsession with the problem of self-identity and the ontology of the individual that has been a distinctive feature of Chinese modernity for at least a century, and this obsession is not equally prominent in all post-colonial contexts.

20. Chris Berry, "Sexual DisOrientations: Homosexual Rights, East Asian Films, and Postmodern Postnationalism," in Xiaobing Tang and Stephen Snyder, eds., *In Pursuit of Contemporary East Asian Culture* (Boulder: Westview Press, 1996): 171.

21. Taiwanese literary critic Sang Zilan ("Cheng Dieyi—Yige Quanshi de Qidian," *Dang Dai*, 1 April 1994, 54–73) has argued against the interpretation that it is the trauma of opera training which creates Dieyi's feminine gender identification. Pointing to Douzi's early attachment to Shitou, and to the shot-reverse-shot between Douzi and the actor playing the King of Chu in the scene in which Douzi and Laizi sneak into the theater, she argues that Douzi/Dieyi accepts the role of concubine because he is already in love with Shitou/the King of Chu. I think that the film is indeed open to this interpretation, and that the ambivalent balance between internalization and externalization in the creation of Dieyi's sexuality is part of *Farewell*'s internationalism. I do, however, think that Sang's interpretation is a specifically Taiwanese one, one which comes out of a history which does include Chinese opera, but does not include the Cultural Revolution.

22. For a more detailed analysis of Mei's career in terms of nationalization and commercialization, see Joshua Goldstein, "Mei Lanfang and the Nationalization of Peking Opera, 1912–1930," *Positions* 7, no. 2 (1999): 377–420.

23. Hu Shih, "Mei Lan-fang and the Chinese Drama," Program for Mei Lanfang's U.S. tour. (New York: The China Institute in America, 1930).

24. For another approach to Dieyi's feminization as national trope, see Wendy Larson, "The Concubine and the Figure of History: Chen Kaige's Farewell My Concubine," in Sheldon Hsiao-ping Lu, ed., *Transnational Chinese Cinemas: Identity, Nationhood, Gender* (Honolulu: University of Hawaii Press, 1997).

25. Mei Lanfang, *Mei Lanfang Wutai Mi Ben* (Taipei: Da Han Chu Ban She, 1977), 19–20.

26. Ding Zhiyun, cited in Zheng Peikai. "'Ba Wang Bie Ji' de Lishi Wenhua Sui Xiang," *Dang Dai*, 1 March 1994, 77–79.

27. James Naremore, *Acting in the Cinema* (Berkeley: University of California Press, 1988), 72.

28. Mei Lan-fang, "The Filming of a Tradition," *Eastern Horizon* 4, no. 7 (July 1965): 13–22.

29. Zhang Jingbei. "Shi Shi Beijing Qian Huodong de Renmen [interview with Chen Kaige]," *Dianying Xinshang* 67 (January/February 1994): 71.

30. Esther C. M. Yau, "Cultural and Economic Dislocations: Filmic Phantasies of Chinese Women in the 1980s," *Wide Angle* 11, no. 2 (1989): 9.

# 11

# Sounding Out the Operatic

## Jacques Rivette's *Noroît*

### *Mary M. Wiles*

> It will be he who, by only half saying things,
> will enable me to graft my dream on to his;
> he who will conceive characters whose story and home
> will not belong to any specific time or place;
> he who will not tyrannically force upon me the "compulsory
> scene" and who will let me, here and there, feel free to be more
> of an artist than he and to complete his work.
>
> —Debussy 1889; description of the ideal poet

I N A 1981 INTERVIEW, JACQUES RIVETTE STATED THAT HE CONCEIVED OF UNIT-
ing his cycle of films, *Les Filles du feu*, through a "progression of complication linked to the intervention of music on action,"[1] expressing his wish to
accord a certain import to music in the production of meaning. In this way,
Rivette moves his art into the realm of operatic dramaturgy, where the relationship or interplay between action and music is the perennial central concern.[2]
From film to film, the audience discerns influences of, and references to, various
musical and dramatic forms, extending from Noh drama and modern dance to
Elizabethan theater and the American Happenings of the 1960s. Of the films
that comprise the cycle, however, *Noroît* is perhaps the most straightforwardly
operatic, the most indebted to opera in its conception. In this chapter, we will
demonstrate that opera resonates throughout *Noroît* on multiple levels.

It is, moreover, through opera—and specifically Claude Debussy's *Pelléas
et Mélisande*—that Rivette pays tribute in this film to his friend and mentor Jean
Cocteau. In 1962, poet and cinéaste Cocteau designed sets and décor for a production of Debussy's *Pelléas et Mélisande* at the Opéra-Comique.[3] Cocteau's
designs were modeled on the original Jusseaume and Ronsin designs produced

for the opera's première performance in 1902, and were, according to one critic, "a very acceptable modernization of the traditional sets."[4] Cocteau confessed that he was working "quickly and with my eyes almost closed," creating sketches based on early adolescent memories of the première production.[5] The following year, shortly before his death, Cocteau disclosed plans for a filmed version of Debussy's opera that was, unfortunately, never produced.[6]

During this time, Rivette enjoyed a particularly close, even filial relationship with Cocteau. Indeed, Rivette has described Cocteau as "le coupable" or the guilty one whose concern and camaraderie brought him to a career in filmmaking.[7] In this context, we may be tempted to characterize Rivette's film as the posthumous completion of Cocteau's final project: the opera-film of *Pelléas et Mélisande*. At the least, *Noroît* discloses the legacy of a theatrical and operatic style passed on to Rivette from Cocteau and, ultimately, from Maeterlinck and Debussy.

The story of *Noroît* is not based solely on the opera *Pelléas et Mélisande*. It is also adapted from Elizabethan dramatist Cyril Tourneur's *The Revenger's Tragedy* (1607). Tourneur provides Rivette with a cast of characters, and particularly the hero(ine) Morag, who is modeled on Vindice, the main character of *The Revenger's Tragedy*. Like Vindice, Morag seeks vengeance for the death of a loved one, and in her quest is, like Tourneur's male hero, carried to her fate through and against the resistance of external forces.[8] *The Revenger's Tragedy* also provides *Noroît* with an Aristotelian beginning, climax, and conclusion, all three of which incorporate explicit references to the play.[9]

In the film's opening scene, we first meet Morag (Geraldine Chaplin), who is lying prostrate on the beach, bent over her lover Shane's body. She exclaims in French, "Shane, my brother, I looked for you. I found you in the ocean on the rocks torn apart, shredded, with my breath, with my hands, I have gathered you again. . . . I'm the last one, now. Our blood has run dry. It runs to avenge you!" Framed against an unforgiving horizon, a disconsolate Morag declares her desire for revenge. Then, she recites a passage in English from the opening of Tourneur's play that mirrors the revenge theme proclaimed in her opening monologue: "O thou goddess of the palace, mistress of mistresses/to whom the costly-perfum'd people pray. . . ." As she speaks these lines, she assumes the theatrical role of the Revenger Vindice. At this point in the play, Vindice dons a disguise that will enable him to seek revenge in secret for his mistress's death. Tourneur's play determines our reading of this opening scene. Like Vindice, Morag will engage in complex schemes of revenge to avenge the murder of her lover, Shane.

The film also borrows the play's climactic scene in which the Revenger Vindice disguises his dead mistress's skull as a tempting seductress and tricks the philandering Duke, who was responsible for her death, into kissing its poisoned lips. In *Noroît*, the murder scene acquires dual reference points in two separate scenes. In the first, the Revenger Morag ensnares the faithless duchess Régina by trapping her within a seduction scene with her sleeping lover, Jacob. Régina kisses his lips that Morag has laced with poison, and then she dies. This scene is then replayed in the following scene, in which Morag and her conspirator Erika perform it before an audience composed of Morag's nemesis Giulia and her court. This scene represents the sole onstage performance of Tourneur's play that uses both theater costumes and props. As the performance begins, the actress Morag enters wearing a blond wig that disguises her as the blond Régina. The film spectator can surmise that here Morag is simultaneously playing the role of "Régina" as well as Régina's role in Tourneur's play: the duped Duke. The spectator may read the performance as the theatrical restaging of Régina's murder, or Régina's murder in the previous scene as a mere theatrical rehearsal for the play's performance. The duplication of scenes does not permit the film spectator to view the Tourneur drama as simply an event occurring within a pro-filmic, fictional world, but to view the play simultaneously as an intertextual reference, a filmed play that is staged by the film characters who become theatrical players.

The final revenge-masque of *Noroît* is also an adaptation of the play's conclusion. At the close of *The Revenger's Tragedy*, the disguised Vindice joins the revengers' ritualistic dance at the masque, the visceral prelude to the murder of all those gathered there. The final scene in both texts provides closure to the earlier climactic scene of the Duke's murder. In the Tourneur play, the Revenger, having just tricked and murdered the Duke, then plots the murder of the Duke's son, who is heir to the throne. The Revenger's successful scheme precipitates a fight for power among his victim's remaining brothers at the masque, where each mortally wounds the other. The only one left standing, an old nobleman, ascends the throne and ironically demands the Revenger's execution. To enhance the drama's tragic tone, Tourneur called for the "sounding of music" to accompany the masquers' dance, while in the film, atonal music counterpoints Giulia's staccato monologue during the masquers' expressionistic dance. Her ceremonial chant presages her final apocalyptic duel with the Revenger Morag on the ramparts.

## FROM MAETERLINCK TO DEBUSSY: *PELLÉAS ET MÉLISANDE*

Rather than the Aristotelian trajectory of Tourneur's play, we have in *Noroît* a field of intertextual forces where intersections of theater and opera with film disturb stable signification, leaving moments of incoherence in the construction of meaning. Predictably, film scholars have focused exclusively on Rivette's use of *The Revenger's Tragedy*.[10] Yet the story of *Noroît* is prismatic rather than teleological because it is informed not only by *The Revenger's Tragedy*, but also by the theatrical and operatic worlds and discourse of Maeterlinck and Debussy. One of these worlds is that of Celtic myth, which is unsurprising given that Maurice Maeterlinck, author of the play, had been inspired by Celtic legend.[11] As the film's story unravels, the spectator discovers a medieval Celtic world inhabited by female deities.

The film story takes place in a mythic past on a Celtic seacoast—hence its title *Noroît* that translates as *Northwest Wind*, indicating its geographical coordinates vis-à-vis the central Rivettian locale of Paris. *Noroît* commences with the last moon of winter and closes with the first moon of spring, a magical forty-day festival period during which goddesses can appear on earth and converse with mortals. As the film opens, the mysterious Morag mourns the death of her comrade Shane and vows to avenge his death. To accomplish this, she seeks to infiltrate into the castle ruled by Giulia (Bernadette Lafont), the goddess of the sun. Morag solicits the help of Erika (Kika Markham) who agrees to serve as her accomplice. As goddess of the palace, Giulia heads a band of pirates and is assisted by her lieutenant Arno, who carries on occasional raids. Other characters who inhabit Giulia's court include Régina, Giulia's foster sister and rival, Régina's daughter, Elisa, and Régina's followers, Charlotte, Celia, and Fiao, the court jester.

Leader of the pirate band, Giulia fears sabotage from forces abroad as well as from her lovers, Ludovico (Larrio Ekson) and Jacob (Humbert Balsan). Giulia confesses her darker suspicions to Erika, who advises her to hire a bodyguard. Giulia promptly employs Morag as her shadow. Following Morag's infiltration into the court, Morag and Erika seek vengeance. They attempt to sabotage a pirate attack led by Giulia, which succeeds in spite of their efforts. Following this raid, those around Giulia, specifically Ludovico, try to discover where her treasure is hidden. The two young lovers, Ludovico and Elisa, together sing about their search for Giulia's treasure and, with Morag's assistance, finally discover it hidden in a grotto.

Meanwhile, Morag and Erika have been secretly staging rehearsals for their performance of *The Revenger's Tragedy*. Their theatrical "plot" intersects with Giulia's own sinister plot to murder Régina, a scheme in which Morag acts as Giulia's accomplice. The scene in which Morag murders Régina is later incorporated into Morag and Erika's performance of *The Revenger's Tragedy*. Giulia soon discovers that Morag is not actually her protector but her divine adversary: the goddess of the moon. Giulia then solicits Erika's help, who she finds singing in the castle tower. Hoping to trap Morag, they plan a masquerade, a masked ball, and a final duel. This duel between the two goddesses, Giulia and Morag, takes place on the ramparts, where they slay each other. Régina's daughter, Elisa, is selected by the goddess of the sun Giulia to be her heiress.

While the entire film draws heavily upon the Celtic world created by Maeterlinck and Debussy, the final revenge-masque is infused with Celtic imagery and myth. The scene opens with an image of black clouds passing over a full moon, demarcating the close of the festival period. The magical temporal zone of the masque is based on the mythic Celtic battle Samhain, which Miranda Green has described as "a liminal, dangerous occasion when time and space are suspended, and the barriers between the supernatural and earthly worlds are temporarily dissolved. . . ."[12] As previously discussed, this duel sequence does, in fact, provide *Noroît* with an Aristotelian conclusion when the film is viewed simply as a Tourneur adaptation. Yet the film's story is multidimensional, drawing on diverse sources that overlap and, thus, foreclose the possibility of stable signification. Within this closing sequence, the rules governing cinematic time and space are temporarily suspended, as montage series are periodically replicated and later replayed as red- or sepia-tinted duplications. The uncanny, mirroring effect produced by the repetition of images creates the highly fantastic dimension of the masque, which entails the collapse of boundaries between supernatural and earthly worlds. Shifting into their respective roles as Celtic goddesses of sun and moon, Giulia and Morag remain poised throughout the masque between two worlds: that of humans and of the spirits.

Maeterlinck's fascination with Celtic myth is evident in the composition and appearance of characters in *Pelléas et Mélisande*. Opera historian Richard Langham Smith observes that Celtic imagery had provided the inspiration for Maeterlinck's character Mélisande, adding that even the spelling of the other characters' names (Yniold, Arkel, and Golaud) added Celtic color.[13] According to Smith, Maeterlinck had been especially taken by the visual art of second generation Pre-Raphaelites Sir Edward Burne-Jones and Walter Crane. He draws this comparison between Mélisande and the figures of Burne-Jones (see Figure 11.1): "The haunting figures of Burne-Jones's pallid damsels, their dilated eyes on the verge of tears, distilling the world's sorrow, were clearly implicated in the genesis of Mélisande. . . ."[14]

Figure 11.1. Sir Edward Coley Burne-Jones's The Love Song. The Metropolitan Museum of Art, The Alfred N. Punnett Endowment Fund, 1947. (47.26)

*Noroît*'s characters bear similar trappings of Irish legend. Rivette's representation of Morag draws heavily on Maeterlinck's Pre-Raphaelite figure, Mélisande. Both the *mise-en-scène* of *Noroît*'s opening sequence and composition of the character Morag bear striking similarity to the corresponding scene from *Pelléas et Mélisande*. As the opera opens, we meet Golaud, prince of Allemonde, who has been out hunting and who has lost track of the boar he has wounded. Golaud hears sobbing and turns to discover the mysterious Mélisande crying by the water's edge and remarks, "I hear crying. Oh! Oh! What is this by the water's edge? A little girl who is crying at the water's edge." Golaud's glance is similar to the point-of-view of Rivette's camera that at the film's opening sweeps across the horizon to discover Morag in mourning. Mélisande's origins remain unknown both to herself as well as to the spectator, like Morag's inexplicable appearance on the shoreline: both characters are enigmas by design. Mélisande's

Figure 11.2. Mary Garden as the msyterious Mélisande, at Théâtre National de l'Opéra Comique, April 30, 1992.

musical motif is soft, calm, and slightly sad, as is the melancholy flute refrain that defines Morag in this scene.

Like Morag, who incarnates the Celtic notion of sovereignty as moon goddess, Mélisande wears a mysterious gold crown. Following Golaud's initial encounter with Mélisande, he spots her shiny gold crown at the bottom of a well. The crown had been a gift, and although Golaud volunteers to retrieve it for her, she refuses his assistance. The source and signification of the crown remain an enigma, as does the character herself (see Figures 11.2 and 11.3).

Indeed, both characters, Morag and Mélisande, project the allegorical presence of the enchantress, which, for Jean Starobinski, symbolizes the seduction and mystery of operatic spectacle itself: "The gardens that open to an endless view, the enchanted palaces that take leave of the earth, the caves that offer a secret retreat are the marvels that respond to the call of the enchantress.. . . .".[15] Rivette's characters share with those of the opera the capacity to transport us to other worlds: those of enigma and seduction. Rivette was perhaps drawn to Maeterlinck's Symbolist drama *Pelléas* for reasons similar to those expressed by Debussy, who declared after having attended the play's stage première at the Théâtre des Bouffes-Parisiens, "It [*Pelléas*] has an evocative language whose sensitivity could find its extension in music and in orchestral setting."[16] On the surface, the capacity of Rivette's characters to seek revenge and to persist in diabolical schemes places them closer to those of Tourneur; however, their underlying power resides in their capacity to convey the atmosphere of dreamlike incertitude that pervades Debussy's opera *Pelléas*.

It seems useful briefly to review the plot of *Pelléas* before we examine the similarities between it and Rivette's film. The opera opens with Golaud's discovery of Mélisande weeping by the side of a well. Unable to discover who she is, Golaud convinces her to follow

Figure 11.3. Geraldine Chaplin as Morag: the original poster at the release of *Northwest Wind*.

him, although he is as lost as she. Golaud marries Mélisande with the consent of both Geneviève, his mother, and the old king of Allemonde, Arkel. Some time after her marriage to Golaud, Mélisande seeks relief from the gloomy, dark environs of the castle, and joins Geneviève on its seaward side in search of light. The two women are joined there by Pelléas, Golaud's younger half-brother. Following this initial meeting, Pelléas brings Mélisande to the well where Mélisande begins to play with Golaud's wedding ring, throwing it into the air. Suddenly, the ring falls into the well and is lost. They return to the castle, where they find Golaud recuperating from a fall from his horse. Upon seeing Golaud, Mélisande inexplicably begins to cry. Attempting to soothe her, Golaud caresses her hand and discovers that her ring is gone. He demands that she go and find the ring immediately, with Pelléas if necessary. Pelléas accompanies her to the grotto where they pretend to search for the ring, which, of course, is lost forever.

We later find Mélisande seated at the tower window of the castle, singing a simple lament. Pelléas passes beneath her window and, suddenly, becomes enmeshed in her hair as it cascades across his face. Golaud sees them flirting and becomes jealous. He wanders through the castle's cavernous vaults, encouraging

Pelléas to smell the stench of death. Anguished, Pelléas leaves the château and once again finds fresh air, rediscovering the sea and flowers by the terrace. Golaud no longer trusts Pelléas or Mélisande, however, and uses his son Yniold to spy on them. The boy peers through a castle window but sees nothing; it seems that the horrors are in Golaud's mind. With his future uncertain, Pelléas makes plans to leave the castle forever, yet before his departure, he decides to meet Mélisande for a final rendezvous at the well. Pelléas and Mélisande meet, embrace, and declare their love for each other. Hidden in the woods, Golaud is watching them in secret. He unsheathes his sword, strikes Pelléas down by the edge of the well, and then silently pursues Mélisande into the forest. Later, we find Mélisande, who lies dying. At her bedside, Golaud attempts to question her about her relation to Pélleas, but to no avail. She dies quietly, without saying anything, a tranquil, mysterious creature. Arkel holds up her newborn daughter, who must be removed from the death-chamber so that she can take her mother's place and ascend the throne.

The décor of *Noroît* is unmistakably indebted to Cocteau's décor from the 1963 production of *Pelléas et Mélisande,* which gives expression to the poet's earnest wish to reinvent the original Jusseaume/Ronsin designs. Indeed, *Noroît* represents the culmination of a chain of homage: Rivette pays homage in his film to Cocteau's *Pelléas*, who, in turn, pays tribute to Debussy's production. Given Rivette's filial relationship to the elder *metteur-en-scène* Cocteau, we can surmise that he had not only studied his designs, but had viewed the Jusseaume/Ronsin originals as well. From the film's scenes of dark forest, grotto, garden, and coast, to the interiors of the castle, resemblances to those of Debussy's opera are striking.

Debussy's dark outdoor environments, which include forest and grotto scenes, closely resemble those of Rivette's film. In the opera, the forest remains a dark mythic place of secrecy that presents the possibility of danger and sabotage; in the film, the significance of the forest seems split between its symbolic resonance and its potential as spectacle. The opera opens with the horseman Golaud emerging from a dark forest after an aborted hunting excursion; he then hears sobbing and spots Mélisande. At the opening of *Noroît,* the sequence of events is inverted. After our introduction to the tearful Morag, we are privy to the second scene of the film in which mounted horsemen emerge from the dark forest and ride past. This unexpected moment that follows *Noroît*'s opening scene is completely unmotivated with respect to the film's story. It stands adjacent to the plot: a gratuitous spectacle and an oblique reference to Debussy's opening scene. In this scene, and in others from the film and the opera, the forest remains a symbolic place of secrecy and sport, implying a vaguely medieval world. Its darker potential is evident in *Pelléas* during the scene of the lovers' final rendezvous, in which Golaud hides by the forest's edge, waiting for his moment of murderous revenge. In *Noroît,* we again witness the forest's potential to symbolize darker forces. As the scene of pirate sabotage begins, we find ourselves peering out from the forest over the bay as a pirate vessel approaches. This opening panoramic shot becomes retroactively identified with Erika's clandestine point of view from the woods, which a reverse shot later confirms. No establishing shot, however, structures spatial relations between the objects, figures, and setting in the scene. The lack of spatial orientation forces us to become aware of our position vis-à-vis Erika's point of view and therefore, to reflect on our own role in the network of sabotage and secrecy that the scene constructs. We are distanced from the saboteur's point-of-view and, thus, are forced to contemplate the symbolic resonance of the forest and the vaguely medieval world it represents (a temporal frame that is contradicted in *Noroît*, however, by the outboard motors that drive the pirate ships!).

While the dreamlike atmosphere of Debussy's opera was captured by the dark and light elements of its *mise-en-scène*, shadow and light define two poles of dramatic action in *Noroît* as well. In both film and opera, landscape elements such as the sun and the moon presage the forces of destiny. The moonlit grotto is a magic landscape in both film and opera, which determines the fate of the characters. Like Pelléas and Mélisande in search of Golaud's lost ring, Elisa and Ludovico approach the sea cave in search of Giulia's lost treasure. A long, low-angle shot captures Elisa cautiously crossing a frighteningly narrow precipice, framed within a shaft of moonlight. Here, Elisa's approach to the grotto seems to draw on Pelléas's description of the cave's entrance: "Let's wait for the moonlight to break through that big cloud; it will illuminate the entire grotto and then, we can enter without danger. There are treacherous spots, and the path is very narrow, between two deep lakes." The film's *mise-en-scène* resembles the opera's décor in which the grotto is draped in blue shadows from moonbeams.

The dark and light symbolism that is so striking in the film is very significant for Maeterlinck. In his essay on "Mystic Morality" from *Le trésor des humbles,* a passage dealing with Man's unsuccessful attempt to voyage into his own soul uses imagery strikingly reminiscent of that of *Pelléas* and of *Noroît*:

> We believe we have dived down to the most unfathomable depths, and when we reappear on the surface, the drop of water that glistens on our trembling finger-tips no longer resembles the sea from which it came. We believe we have discovered a grotto that is stored with bewildering treasure; we come back to the light of day, and the gems we have brought are false—mere pieces of glass—and yet does the treasure shine on, unceasingly in the darkness.[17]

Indeed, in *Noroît* the treasure discovered by Ludovico and Elisa literally glows, illuminating the dark grotto with its red radiant light. The sea-cave scenes from both *Noroît* and *Pelléas* profit from a dreamlike atmosphere in which a poetic moment is grafted onto the dramatic, producing in both an instantaneous translucence.

The characters of both *Pelléas* and *Noroît* inhabit an old castle that is surrounded by gardens and forest, bordered by the sea on one side. Clearly, Rivette borrows his *mise-en-scène* from Maeterlinck, for whom the sea is associated with past and future journeys away from the destiny of Allemonde. In both film and opera, the sea is viewed as a source of mystery, an agent of destiny that brought Mélisande to Allemonde and Morag to the island kingdom. Characters in both texts are attracted to the space and light of the sea on a clear day (see Figures 11.4 and 11.5).

Figure 11.4. Jusseaume's original set for Act II scene I, Mélisande meets Pelléas at the well by the water. Cliché Bibliothèque nationale de France, Paris.

Many scenes from *Noroît* are structured around elements of space, light, and sea. Several other scenes from the film also stand out in this regard, but perhaps the most visually stunning is the sword duel scene between Ludovico and Jacob on the castle ramparts. There, sea, sky, and sun are transformed into a symbolic force field that is brought to life by the instrumental music of the Cohen-Solal brothers (flute, bass, and percussion), who, according to sound engineer Pierre Gamet, improvised the entire scene with utter spontaneity and freedom.[18] While shooting the scene, Rivette allowed the music to inspire his actors. Consequently, Rivette confessed that the best takes for the musicians inevitably became the best takes for the actors.[19] During this scene, the castle ramparts are transformed into a theater proscenium, while the improvised music introduces a momentary pause in the story's development (see Figures 11.6). Meaning is deferred while the spectator is forced to attend to the sensuality of sounds, movements, and visual symbolism. One focused interval occurs when Rivette zooms in on the sun, a long take that both interrupts the performance and induces a moment of pleasurable dilation, which is distanced from the dancers' expressionistic movements. Rivette's objective here is to translate the opera's atmosphere, permitting the forces of the sun and sea to resonate. The air, water, and light from the sea are regenerative forces in the film that contrast with the dark symbolism of the forest, grotto, and castle. In *Noroît*, Rivette not only borrows

Figure 11.5. *Noroît*, the castle by the water.

the playwright's *mise-en-scène* but also adopts a Maeterlinckian approach to the significance of the *mise-en-scène*.

Rivette's scene is similar to Debussy's, insofar as both artists compose narratives where a pause or an ellipsis provides a moment for prolongation into music. Two insert shots of the sea follow the Cohen-Solal brothers' performance, punctuating it. The first, a long shot of the castle surrounded by the sea (shown in Figure 11.5), is silent. The second shot opens on waves breaking and then pans laterally to a panoramic shot of the castle from a much further distance. The silence of the first shot acquires a musical significance; its duration resembles an ellipsis (suspension points) sandwiched between the Cohen-Solal brothers' music and the roar of ocean surf, which saturates the soundtrack in the second shot. Both the silent ocean vista and the sonic persona of waves that had initially served as the backdrop of the instrumentalists' music are foregrounded here; in this manner, the sea itself plays a participatory role in the total musical performance.

Fig. 11.6. Pelléas et Mélisande, the castle ramparts. Cliché Bibliothèque nationale de France, Paris.

While there seems no question that the film's décor and general atmosphere are indebted to that of *Pelléas et Mélisande*, Rivette also used specific scenes from the opera. Rivette transposes the scene in which Mélisande sings a sad lament as she undoes her hair, allowing it to fall from the balcony window onto Pelléas below. Sung without orchestral accompaniment, Mélisande's song "Mes longs cheveux" carries no symbolic resonance, portraying her as an innocent soul beyond ulterior motives. Erika, who, like Mélisande, is found seated alone in the tower singing a melancholy ballad, sings the only substantial solo in *Noroît*. At the close of the song, Erika's glance scans the ocean horizon, indicated by a whip pan from the tower window. This brief shot from the tower window is followed by a slow lateral tracking shot across the castle chamber that finds and frames the Cohen-Solal brothers, who take up her sad refrain on flute. Both the ballad-like quality of the song's lyrics and its invocation of Celtic lore are reminiscent of Maeterlinck. Yet her song also invokes Tourneur, because its lyrics reflect the tone of betrayal that pervades the castle: "Old friends and faith have left me." At the close of the musical interlude, Giulia enters Erika's chamber to conspire with her, asking her to betray Morag by inviting her to the final masque.

In both *Noroît* and *Pelléas*, the song from the tower signals a moment of transition in the singer's life. In *Noroît*, Erika's solo performance signals her movement away from her previous role as Morag's longtime co-conspirator to an ambiguous position between Morag and Giulia. During her opera solo, Mélisande, like Erika, is pulled in opposite directions, insofar as she too is caught between her loyalty to her husband Golaud, who literally calls her away from the tower window, and her love for Pelléas, who will become her amorous confidante. In both opera and film, the solo passages signal significant transitional moments in their respective stories.

DUPLICITOUS STAGING: *THE REVENGER'S TRAGEDY* AND *PELLÉAS ET MÉLISANDE*

Debussy's opera also provides *Noroît* with dramatic definition, a beginning, climax, and closure that parallels that of *The Revenger's Tragedy*. The Aristotelian form provided by Tourneur that structures *Noroît* is obvious, while that of Debussy's opera is veiled. Indeed, the film is informed by a double voice that is composed of theatrical and operatic intertexts. While these two voices begin and end in unison, they diverge in between the opening and closing scenes, counterbalancing each other. This duplicity is perhaps most evident in its opening scene. As we previously demonstrated, *Noroît's* opening scene foregrounds Tourneur's story that introduces us to the Revenger Vindice. The film's citation of Tourneur's script in the opening scene effectively masks its phantom source in the opera's tale of Mélisande. As Morag assumes her "theatrical" persona as Vindice the Revenger, marked by her artificial English monologue, the film is simultaneously assuming the Tourneur script like a theatrical mask that hides its duplicitous identification with theater and opera. The "natural" sounds of the ocean surf accentuate the artificiality of Morag's recitation of Tourneur. Rivette had insisted on direct sound in this scene, overriding the numerous objections of his sound engineer Gamet. At Rivette's request, the level of the ocean sound was consequently never adjusted later in a sound mix, as would normally have been the case, and so it remains disproportionately loud with respect to the theatrical monologue. Real sound, as François Thomas points out, paradoxically underscores the unreal in *Noroît*.[20] In the opening scene, the ocean waves generate their own musical persona, which is perceived as auditory excess grafted onto the drama. In this manner, the unreal dimension of *Pelléas* paradoxically translates as real sound, which moves the film spectator away from the stasis of a linguistic signified to integration in the totality of spectacle.

As we have seen, the beginning of *Noroît* incorporates the respective opening scenes from both theater and opera productions. The final masque sequence of *Noroît,* which includes spectacle, instrumental music, and dance, is most obviously an adaptation of the corresponding scene from *The Revenger's Tragedy*. Yet one crucial detail differentiates the final film scene from Tourneur's drama. While the play ends with all familial heirs to the dukedom dead, the film closes as Elisa ascends the throne as Giulia's successor and heiress. This ceremonial initiation rite is inspired, not by Tourneur's drama, but by the opera *Pelléas*. During the opera's final scene, the tragic death of Mélisande makes possible a new regime, because her daughter is heiress of Allemonde. Similarly, in *Noroît's* final scene, the deaths of both maternal goddesses during the duel make possible the coronation of Elisa.

The masque opens with an initiation ritual that takes the form of a moon-lit, somnambulistic dance in which Giulia and two masquers chant while encircling Elisa. The goddess of the sun, Giulia, and her heiress, Elisa, dance before a burning fire resembling a funeral pyre and are cyclically reproduced in red-colorized images. In contrast, the Revenger—moon goddess Morag—is represented in sepia-colored images against a black sky. Their battle for control over Elisa is articulated across the oscillation of colorized images during the final masque, while Elisa is shuttled back and forth between them. In a verbal exchange, Morag encourages Elisa to save herself and run away. Giulia is waiting, however, and catches her in flight. With a blinding flash of light, Giulia bestows on Elisa a magic amulet, and ceremoniously says, "Now you are the heiress!"

During the final duel, dialogue between Giulia and Morag is reduced to elliptical exclamations. As Giulia slays Morag, she proclaims, "Courage, Morag. Tonight I am doubled." Morag responds, "Then I will kill you twice!" As Celtic goddesses, Morag and Giulia are able to shift back and forth between divine and human forms, assuming double personas. Similarly, the dramatic shape of the film shifts between its adherence to a theatrical script that calls for the Revenger to slay and be slain by the maternal "Goddess of the Palace," on one hand, and its fidelity to an operatic libretto that calls for Mélisande to become and then to beget the maternal "Goddess of the Palace," on the other hand. *Noroît* is informed by a double voice that is composed of theatrical and operatic intertexts, which begin and end in unison. Similar to the film's duplicitous opening scene, the final scene foregrounds Tourneur's story, disguising its double source in *Pelléas*'s tale of the medieval queen Mélisande.

*Pelléas* also provides *Noroît* with a climax, the duet between Ludovico and Elisa in which the actual dialogue is half-spoken and half-sung in metric repetitions. In a dazzling field of pink blossoms, Ludovico and Elisa chant their sibylline declarations as they continue their search for Giulia's treasure:

> The treasure is more than that/Le trésor est plus que ça
> I am here and there/Moi, je suis ici et là
> A little farther/Encore plus loin, voilà
> I have all the time I need/I have all the time I need/ Et j'ai tout mon temps à moi
> I am you and me /Je suis toi et moi
> Me? /Moi?
> Yes, twice me. /Oui, deux fois moi.

The multiple repetition of the word "moi" at the close of this songlike speech recalls Pelléas's response to Mélisande, which follows her ballad from the tower window. She queries Pelléas who is passing below, "Qui est là?/Who is there?" He responds, "Moi, moi, et moi! Que fais-tu là à la fenêtre en chantant comme un oiseau qui n'est pas d'ici? /Me, me, and me! What are you doing there at the window singing like a bird far from home?" Ludovico and Elisa's chant marks a climactic moment in the film because it mobilizes not only Mélisande's singular solo passage from *Pelléas,* but two other scenes from the opera as well, which both focus on Golaud's lost treasured ring. The first, Act II scene I from the opera (shown in Figure 11.4), depicts Mélisande and Pelléas by the well where she loses Golaud's ring by tossing it into the air. In the corresponding scene from *Noroît,* Rivette reinvents the opera's *mise-en-scène* by recasting the amorous figures Ludovico and Elisa against the bright sea-air, where they conspire together while playing flirtatious games that involve a ring. The ring scenes from both the film and the opera are designed to establish the lovers' amorous complicity. The theme of Ludovico and Elisa's duet not only mobilizes this initial scene from the opera in which Pelléas and Mélisande lose Golaud's treasured ring, but the later scene as well, in which both lovers return together to the grotto to search for it.

While the thematic content of Ludovico and Elisa's duet is lost treasure, the scene's spectacular *mise-en-scène* of pink blossoms borrows directly from Act III, scene iii of the opera in which Pelléas takes leave of Golaud and finds rebirth in the fresh sea air and the smell of roses. After his ascent from the castle vaults below, Pelléas exclaims, "And now, sea air! . . . There is a fresh wind, fresh as a bud opening on little green blades. . . . Wait! They have just watered the flowers at the edge of the terrace and the odor of the greenery and of wet roses fills the air."

Could it be mere coincidence that both *Pelléas* and *Noroît* include a pink-blossom scene, and that both film and opera narratives include the lovers' search for a lost treasured object? It is certain that in both productions, the pink-blossom scene stands out as the most sensual and colorful, transporting the spectator through song and a celebration of the senses. In both *Pelléas* and *Noroît,* the pink-blossom scene represents an ascent into light and sensual pleasure, a rising movement that in both opera and film precedes a final descent into a dark, tragic moment where the hero and/or heroine(s) perish. Indeed, Rivette uses dark and light contrast in the film to give form to the opposing forces of vengeance and love, of death and regeneration.

The significance of Rivette's *mise-en-scène,* in which renewal is cast in terms of light and dark, draws directly from Maeterlinck, who proclaims, "We can be born more than once: and each birth brings us a little nearer to our God. But most of us are content to wait till an event, charged with almost irresistible radiance, intrudes itself violently upon our darkness and enlightens us in our despite."[21] In *Noroît,* the pink-blossom scene discloses the hope of romantic love, the retrieval of Giulia's treasure, and the ultimate restoration of the kingdom with the ascent of its heiress Elisa. Rivette's use of intense light and lush imagery in this love scene is consistent with Maeterlinck's vision, which corresponds to his own conception of a cinema in which "the principal priorities on the screen would be purely spectacular ones, in the strict sense of the word."[22]

The duet between Ludovico and Elisa remains the only sung exchange in *Noroît,* yet it is representative of other dialogues in the film, which are also brief, indefinite, consisting of unanswered questions, unmotivated comments, and unfinished phrases connected by ellipses. In the pink-blossom scene, the film's fantastic dimension is intentionally cultivated through the doubling of dialogue lines, which produces an uncanny, mirroring effect. In fact, Ludovico and Elisa's exchange is representative of others in the film in which the underlying significance of the conversation is understood by the interlocutors, but not by the film spectator who, as François Thomas points out, does not possess the "complete picture" through which he can understand the mysteries.[23] This tone of ambiguity, intentionally cultivated in *Noroît,* recalls the style of *Pelléas* in which incompleteness and indirection were maintained, even justified by the nature of the music. Critic Jacques Dubois has remarked that the characters of *Pelléas* almost never engage in a completed conversation.[24] Indeed, the echoing of dialogue in *Noroît* is everywhere evident in the opera's libretto, in which characters continually repeat the same line twice: "J'attendrai, j'attendrai . . ." "C'est le dernier soir . . . le dernier soir . . ." (Pelléas, Act III scene I, Act IV scene iv), "cette pierre est lourde! . . . Elle est plus lourde que moi . . . Elle est plus lourde que tout le monde. Elle est plus lourde que tout." (Yniold, Act IV scene iii), "Ouvrez la fenêtre . . . ouvrez la fenêtre. . . ." (Mélisande, Act V scene I). As Paul Griffiths has observed, modes of suggestion and uncertainty are essential to the opera's characters that reveal themselves only indirectly.[25] Debussy's music, full of harmonic ambiguity, reflects and extends the characters' uncertainty.

*Noroît* translates *Pelléas's* sense of mystery. Like Maeterlinck, Rivette intentionally cultivates a fantastic, mysterious atmosphere through the doubling of dialogue lines, oblique elliptical dialogue, and repetition of lines; like Debussy, Rivette uses music to heighten the sense of mystery further. As Richard Langham Smith notes, Debussy created mystery through harmonic means: "'Vagrant' progressions or chord-pairs with allegiance to no clear tonal centre are used to portray particularly mysterious moments, often providing a void in which a literary symbol may resonate."[26] Paul Griffiths situates *Pelléas* historically as one possible response to the crisis in operatic form that coincided with the revolution in harmony in the decades prior to the first World War. Opera had previously relied on harmonic forces. In both Mozart and in Wagner, resolution in opera had meant harmonic and dramatic resolution, which Griffiths characterizes as follows: "Harmony provides narrative with an engine; narrative provides harmony with an explanation."[27] The increasing irresolution of tonal harmony in the early twentieth century was depleting the narrative of its momentum. One possible response to this ongoing crisis was Schoenberg's, which was to abandon tonality. Debussy's reaction was to embrace the non-directional nature of harmony and to compose, with *Pelléas,* an opera of uncertainty. Debussy's opera, a profound if subtle response to the crisis in musical representation, points to a decidedly French musical modernism quite distinct from and, in some respects, directly opposed to the more aggressive modernist project of Schoenberg.[28] To borrow a useful distinction made by Tony Pinkney, we might say that Debussy's modernism is one of "evanescent subjectivity" rather than "extreme objectivity."[29]

## FROM GERMAN AND FRENCH OPERA TO CINEMA

It was perhaps Debussy's subtle, though nonetheless radical, modernism that appealed to Rivette in the context of Brechtian tendencies that were being explored in cinema of the late 1960s and 1970s. Central to this debate was the Brechtian strategy of *Verfremdung,* which is translated as "distanciation" or "alienation," and is counterposed to the identification of the spectator with the work and with characters in traditional theater.[30] Brecht distinguishes his epic theater from the Aristotelian dramatic theater and its reliance on the psychological effects of empathy and emotional catharsis. Filmmakers Rainer Werner Fassbinder, Alexander Kluge, Jean-Luc Godard, Jean-Marie Straub and Danièle Huillet are generally regarded as central borrowers from and as main translators of Brecht.[31] These directors attempt to translate Brechtian strategies into cinematic form, using an anti-illusionistic style of presentation. The epic film replaces the conventional suspense story and its Aristotelian dramatic structure with a didactic presentation, using consecutive tableaux. Written intertitles and voiceover commentary simulate the effect of marginal footnotes, which call attention to image-sound relations, producing a radical separation of the elements. Filmmakers adapt this process of "literarization," which Brecht describes as "punctuating representation with formulation," to destroy the aesthetic illusion.[32] The intent of the epic film remains identical to that of the epic theater, which Brecht claims is "to develop the means of pleasure into an object of instruction, and to convert certain institutions from places of entertainment into organs of mass communication."[33]

Jean-Marie Straub and Danièle Huillet's film production of Schoenberg's opera *Moses und Aron* (1975), based on an Old Testament tale, represented the zenith of the Brechtian anti-aesthetic trend in cinema. Straub and Huillet's austere approach to Schoenberg's opera libretto is resolutely Brechtian; as Jeremy Tambling has observed, the directors had recourse to the separation of elements that stripped away anything mythic or mystificatory. The singers sang on the set, an open-air amphitheatre in which the stationary, empty oval space of ancient theatrics drew attention to the non-naturalism of the work, foregrounding its character as artifact.[34] The Brechtian direct sound and imaging strategy in *Moses und Aron* represented the strongest form of materialist cinema, which was heralded on its release in full-page spreads of *Cahiers du Cinéma.* Maureen Turim speculates as to possible reasons for this accolade: "Straub and Huillet are the filmmakers that film theory... desired, for they develop an ideologically motivated process of signification."[35] The discursive flowering of *Moses und Aron* during the mid-1970s would ultimately calcify, however, leaving Brechtian cinema pressed between the pages of the intellectual press, a wall that would serve to further obscure the veiled operatic style of *Noroît.*

The operatic tendency exemplified in *Noroît* runs counter to the Brechtian tendency that was surfacing in the European art cinema. In a 1968 interview with *Cahiers du Cinéma*, Rivette himself openly dismissed the political potential of a Brechtian cinema:

> I wondered quite a bit whether one could create a "distanciated" cinema, and basically, I don't think so. The cinema is necessarily fascination and rape, that is how it acts on people; it is something pretty unclear, something one sees shrouded in darkness, where you project the same things as in dreams: that is where the cliché becomes true.[36]

In this passage, Rivette seems to touch on the fundamental difficulty of transferring Brechtian theory to film. As Richard Wolin points out, epic theater sought to "freeze the normal flow of events in life in order to subject them to an intensive process of critical scrutiny."[37] This structuring device of interruption is designed to achieve an effect of astonishment, which as Walter Benjamin reminds us, is opposed to the immersion of the spectator in traditional auratic works of art.[38] Yet it becomes impossible to "freeze the normal flow of events in life" at the cinema where the event is imprinted on a filmstrip. The alienation effect was originally conceptualized around the copresence of the actor and of the spectator in the same space and time; whereas, at the cinema, the object and actors are already distanced as representations.

In "What is Epic Theater?," Benjamin moves beyond this notion of presence used to distinguish between the two art forms to insist that there does, in fact, exist a preestablished harmony between cinematic technique and the Brechtian epic. Indeed, the experience of shock that the Brechtian drama sought to impart to the audience through the strategy of interruption was, as Benjamin points out, already integral to film form. Benjamin claims:

> Like the pictures in a film, epic theater moves in spurts. Its basic form is that of the shock with which the single, well-defined situations of the play collide. The songs, the captions, the lifeless conventions set off one situation from another. This brings about intervals which, if anything, impair the illusion of the audience and paralyze its readiness for empathy.[39]

The precise nature of the relation between epic theater and film form pinpointed by Benjamin underscores the futility of filmmakers' attempts to translate the Brechtian device of interruption.

Seeking an opening through this impasse, Ishaghpour theorizes an alternative form, which he refers to as the Aristotelian epic film, which would not have to disengage itself through interruption from and against dramatic form.[40] The operatic style of *Noroît* conforms to Ishaghpour's new form. Rivette's film borrows its Aristotelian dramatic form from both Tourneur's *The Revenger's Tragedy* and from its veiled source *Pelléas*, both sources determining a beginning, a climax, and a conclusion from within their respective theatrical registers. While these two voices of theater and opera begin and end in unison, they diverge in between the opening and closing scenes, working both with and against each other. This dynamic interaction of double voices in *Noroît* invites the spectator to move back and forth between separate theatrical registers, opera or theater. Thus, in contrast to the unified effect of traditional Aristotelian drama, the film retains an epic quality, which Brecht defines in the following passage:

> The bourgeois novel in the last century developed much that was "dramatic," by which was meant the strong centralization of the story, a momentum that drew the separate parts into a common relationship. . . . The epic writer [Alfred] Doblin provided an excellent criterion when he said that with an epic work, as opposed to a dramatic, one can as it were take a pair of scissors and cut it into individual pieces, which remain fully capable of life.[41]

As in epic dramaturgy, in *Noroît* the intertextual tableaux of opera and theater can be extracted from the complete work and read as discrete and autonomous entities. Although the film conforms to a traditional tripartite dramatic structure, it is not driven by the dynamics of Aristotelian dramaturgy, which elicit an emotional catharsis and empathetic identification with the characters and the work.[42] Rather than linear Aristotelian teleology, in *Noroît* we have a field of intertextual forces in which the sheer physicality of sound and spectacle supersedes narration and induces an entranced participation, a pleasurable investment in the text.

To suggest an operatic style, the image of a monumental world of objects and events is solicited for itself in the film. Indeed, Rivette has affirmed that the cinema's mission should be to recapture monumentality through spectacle:

> I'm impressed by films that impose themselves visually through their monumentality. There is a weight to what is on screen, and which is there on the screen as a statue, a building, or a huge beast might be. . . . These are films that tend towards the ritual, towards the ceremonial, the oratorio, the theatrical, the magical, not in the mystical so much as the more devotional sense of the word as in the celebration of mass. Rite or ceremonial or monumental. In films, in texts, and in theatrical performances, the accent should be placed on the elements in which the spectacle itself (or the fiction) is represented.[43]

In *Noroît*, the power of plastic expression moves the spectator away—without the distancing of Brecht—from the immediate action while integrating him/her into a totality of spectacle. What the operatic tendency of *Noroît* offers is an aesthetic of "spectacular" presence that pays homage to the unfinished opera-film of poet-cinéaste Cocteau.[44]

While *Noroît* is usually read as the adaptation of Tourneur's *The Revenger's Tragedy*, it also assumes an operatic style of uncertainty and mystery. Debussy's *Pelléas et Mélisande,* which had represented a radically innovative response to the crisis in tonality at the turn of the century, provided Rivette with a stylistic idiom that offered an alternative to Brechtian cinema, the cinematic *Zeitgeist* of the 1970s. The French and German debate in the realm of cinema aesthetics paralleled that of music. Just as the operatic style of Debussy profoundly opposes the negative aesthetic of Schoenberg, which necessitated the complete rejection of tonal harmony, so does the operatic style of *Noroît* oppose the anti-aesthetic tendency of Brechtian cinema, which was formulated in conscious opposition to the affirmative character of high capitalist Hollywood cinema. Debussy shaped Rivette's operatic style, and in similar fashion, Schoenberg profoundly influenced filmmakers Straub and Huillet's conception of their Brechtian work *Moses und Aron.*

Rivette's adaptation of Debussy's opera reflects his enduring preoccupation with the relation between theater and cinema. In this passage, Rivette affirms:

> All films are about the theatre, there is no other subject. . . . If you take a subject which deals with the theatre to any extent at all, you're dealing with the truth of the cinema: you're carried along.. . . . Performance as the subject.[45]

The essence of mystery and ambiguity found in *Pelléas* and captured in *Noroît* remains consistent with Rivette's theoretical speculations. In 1959, he affirmed that an ontological mystery forms the essence of cinema and of all the arts:

> To the extent that there is mystery at the heart of the cinema (as there is mystery at the center of everything, in general, and of all the arts, in particular), . . .
> I believe that the mystery at the heart of cinema is, to use the expression of André Bazin, ontological: in the cinema, there is a process through which one can apprehend reality that, on the one hand, will only be able to apprehend appearances, but that, on the other hand, through appearances, can also apprehend an interiority.[46]

The tone of *Noroît* that intentionally maintains a sense of mystery is attributable, in part, to Rivette's theoretical convictions; the film's fantastic dimension that is created through verse and music is inspired by *Pelléas*, Debussy's opera of uncertainty.

## NOTES

1. Jacques Rivette, "Entretien avec Jacques Rivette," *Cahiers du Cinéma* 323–24 (May 1981): 48. Rivette borrowed his film tetralogy's title from Gérard de Nerval's publication *Les Filles du feu* (Paris: Flammarion, 1994) in which the celebrated poem *El Desdichado* (*The Disinherited*) appeared in 1854.

2. Joseph Kerman, *Opera as Drama* (Berkeley: University of California Press, 1988), 58.

3. Roger Nichols, "*Pelléas* in performance I—A History," chapter 6 in *Claude Debussy: Pelléas et Mélisande*, ed. Roger Nichols and Richard Langham Smith (Cambridge: Cambridge University Press, 1989), 140. As Nichols points out, Cocteau designed the décor and costumes for the Marseille production of *Pelléas*, which went on to Metz and Strasbourg, and then in 1963 replaced the centenary production at the Opéra-Comique.

4. Jean Mistler, *La Revue de Paris* (January 1963) quoted in Nichols, "*Pelléas* in Performance," 163.

5. Jean Cocteau quoted in Jacques Longchampt, *Le Monde*, 25 September 1962, quoted in Nichols, "*Pelléas* in performance," 163. At first glance, Cocteau's absolute fidelity to Debussy's original vision would seem inexplicable in view of his harsh criticism of "debussyisme" published in *Le Coq et l'Arlequin* (1918). Yet Cocteau later confessed to his close friend Jacques Maritain his own profound sense of regret for his attack on Debussy in *Correspondance* (1923–1963) *avec la Lettre à Jacques Maritain et la Réponse à Jean Cocteau* (1926) (Paris: Editions Gallimard, 1993), 301.

6. Jean Touzot, *Jean Cocteau* (Lyon: la Manufacture, 1989), 403.

7. Jacques Rivette, interview by author, tape recording. Paris, France, 16 June 1999.

8. Tourneur's themes of revenge and betrayal are well suited to Rivette, whose profound interest in the conspiracy narrative as well as in theatrical or filmic fictions as forms of conspiracy can be traced to his first New Wave film *Paris nous appartient* (1958–60).

9. Aristotle, *Aristotle's Poetics* trans. S. H. Butcher (New York: Hill and Wang, 1961), 65.

10. Rivette's use of Tourneur is noted within varied contexts, such as Jonathan Rosenbaum and Michael Graham's analysis of *Noroît* in *Sight and Sound* (autumn 1975): 234–39 and François Thomas's discussion of direct sound practice in *Noroît* in "Les Films 'parallèles,'" in *La Règle du jeu*, ed. Jean Esselinck (Turin: Centre Culturel Français de Turin, 1991), 71–8.

11. When assessing the impact of theatrical styles on his work (interview by author, 16 June 1999), Rivette never openly credits Maeterlinck. He does, however, acknowledge his profound debt to Antonin Artaud, whose own admiration for the Symbolist dramatist Maeterlinck is unequivocally attested to in an essay from the 1920s entitled, "Maurice Maeterlinck" in *Artaud on Theatre*, ed. Claude Schumacher (London: Methuen Drama, 1989), 9–12. Artaud's expression of respect for Maeterlinck undoubtedly provided Rivette with yet another possible source of motivation for his adaptation of *Pelléas*.

12. Miranda Green, *Celtic Goddesses: Warriors, Virgins and Mothers* (London: British Museum Press, 1995), 44. Green explains that Celtic goddesses had the ability to "shape-shift" and thereby adopt a human or animal form at will as a way of displaying their power, see p. 42.

13. Richard Langham Smith, "The Play and its Playwright," chapter 1 in *Claude Debussy: Pelléas et Mélisande,* 4–15.

14. Smith, "The Play and its Playwright," 4.

15. Jean Starobinski, "Opera and Enchantresses," in *Opera through Other Eyes,* ed. David J. Levin (Stanford: Stanford University Press, 1994), 20–21.

16. Claude Debussy quoted in David Grayson, "The Opera: Genesis and Sources," chapter 2 in *Claude Debussy: Pelléas et Mélisande,* 32.

17. Maurice Maeterlinck, *The Treasure of the Humble,* trans. Alfred Sutro (London: 1897), 61–62 quoted in Richard Langham Smith, "Tonalities of Darkness and Light," chapter 5 in *Claude Debussy: Pelléas et Mélisande,* 110.

18. Pierre Gamet, "Image du Son: Entretien avec Pierre Gamet, interview by François Thomas," in *Jacques Rivette: La Règle du jeu,* ed. Jean Esselinck (Turin: Centre Culturel Français de Turin, 1991), 71.

19. Jacques Rivette, "Entretien avec Jacques Rivette: Présentation par Jean Narboni," *Cahiers du Cinéma* 327 (September 1981): 18. Rivette found inspiration for his music and *mise-en-scène* in American dancer Carolyn Carlson's choreography, whose rehearsals he had attended at l'Opéra de Paris. Larrio Ekson (Ludovico) performed with Carlson in a duo *Il y a juste un instant* (1975). See Marcelle Michel and Isabelle Ginot, *La Danse au XXe siècle* (Montreal: Larousse-Bordas, 1998).

20. François Thomas, "Les Films 'parallèles': musique et son directs," in *Jacques Rivette: La Règle du jeu,* ed. Jean Esselinck (Turin: Centre Culturel Français de Turin, 1991), 166.

21. Maeterlinck, *The Treasure of the Humble,* 174 quoted in Smith, "Tonalities of Darkness and Light," 111.

22. Rivette, "Interview with Jacques Rivette by Bernard Eisenschitz, Jean-André Fieschi and Eduardo de Gregorio," *La Nouvelle Critique* 63, no. 244 (April 1973) in *Rivette, Texts and Interviews,* ed. Jonathan Rosenbaum (London: BFI, 1977), 49.

23. Thomas, "Les Films 'parallèles': musique et son directs," 169.

24. Jacques Dubois, "La Répétition dans *Pelléas et Mélisande,*" *Revue des langues vivantes* 28, no. 6 (1962): 487.

25. Paul Griffiths, "The Twentieth Century: To 1945," chapter 8 in *The Oxford Illustrated History of Opera*, ed. Roger Parker (Oxford: Oxford University Press, 1994), 284.

26. Richard Langham Smith, "Motives and Symbols," chapter 4 in *Claude Debussy: Pelléas et Mélisande,* 99.

27. Griffiths, "The Twentieth Century: To 1945," 280.

28. Ibid.

29. Tony Pinkney, introduction to *The Politics of Modernism: Against the New Conformists,* by Raymond Williams (London: Verso, 1989), 6. Expanding upon Roland Barthes' observations in *Writing Degree Zero* (New York: Hill and Wang, 1977), Pinkney adds that after the revolutions of 1848, realist dialectics split apart

into an "evanescent subjectivity" or the "extreme objectivity" of photo-realism, see p. 6.

30. Bertolt Brecht, *Brecht on Theater: The Development of an Aesthetic* trans. and ed. John Willet. (New York: Hill and Wang, 1964), 91–100.

31. Maureen Turim, *The Films of Oshima Nagisa: Images of a Japanese Iconoclast* (Berkeley: University of California Press, 1998), 45. Turim provides an incisive discussion of Brecht's theories of theater and their translation into cinema by European and Japanese avant-garde directors.

32. Brecht, *Brecht on Theater,* 43–47.

33. Brecht, *Brecht on Theater,* 42.

34. Jeremy Tambling, *Opera, Ideology and Film* (New York: St. Martin's Press, 1987), 148–9.

35. Maureen Turim, "Oblique Angles: The Film Projects of Jean-Marie Straub and Danielle Huillet," in *The New German Filmmaker*, ed. Klaus Phillips (New York: Ungar, 1984), 337.

36. Jacques Rivette, "'Time Overflowing': Rivette in interview by Jacques Aumont, Jean-Louis Comolli, Jean Narboni, Sylvie Pierre," *Cahiers du Cinéma* 204 (September 1968) in *Cahiers du Cinéma 1960–1968: New Wave, New Cinema, Reevaluating Hollywood,* ed. Jim Hillier (Cambridge: Harvard University Press, 1986), 322.

37. Richard Wolin, *Walter Benjamin: An Aesthetic of Redemption* (New York: Columbia University Press, 1982), 152. In chapter 5 "Benjamin and Brecht," Wolin provides an excellent overview of Brecht's theory of theater in the context of his analysis of the Brecht-Benjamin alliance.

38. Walter Benjamin, "What is Epic Theater?" in *Illuminations,* ed. Hannah Arendt (New York: Schocken, 1968), 151.

39. Benjamin, "What is Epic Theater?" 153.

40. Youssef Ishaghpour, *D'Une Image à L'Autre: la représentation dans le cinéma d'aujourd'hui* (Paris: Petite Bibliothèque Méditations, Denoel, 1982), 39.

41. Brecht, *Brecht on Theater,* 70.

42. David Roberts, "Brecht and the Art of Scientific Theatre," in *Brecht Performance*, vol. 13 of *The Brecht Yearbook*, ed. John Fuegi et al. (Detroit: Wayne State University Press, 1984), 41.

43. Rivette, "Interview with Jacques Rivette by Bernard Eisenschitz," 49.

44. The mythic, fairy tale dimension of *Noroît* is traceable not only to Cocteau's décor for the 1963 production of *Pelléas* but to his masterpiece *La Belle et la Bête* (1946). Indeed, the circumstances surrounding the reception of Cocteau's film closely resemble those of *Noroît*. Cocteau's fairy tale ran counter to the post-Liberation taste for realism. As Susan Hayward has observed in "La Belle et la Bête," *History Today* 46, no. 7 (July 1996): 44, Cocteau's scenario seemed an irrelevance within the climate of postwar concerns; *La Belle et la Bête* was regarded as detached from the sociopolitical climate of the time. In essence, Cocteau's film presented a challenge to

the cinematic *Zeitgeist* of its time, patriotic realism, in the same way that Rivette's *Noroît* would challenge Brechtian cinema of the 1970s.

45. Rivette, "'Time Overflowing': Rivette in interview by Jacques Aumont," 317.

46. Jacques Rivette quoted in Jean Collet, *Le Cinéma en Question* (Paris: Editions du Cerf., 1972), 57–8.

# Afterword
# In Appreciation
*Stanley Cavell*

P ERHAPS THE BEST WAY I CAN EXPRESS MY GRATITUDE FOR THIS COLLECTION of texts is through recounting experiences of my own in recent years following upon my dawning recognition of the fascinating and pervasive relationships between opera and film and finding myself wishing for the appearance of just such a volume.

Still in the first decade of sound film—talking pictures they were called, though the famous first one was a singing picture, Al Jolson's *The Jazz Singer*— one of Hollywood's most significant directors, Frank Capra, in his classic comedy *Mr. Deeds Goes To Town* (1936, with Gary Cooper and Jean Arthur), confesses a sense of affinity between film and opera, expressed as an impulse toward competition with opera. The narrative of this enduringly admired, even beloved, film concerns the consequences, from the ludicrous to the sublime, of its innocent, provincial hero's unexpected inheritance of an enormous fortune upon the sudden death of his rich uncle. As soon as Mr. Deeds moves into his uncle's mansion in New York, he is assaulted by proposals for ways to spend his fortune. One proposal is from a group informing him that they have elected him to replace his uncle as President of the Friends of the Opera, entailing for him the privilege of continuing his uncle's annual subsidy of the opera's productions. Mr. Deeds, however (whose name suggests allegory, daring us to enlarge upon his actions), seems to be one in a long line of fictional country bumpkins who outwit the schemes of the sophisticated rich. He asks why the opera company needs so much help, why it doesn't sell more tickets. When told that its season is always sold out and that everybody understands that ticket sales alone cannot support the undertakings of opera productions, he replies, "You must be putting on the wrong kind of shows."

It seems plain enough to my mind that the film is proposing that the right kind of shows for them to put on are movies, and that it is offering itself as a candidate. Considering that this is a film in which its title character will refer reverently to the philosopher Henry David Thoreau, and that it is made by a director whose leading characters in another of film of the period (the grandfather in *You Can't Take It With You*) refers fervently to Ralph Waldo Emerson, I am not willing to reduce the proposal of a different kind of "show" to the incontestable idea that movies are in some obvious sense economically more viable than operas. What is this film about, that offers itself in the place of opera?

Consider that it is to be understood, so I claim, not simply as depicting a fantasy of inheritance, but that it is *about* the idea of inheritance: the invocation of Thoreau takes place in front of a monument in remembrance of the American Civil War, the tomb of President Grant, a tourist attraction in New York City, where Mr. Deeds is moved to the recognition that America, for all its big buildings, has failed to live up to its promise, its inheritance of noble ideas. Consider further that the film climaxes with a sequence about the idea of expressiveness: the hero Mr. Deeds has, because of his apparent betrayal by the woman he has fallen in love with in New York, fallen into a silent melancholy; and consider how he regains his voice, or how what his voice is becomes the subject of the drama. I have elsewhere proposed understanding the origins of opera in the first decade of the $17^{th}$ century, namely the same decade that saw the creation of Shakespeare's major tragedies, as marking a cultural trauma having to do with a crisis of expression, with a sense that language as such, reason as such, can no longer be assured of its relation to a world apart from me or to the reality of the passions within me. Nothing less than such a trauma could meet the sense of language requiring a rescue by music.

This traumatic crisis of expression will be articulated philosophically in the generation after Shakespeare, belatedly—as philosophy is belated—in Descartes's process of doubt, that radical skepticism which heralds the modern era in philosophy. I cannot here go into the readings I have given of Shakespearean tragedy that are meant to demonstrate its working out, in other terms, at other levels, what philosophy knows as the problematic of skepticism, nor can I do more than mention the connection between Shakespearean comedy and a central genre of American film comedies, those I call comedies of remarriage. So I must merely assert that such ideas underlie the powers I attribute to film and to opera when I read a moment in Hollywood comedy, the moment of Mr. Deeds refusing the use of his inheritance to support opera, as an argument of film with opera generally: namely about its claims to inherit from opera the flame that preserves the human need, on pain of the madness of melancholy, for conviction in its expressions of passion.

It is out of such preoccupations that I was first moved some ten years ago to offer a course on opera and cinema. It seemed reasonable to try the material first as a graduate seminar where students with experience from various fields might find profit in thinking about philosophical implications of the interactions or affinities of these arts, or genres, or media, affinities registered most generally in the sheer fact that music, one might even say operatic music, has been part of the presentation of films throughout their history, most particularly in the appearances of specific operas, in their spectacle and their sound, as integral in specific films. More personally, in writing about film I had more than once recurred to my sense that the transfigurative power of the motion picture camera on human beings and their utterances bore comparison, in the absoluteness of its rule, with the transfigurative role of music in opera's presentation of human beings and their utterances, powers essential to the narrative, to the poetry, to the sometimes inhuman extremity of emotion invited and sponsored by each. How could one not wish to understand these affinities and to consider what happens when they interact?

The urgency of the question, and its pedagogical impulse, became irresistible with the sense (perhaps I was only catching up with a fact better known to others) of a concentrated production of opera films, or of opera in films, or of filmed operas, or relatedly of operas presented for television, together with the expanding institution of the video cassette, which revealed new forms of pleasure and instruction in experiencing opera, as if a video maintains the dimension of intimacy in the experience which the accustomed grandeur of opera's spectacle (even its spectacles of isolation) occludes. (This contrasts with the experience of a film on video, which is massively convenient but which contains no aesthetic compensation for the loss of, let's say, presence.)

Two films in particular seemed most directly to exemplify what I called the competition of film with opera (that of opera with film is, I would say, fairly recent, or rather more intermittent), namely *Moonstruck* and *Meeting Venus*. In the case of *Meeting Venus*, enough of the related opera's music is quoted, often in the settings of rehearsals for a production of *Tannhäuser* that is never actually presented, and is in fact narratively prohibited from occurring, and its circumstances are clearly enough alluded to in the casting and plot, for the film to count as a kind of stylized production of, or commentary on, the opera. The relation between *Moonstruck* and *La Bohème* is less systematic (anyway the music of the opera is less extensively quoted), but no less direct in its consequences for the film. In *Meeting Venus,* the principal woman (the diva, played by Glenn Close) sings the part of Eva, but in the film she is the goddess of love (the identification of the two women has been accomplished within productions of the opera by casting the same singer in both parts). In *Moonstruck*, the principal woman (Cher) is identified with Musetta's music —the flouncing-along-the-street motif that introduces her famous Waltz—whereas Mimi's frozen hand belongs to the principal man (Nicholas Cage). (While less extensively quoted, the music in *Moonstruck* is also tested by being played in the company of a quasi-Italian song, "That's Amore," sung by one of the famous Italian singers of the recent past, Dean Martin. It was, I add, a revelation to me to discover that Mimi's motif of breathlessness or suffocation sounds wonderful, anyway at home, played on the concertina. Unless, that is, I hallucinated the instrumentation, which occurs pianissimo after Cage's early aria to his missing hand. It would not afford a revelation if all it meant is that Puccini's music is no better than conventionally understood popular music; it should rather make one consider what Italian popular music is.) It is an interesting connection between the films that each reconstitutes elements of its companion opera so as to divert death and arrive at a happy ending, roughly the recommendation of Freud in *Beyond the Pleasure Principle*. (This consequence or condition of a transformation from stage to screen had also been managed, or fantasized, fifty years earlier by the Marx Brothers in *A Night at the Opera.*)

But despite such an array of provocative topics to think about, that experimental seminar of mine was pedagogically a fiasco, in comparison with its philosophical and aesthetic promise, most dramatically because of my failure to get the talented musicians and philosophers present to be willing to talk together. (Music and philosophy are both famously terrorist territories, where those who are anxious about their powers of sense or intelligence are easily prompted to suspect that they are not discriminating something.) Reading through *Between Opera and Cinema* has put me in mind of such rueful memories, out of the realization that if this present collection of texts had been available for our use then, a certain level of success for the work of the seminar would have been assured.

The topics resourcefully touched on by one or another of its authors amount to an education in the evidently burgeoning topic of opera and cinema, with ideas, examples, and bibliography to launch one in thinking about everything from the concrete and detailed interactions of music and *mise-en-scène* in a specific sequence to the most general speculations concerning the interaction of specific films (throughout the history of the new art of cinema) with opera. I take it to indicate no small affinity between opera and cinema that the study of their individual works so often irresistibly prompts philosophical speculation about what these media are, what human or ontological or epistemological purposes they serve. This is perhaps furthered by the fact that the events that marked the entry of these arts into Western culture are datable, the results of decisions and inventions at particular times and places that are fully knowable—unlike the origins of, say, writing or painting—so that the fact that they remain mysterious has its own mystery. With literature we had to be forced to recognize the importance of "theory," which, for better or worse, became its own subject, whereas in thinking about opera and film, theory seems always to have been part of the daily fare, easy to start doing, making it easy to settle for too little. The hard and inspiring work of the essays in *Between Opera and Cinema* is something to build on.

I cannot say what stirrings within the discipline of musicology have produced this new degree of concentration on what happens between opera and cinema, but it is obvious that responsible musicians will rely on the current dispensation of the discipline of film studies for guidance across the bounds of medium and expertise. Considering that film studies also has its stirrings and historically shaped preferences, there is a risk that its necessary guidance at the same time incurs the risk of adopting certain unnecessary biases. For example, in reading the present essays, it seemed to me that I was encountering judgments of a film that I felt partook of a certain condescension that American film studies has encouraged toward classical Hollywood films of the era of sound. Or perhaps it is a tendency to regard the Hollywood contribution to the art of cinema as more monolithic, more ideologically unaware of its sins than it deserves. I recall the reading, in so many ways informed and nuanced, of the moment in *The Shawshank Redemption* of the broadcast of the Letter Duet from *The Marriage of Figaro* as in effect asserting a "brotherhood of listeners" (p. 143) whose political point is to slight the savage power of institutions over moral and emotional power. This is taken to be demonstrated in the fact that when the voice-over responds to hearing the music by declaring that "for the briefest of moments every last man at Shawshank felt free," the response is "clearly shared by every inmate" (p. 142). But this seems to me to accept an idea that a Hollywood film *cannot* be going beyond such an assertion, cannot, I mean, form some perspective on the events it depicts. For example, the thought that whatever Red thinks he knows, we know nothing of what each inmate and guard feels when he is stilled by the music, and that accordingly the end of the ascending shot of the full prison yard is readable as a painful, deeply ironic tableau of a mock universality, a picture of individuals isolated from one another, perhaps from themselves, forming a kind of homage to music's capacity to imagine redemption, or its lack (as if music is unsynchronized with the secularization of the other arts, more closely retaining its ties to religion). I associate the homage, further, with the issue of the origin of music, since in this case the sound comes surrealistically over a warden's PA system. The origination or source of sound as music is an insistent issue of the world of opera: for example, in the form of the question of whether the singers hear singing, hear their companions to be singing, when the issue is not obviously depicted song. And isn't the elevated invitation to deferred redemption in the prison yard to be put together with the elevated shot as Andy emerges from the prison's sewer pipe and rises up from a cleansing stream into saving rain, lifting his arms and his face in an ecstasy of physical liberation? Is this to mock the former elevation, or is it to acknowledge its sustenance?

Because the period of classical Hollywood film has provided me with pleasures I am not willing to forgo, I might add a few instances of the occurrence of opera in films I have studied from that period, generally as a tip that if I can think without much reflection of a handful of such occurences, there must be a hundred times that many to consider—but more specifically, to emphasize the question of why, though striking in the moment of perception, they are hard to remember afterwards.

I think of the moment in *Now, Voyager* (1942) in which, as Bette Davis and Paul Henreid are lying beside one another fully clothed and wrapped separately in blankets in a mountain cabin, and he kisses her chastely as she sleeps, the sound track is moved to announce the unmistakable harmonic progressions from Act II of *Tristan und Isolde* on the fourfold repetition of the word "Liebe" at the end of the line, "O sink hernieder Nacht der Liebe . . ." It would take some work to capture the mocking, yet after all ratifying, effect of this juxtaposition. And this work should immediately caution us against the temptation to dismiss such moments as "in jokes." The other arts familiarly contain incessant examples of decisions whose significance the bulk of an audience will not pick up from an initial encounter. (Otherwise the institution of literary criticism, born with philosophy, would not have been born.) The dismissal in the case of film I assume to be a holdover of the surprisingly stubborn idea that films are made to be viewed just once. (Many are; surprisingly many more are not.) The idea encourages the discouraging thought that film criticism can play no role in a serious film culture, but is merely a grading operation.

And I think of the occurrence in George Cukor's *Gaslight* (1944) of a famous tag from *Lucia di Lammermoor* ("Verrano a te sull'aure," the duet between Lucia and Edgar that closes Act I), a favorite role of the singer (called the "aunt" of the character who is played by Ingrid Bergman), the announcement of whose murder begins the film's narrative. The suitability of the opera tune as music for this movie is one of countless instances in which film in effect declares itself already to be opera, to want the extremity of expression in opera, realized in *Gaslight* as we are shown Bergman, the aunt's inheritor, finding her voice. As she puts it early in the film, she "has no voice" when she sings, but now, at the end, her lucidly deranged outpouring to her husband, exposed as the murderer, demonstrates to him that the woman he has silenced is capable of a full aria of histrionic words and deeds. Another tune associated with the aunt (as her signature encore, "The Last Rose of Summer") is announced by a passing organ grinder as a kind of transition between sequences so the effect of the operatic and the popular align in such a say that we may be inclined to ask what becomes of music when film takes it into its medium.

And I think of Preston Sturges's *The Lady Eve* (1941), in which out of nowhere (but narratively in the sleeping car of a speeding train) The Pilgrim's Chorus (that is, the opening of the Overture) from *Tannhäuser* arises to underlie and undermine a pious speech of "sweet forgiveness," directed with impeccably bad faith by Henry Fonda to Barbara Stanwyck as they begin—and end—their honeymoon. Is this unalloyed mockery? But what is being mocked, this newly wed, dim husband, Wagner's (or Tannhäuser's) impeachable faith (in what?), or the inescapably happy (more or less) ending the film must find? We are asked to think about opera early in the film in the sequence in which the principal pair become acquainted. The woman manages to turn a virtuosic exchange, shuffling parody with seduction (in which the man from time to time enters a monosyllable or minimal sentence), to the question of what ideal woman the man imagines he will marry. In one of her confidential flourishes, she proposes, "I'll bet she looks like Marguerite in *Faust*," to which the man dreamily responds, as if they are talking sense, "Oh no, she's not so . . . bulky," thus automatically taking it as obvious that it is the medium of opera in question, and citing the banal assumption that it is well known what divas look like. But in the course of this long duet, a considerable dialectic on the subject of imaginary (or ego) ideals is put into play, whose substance the hilarity and eroticism of the moment hardly dispels. Something is as if dispelled, or else what happens to these striking references to opera when the film concludes? I would like the experience of such recurring moments to raise issues of what counts as remembering a film, perhaps in comparison with remembering a poem, a novel, a painting, a tune, a voice, a place, a face. Some used to speak of films as if their details were meant to be forgotten. If that were true, how does it happen that the memory of a film, which may remain lazy or rigid in isolation, is so productively jogged into life by a companion's memory?

The collective project of *Between Opera and Cinema* significantly furthers the perception that cinema, for most (or nearly all) of its life, has been something to listen to as well as to watch. At the same time, it demonstrates that professional films scholars should not neglect the impulse to consult colleagues with a professional knowledge of music, centrally of opera, to know all they are listening to, or being inattentive to. For those curious about the phenomenon of film or that of opera, this knowledge will deepen the curiosity. For those in love with both film and opera who have yet to explore the uncountable possibilities of their colloquy, or argument, a renewed admiration is in store.

# Contributors

**Marcia J. Citron** is Lovett Distinguished Service Professor of Musicology at Rice University. She is author of *Opera on Screen* (Yale, 2000), a critical study that interprets major treatments of opera in cinema, television, and video, and offers a theoretical groundwork for the genre. She also specializes in women in music. Publications include the prize-winning book *Gender and the Musical Canon*, now in reprint edition (Illinois, 2000), as well as an edition of Fanny Hensel's letters to Felix Mendelssohn (1987; winner of *Choice* award) and a bio-bibliography of Cécile Chaminade (1988).

**Deborah Crisp** lectures in Musicology at the Australian National University's Institute of Arts. In addition to her collaborative work with Dr. Roger Hillman on music and film, her research interests lie in early romanticism and the history of music in Australia. Recent publications include articles on Liszt's view of J. S. Bach, the nexus between amateur and professional music-making in colonial Australia, and the beginnings of professional opera in Sydney in the 1850s. She is editor of written material for the *Anthology of Australian Music on Disc* series.

**Michal Grover-Friedlander** is Assistant Professor of Musicology and the Interdisciplinary program for the Arts at Tel Aviv University, Israel. She is currently a visiting fellow at Princeton University. Her article "The Phantom of the Opera: The Lost Voice of Opera in Silent Film" appeared in *Cambridge Opera Journal*, 1999. She has published articles on the relationship between Voice and Death in nineteenth- and twentieth-century opera, and is now completing a book on the voices of opera in film.

**Roger Hillman** is Senior Lecturer at the Australian National University, Canberra, with half-posts in Film Studies and German Studies. Heconvened the Film Studies Program there from its inception in 1995 until 2000. He co-edited the volume *Fields of Vision: Essays in Film Studies, Visual Anthropology, and Photography* (University of California Press, 1995). His recent publications focus on the use of classical music in postwar German and Italian films.

**Mary Hunter** is Professor of Music at Bowdoin College. She is the author of *The Culture of Opera Buffa in Mozart's Vienna* (Princeton University Press, 1999), co-editor, with James Webster, of *Opera Buffa in Mozart's Vienna* (Cambridge University Press, 1997), and is currently the Editor of *Cambridge Opera Journal*. Her current work concerns the ways in which classical music is represented in popular films.

**Jeongwon Joe** is Assistant Professor of Music at the University of Nevada, Reno. She received her Ph.D. from Northwestern University in 1998 with a dissertation entitled "Opera on Film, Film in Opera: Postmodern Implications of the Cinematic Influence on Opera." She has published essays on opera-film, 20th-century opera, postmodernism, and film music. Her current projects include the voice of the *Noir* Sirens and the discursive interplay between the singing voice and the speaking voice in Korea opera-film.

**David J. Levin** is Associate Professor in the Department of Germanic Studies and on the Committee on Cinema/Media Studies at the University of Chicago. In 1994, he edited *Opera Through Other Eyes* (Stanford University Press); his *Richard Wagner, Fritz Lang, and the Nibelungen: The Dramaturgy of Disavowal* was published by Princeton University Press in 1998. He is currently at work on a book on opera and *mise-en-scène*. In addition to his academic work, Professor Levin has worked extensively as a dramaturg for various opera houses in Germany.

**Teri Silvio** is Lecturer in Chinese Studies at the University of New South Wales in Sydney, Australia. She received her Ph.D. in anthropology from the University of Chicago in 1998. The topics of her current projects are "Televised Puppetry in Taiwan" and "Drag Melodrama/Feminine Public Sphere/Folk Television: 'Local Opera' and Identity in Taiwan."

**Lesley Stern** is Professor of Visual Arts at the University of California, San Diego. She is the author of *The Scorsese Connection* (1995) and *The Smoking Book* (1999) and co-editor of *Falling for You: Essays on Cinema and Performance* (1999). She has written extensively in the areas of film, performance and cultural studies, and is currently working on the gestural element in cinematic performance.

**Rose Theresa** is Visiting Assistant Professor at the University of North Carolina at Greensboro. She has also taught at the State University of New York at Stony Brook and at the University of Pennsylvania, where she recently completed a Ph.D. in Music. Her dissertation, "Spectacle and Enchantment: Envisioning Opera in Late Nineteenth-Century Paris," explores the nature of opera and operatic spectating at the Palais Garnier. She is currently working on a book-length study of Gounod's *Faust*.

**Marc A. Weiner** is Director of the Institute of German Studies, Professor of Germanic Studies, Adjunct Professor of Comparative Literature & Communication and Culture (Film Studies), and Finkelstein Fellow in the Humanities at Indiana University, Bloomington. He is the author of *Arthur Schnitzler and the Crisis of Musical Culture* (Heidelberg: Carl Winter, 1986), *Undertones of Insurrection: Music, Politics, and the Social Sphere in the Modern German Narrative* (Lincoln: University of Nebraska Press, 1993), and *Richard Wagner and the Anti-Semitic Imagination* (Lincoln: University of Nebraska Press, 1995; Paperback 2nd ed., 1997), which won the Eugene M. Kayden National University Press Book Award for best book in the Humanities in 1996 and was recently published in German as *Antisemitische Fantasien: Die Musikdramen Richard Wagners*, trans. Henning Thies (Berlin: Henschel Verlag, 2000). He has published numerous articles on the musical aesthetics and ideology of nineteenth- and twentieth-century German-speaking Europe, and is currently working on a book entitled *Hollywood Goes to the Opera*.

**Mary M. Wiles** teaches in the Film Studies Division of the Communications Department at Florida Atlantic University. She has recently completed her dissertation entitled "Theatricality and French Cinema: The Films of Jacques Rivette" in the Film Studies Program at the University of Florida. She has published on avant-garde theatricality and adaptation in contemporary French and New German Cinemas. Her recent work explores the manner in which the coming-of-age narrative of girlhood overlaps with themes of race and nationalism in French and American fictions of the 1990s.

# Index